商务话语与文化研究丛书

总主编 郭桂杭　副总主编 胡春雨

A Discourse Study of Insurance Sales Agent-Client Interactions in Transformational China's Rural Areas

转型期中国农村保险销售互动话语研究

汪谓超 著

科学出版社

北京

内容简介

本书使用人类学方法收集数据，通过对国内外话语研究现状及趋势的分析建构语篇系统分析理论框架，整合话语分析理论、批判话语分析及社会文化研究，总结中国当代农村商业保险销售中的语言使用策略和方法，并对其内在动因进行探索。本书对农村保险销售语体特征、模式、劝说策略、身份建构及其内在社会文化动因的描写和分析，丰富了对中国农村现实语言事实的描写，厘清了语言、身份建构、社会文化动因之间的内在关系，也拓展了社会语言学、跨文化交际、商务英语方面的相关研究。

本书适合话语语言学、商务英语研究、对外汉语教学及服务营销等领域的研究人员和研究生阅读，尤其适合社会语言学、跨文化研究、商务英语研究及对外汉语教学等领域的学者参考使用。

图书在版编目（CIP）数据

转型期中国农村保险销售互动话语研究＝A Discourse Study of Insurance Sales Agent-Client Interactions in Transformational China's Rural Areas：英文 / 汪谓超著. —北京：科学出版社，2018.8

（商务话语与文化研究丛书/郭桂杭总主编）

ISBN 978-7-03-058637-7

Ⅰ. ①转… Ⅱ. ①汪… Ⅲ. ①农村保险–销售–研究–中国–英文 Ⅳ. ①F842.66

中国版本图书馆 CIP 数据核字（2018）第 199511 号

责任编辑：常春娥 / 责任校对：贾娜娜
责任印制：张欣秀 / 封面设计：铭轩堂

科学出版社 出版
北京东黄城根北街 16 号
邮政编码：100717
http://www.sciencep.com

北京建宏印刷有限公司 印刷
科学出版社发行　各地新华书店经销

*

2018 年 8 月第 一 版　开本：B5（720×1000）
2018 年 8 月第一次印刷　印张：14
字数：250 000

定价：88.00 元
（如有印装质量问题，我社负责调换）

总　　序

自 2007 年教育部批准设置商务英语本科专业至今，随着国家"一带一路"倡议的提出，我国国际贸易、国际投资等国际商务活动快速增长，设立商务英语专业的学校也得以迅猛发展，截至 2018 年，共有 367 所高校开办商务英语本科专业，探索人才培养模式，服务于国家和区域经济发展需要。商务英语在国外不作为一个独立专业和学科，但在我国，随着国家高等教育大力发展新兴交叉学科总体战略目标的提出、人才培养需要以及商务英语教学实践的深入，商务英语学科理论研究日益受到国内专家学者的重视，并已经取得一些研究成果。一些论文在国内外有影响力的期刊上发表，也有若干涉及商务英语教师发展的著作相继出版。

在人才培养和学科建设方面，广东外语外贸大学国际商务英语学院也在一直努力探索开拓。继 2007 年申办商务英语本科专业之后，我们先后率先在外国语言文学一级学科下开设了商务英语研究二级硕士学位授权点和博士学位授权点，形成了完整的本科、硕士和博士人才培养体系和学科层次。商务英语研究的独特性和学科交叉性、研究内容的包容性、研究方法的多样性已突破了外国语言学及应用语言学学科的限制，它融合了语言学、经济学、管理学、社会学、教育学等多个学科类别，具有鲜明的跨学科性质。我们这次编辑出版"商务话语与文化研究丛书"，就是一种交叉学科研究的尝试。在国内学界享有盛誉的科学出版社高瞻远瞩，大力扶持商务英语研究，欣然同意出版这套丛书。丛书为国内商务英语话语与文化研究者提供一个平台，较为系统地展示国内学者在商务话语与文化领域的研究新成果，供广大同行分享。

本丛书由商务话语与商务文化两类研究话题构成，首批著作主要涉及以下话题：多模态广告话语研究、英语商业广告语篇隐性连贯的识解机制研究、社会-认知视角下BELF交际中的元语用话语研究、中美上市公司年报MD&A中语言策略对比研究、转型期中国农村保险销售互动话语研究、商务会议冲突管理中的高效信息交换研究、中外会计文化对比研究、语言博弈论视角下的跨文化商务谈判互动研究、基于认知视角下的跨文化商务传媒语篇研究。本丛书的作者均为商务话语或商务文化研究领域的学者，相信本丛书的出版将进一步促进国内商务话语与文化研究的发展。

本丛书是一个开放的平台。鉴于商务英语研究的跨学科性质，我们希望本丛书以外国语言学及应用语言学为坚实的学科基础，旁及其他学科，并在中外比较研究中、在不同视角中、在学科交叉中、在观点碰撞中去从事学术研究。欢迎广大同仁提供自己的新作，和我们一起紧扣时代需要，探索和拓展新领域，发现和研究新问题，为国家社会经济文化建设服务。

本丛书的出版得到广东外语外贸大学高水平学科建设项目的大力支持，也得到科学出版社编辑们的鼎力相助，在此对他们表示衷心的感谢。本丛书的首批著作是近年来广东外语外贸大学商务英语学科领域的部分研究成果，"路漫漫其修远兮，吾将上下而求索"，我们深知学术求索之艰辛，丛书中可能存在有待商榷的学术问题，敬请专家学者给予批评指正。我们也热忱欢迎同行学者不吝赐稿，为本丛书的成长壮大添砖加瓦。我们愿与国内同行一起，为商务英语学科的发展壮大而努力。

郭桂杭
2018年6月于广东外语外贸大学

前　　言

  基于真实对话录音及访谈，本研究从社会文化的角度通过对处于转型期的中国农村保险销售过程中保险销售员（代理）与客户之间十个互动对话材料的分析，研究了中国农村保险销售会话的语篇特征，进而揭示了双方身份的建构和利用过程；与此同时，运用观察日志及后续访谈方法对分析结果做出验证。通过整合 R. Scollon 和 S. W. Scollon（2001）的语篇系统、Swales（1990）和 Bhatia（2005）的体裁分析及 Livari、Kinnula 和 Kuure 等（2014）的身份建构框架对保险代理及客户之间的会话进行分析。首先，通过对保险代理与客户之间的对话进行体裁分析得出其具体、普遍的语篇特征；然后针对保险代理及客户对话题的控制、管理来分析不同框架之间的调适过程。在农村的保险销售过程中，保险代理的销售主要是通过传统社会中熟人关系来开展销售活动并达到推销产品的目的，即通过对人际意义的利用来达到控制、利用对方之交际目的。

  具体而言，本研究详细分析、讨论了保险代理与客户沟通过程中关键的第一语步，即热身的分类及作用，借此探讨农村保险销售代理与客户之间沟通的内在运作机制；鉴于信用和信任在农村保险销售过程中的重要作用，在分析另一关键语步，即建立信用及信任时，本研究探讨了信任在转型期中国农村存在的情况和作用，这些可以从保险代理及客户的访谈中得到验证。

  与社会通常理解的关系相对，保险代理与传统企业员工的社会化过程不同，他们的社会化过程更强调自由、融洽、和谐和独立。一直以来，人们对保险及其销售的理解有些负面性。对保险代理的访谈反映了在保险销售这一促销型语篇中"关系（Guanxi）"对人际意义的利用是一致和相容的。

A Discourse Study of Insurance Sales Agent-Client Interactions in Transformational China's Rural Areas

对保险代理和客户之间的互动进行分析的目的是理解双方在社会变革过程中各自的角色。保险代理与潜在客户之间的关系存在模糊不清且充满冲突的特征。一方面，在保险销售过程中对融洽与和谐的强调反映了双方的朋友（熟人）关系；另一方面，因保险代理的利润和收入来源依赖于潜在客户决心购买保险的意愿，所以保险代理必须通过成功签单达到销售目的。但由于他们缺乏管理和控制潜在客户的权力、权威，因此他们必须经常启用不同身份及在不同话题之间频繁切换以进行冲突管理、建立合理性和达到控制之目的。在对三种会话类型——友情谈话、机构性谈话及任务导向型谈话——进行分析后，本研究展示了因不同身份的内在不相容性而引发的持续不断的对立、冲突和调适。

保险代理与潜在客户之间的互动揭示了为实现对关系的动态协商这一目的，他们通过展示、利用对关系的社会期望以及对面子需求的互动管理而实现对关系的动态协商。由此可以得知关系并不具备预先指定的特征或性质，而是极具协商性和操纵性的。

通过以上分析结果可以看出，身份是多种语篇系统相互作用的产物，我们的身份都是经过不断协商、调适的结果。在社会变革过程中，人的主观能动性不可忽视。只有通过对社会实践和人的能动性相对平衡的考量和分析才能对身份这一概念得出相对比较公允的理解。

汪谓超

2018 年 1 月 30 日

Contents

总序

前言

Chapter 1　Introduction ·· 1
　1.1　Background Briefing ··· 2
　1.2　From Linguistic Manifestation to Social Transformation ······················· 6
　　1.2.1　Introducing Insurance Sales Discourse ··· 7
　　1.2.2　Discourse System as the Overarching Framework ························ 8

Chapter 2　Mechanism of the Chinese Insurance Sales, Data Collection and Analysis ··· 10
　2.1　Language, Friendship and Persuasion in Insurance Studies ················· 10
　　2.1.1　Language and Friendship in Insurance Studies ···························· 13
　　2.1.2　Persuasion in Insurance Study ·· 16
　2.2　Theoretical Approaches ··· 19
　　2.2.1　Critical Discourse Analysis ··· 19
　　2.2.2　Identity Construction ··· 22
　2.3　Three Key Questions ··· 26
　2.4　Discourse System and Maxims of Friendship Engagement ················· 27
　　2.4.1　Discourse System ·· 29
　　2.4.2　Maxims of Friendship Engagement ··· 33
　　2.4.3　Confucianism and Utilitarianism ··· 35
　2.5　Business Communication and Culture ·· 41
　　2.5.1　The Chinese Business Culture ··· 42
　　2.5.2　*Guanxi* ·· 43
　　2.5.3　The Key Values of Facework and Politeness in the Chinese Society ··· 48
　2.6　Genre Analysis, Participation Framework and *Guanxi* ························ 52

  2.6.1 Genre Analysis: Communicative Purpose, Moves and Steps ········ 53
  2.6.2 Negotiation of Participation Framework through *Guanxi* ······ 55
  2.6.3 Frames, Footing and Contextualization Cues ···················· 59
  2.6.4 *Guanxi* and Topic ··· 61
 2.7 Data Collection and Data Analysis ·································· 64
  2.7.1 Data Collection and Transcription Conventions ··············· 65
  2.7.2 The Sampled Location ··· 67
 2.8 The Research Procedure ··· 69
 2.9 Analysis Procedure ·· 70
 2.10 Summary ··· 71

Chapter 3 Genre Analysis of the Insurance Sales Dialogues ······ 73
 3.1 Different Schools of Genre Analysis ································ 73
  3.1.1 Australian School ··· 73
  3.1.2 Narrative School ·· 74
  3.1.3 American School ··· 75
 3.2 Communicative Purposes ·· 79
 3.3 Moves and Steps ··· 81
  3.3.1 A Sample Analysis of Moves and Steps ·························· 82
  3.3.2 Detailed Analysis of Moves and Steps ··························· 89
  3.3.3 Introducing the Offer ·· 99
  3.3.4 Offering Incentives ··· 102
  3.3.5 Establishing Credentials ··· 103
  3.3.6 Other Moves ··· 106
 3.4 Summary ··· 108

Chapter 4 Topic Management in Insurance Sales Dialogues ······ 112
 4.1 Introduction ··· 112
 4.2 Topic Management ·· 112
 4.3 Phatic Talk and Its Functions ······································ 113
 4.4 Categories of Talk in Insurance Sales Interactions ·············· 116
  4.4.1 Three Types of Talk ·· 117
  4.4.2 Friendship Talk ·· 117
  4.4.3 Institutional Talk ·· 122
  4.4.4 Task-oriented Talk ·· 131

    4.5   Summary ·· 134

Chapter 5   Negotiation of Interactive Frames and Discourse Identities ····· 136
    5.1   Introduction ··· 136
    5.2   Negotiation of Frames and Discourse Identities in Different Types of Talks ·· 136
        5.2.1   The Context of the Interactions ·· 137
        5.2.2   Co-construction of Different Identities in Task-oriented Talk ··················· 138
    5.3   Summary ·· 161

Chapter 6   Epilogue and Discussions ·· 165
    6.1   Summary of Discursive Features, Frame Mediation and Discourse Identity ····· 165
    6.2   Discussions ··· 166
        6.2.1   Theoretical Framework, Analytical Framework, Analytical Concepts
                   and Methodology ··· 166
        6.2.2   A Socio-cultural Perspective ··· 170

References ··· 174

Appendixes ··· 193
    Appendix I   A Reconstructed Dialogue between an Insurance Sales
                        Agent and a Prospective Client ·· 193
    Appendix II   Questionnaire for Insurance Sales Agents ································· 201
    Appendix III   Questionnaire for Clients ·· 202
    Appendix IV   A Sample Answer to the Questionnaire from an Agent ········ 203
    Appendix V   A Sample Interview of an Agent ··· 207
    Appendix VI   A Sample Interview of a Client ·· 208
    Appendix VII Confession of an Agent ··· 209

Index ·· 213

Chapter 1

Introduction

The study aims to explore the dynamics of the insurance sales agent-client interactions in transformational China's rural areas from a socio-cultural perspective. By examining the discursive pattern in the actual dialogues made between the agent-client interactions and the agents' socialization process, it is my hope to depict the transforming nature of the modern Chinese rural society, where old and traditional value system has been, for a large part, demolished, while new value system is yet to be established.

In the actual dialogues between insurance sales agents and their prospective clients, various means are employed by the agents to achieve their goal of concluding business, i.e., making the sales happen. This study attempts to investigate, first of all, the generic pattern of the sales dialogue, i.e., moves and steps, and then the patterns of topic management and discourse identity.

By adopting moves and steps proposed by Swales (1990) and Bhatia (1993, 1997a), the study sets out to summarize the moves and steps of all the samples in insurance sales that are collected and transcribed.

On the one hand, I have tried to not only identify the obvious and surface messages, but also deconstruct the hidden ones in insurance sales discourse—comprised of a total corpus of 10 complete dialogues, with each dialogue lasting for about an hour between insurance sales agents and their prospective clients ranging from 2009 to 2013 in a county of a rural area in Central China (as a sample of the transformational China's rural areas). Due to the nature that the conversations are impromptu, especially on the part of the (prospective) clients, they are spontaneous in nature. The aim is to investigate what specific discursive patterns can be generalized, and thereby to discover whether there are any prominent discursive strategies intended for persuasion in terms of communicative purposes, moves and steps.

On the other hand, this study further investigates topic management by probing into the nature of agent-client interactions, since topic control and shifting can demonstrate the conscious attempt of both parties in controlling the initiative. To be more specific, the agent attempts to persuade the (prospective) clients to make the purchase by consciously and constantly shifting topics between casual talk and business talk, while the (prospective) client is attempting to maintain his/her autonomy by mostly controlling the topic in casual talk (if he/she intends to make the purchase, he/she would mostly ask more detailed questions about the specific terms of the insurance policy).

Furthermore, since insurance sales conducted in transformational China's rural areas are mostly concluded between the familiar people, the agents' role in the discourse and their relationship with the clients are ambiguous and conflicting. On the one hand, they are friends, and they are supposed to support each other and care for the interests of each other; on the other hand, the agents' income and well-being, to a large extent, are based on the clients' willingness to make the purchase. Thus how the complex identities are negotiated and contested is worthy of our attention.

All in all, the study is conducted from a socio-cultural perspective to examine the specific discursive patterns in agent-client interactions and to probe into the underlying operating mechanism in transformational China's rural areas.

1.1 Background Briefing

Like many socialist or former-socialist countries, China's shift from a centralized, planned economy and a state socialist system to a market-oriented, competitive one that centers on economic development has blurred the boundaries of the categories that once recognized people's daily lives. The past few decades (from the 1980s to 2010s) have witnessed tremendous social, cultural and ideological changes in China ever since the introduction and initiation of reform and opening-up policy. Ideology of class struggle was replaced by the idea of the Four Modernizations, namely, modernization of industry, agriculture, national defense and science and technology, in which the emphasis and priority lie in economic development instead of ideology. Meanwhile, in China's rural areas, with the introduction and initiation of the household contract responsibility system in 1979, tremendous impetus had been provided to China's rural economy and the local peasants' enthusiasm had been greatly boosted in developing agricultural produce. Consequently the efficiency of agriculture had been enormously increased, while the increased efficiency in turn had taken the society at large forward to an extent far beyond the imagination of both the policy makers and the ordinary people (Cao and Chen, 1997).

Take insurance for example, China, as the most populous country in the world, possesses the world's largest potential market for insurance, which has experienced rapid expansion over the past decades, with annual life-insurance premiums growing from 10 billion US dollars in 1999 to 46 billion US dollars in 2006 (Zhang and Wang, 2016). Given this steadily increasing demand, some major trends have encouraged the boom of the industry. To begin with, with China's entry into the WTO, the Chinese government lowered its entry barriers to foreign insurance companies under the WTO framework, allowing them to set up joint venture insurance firms in China; and domestic insurance companies strengthened themselves enormously through various market mechanisms such as IPOs (Initial Public Offerings). For instance, China Life Insurance (Group) Company became the second largest insurance company in the world in terms of market capitalization[①] even though the company's value has kept declining since

---

[①] http://article.haoxiana.com/13129.html, accessed on July 21, 2018.

the stock market peak of 2008. The rapid expansion of the insurance industry cannot separate itself from its development in China's rural areas, with the soaring numbers of insurance agents (both part-time and full-time ones). Thus the idea of insurance and the market has been gradually explored into. The total sales of insurance through agents in 2011 reached RMB 1,200 billion yuan, accounting for 86% of the total insurance sales, which indicates the emerging importance of insurance agents as major sales channel[①]. According to *China's Insurance Agent Market Report 2011*, up until the end of 2011, there are in total 2,554 professional insurance agencies in China, with a registered capital of RMB 11 billion yuan, a total asset value of RMB 17 billion yuan, 190,000 agency institutions, and 3.35 million insurance agents. However, given the lower level of development of education level in the rural areas, even with the enormous profit earned by the insurance companies and the agents, an interesting question emerges: At the micro-level and language level, how do agents persuade their prospective clients during the process in current China's socio-cultural context? What's more, for both clients and agents, they confront with a lot of struggles and criticisms in their business dealings and later claims. More specifically, for the agents, they need to face the complexity of concluding business through *Guanxi* (relationship in Chinese pinyin, 关系). While for the clients, they need to face the later claims or conflicts with much stricter conditions and clauses in insurance policies. Since in current China's rural areas, the old system of familiarity has been compromised, and new contractual system is yet to be established[②].

Facing such tremendous economic, social and cultural changes, scholars

---

① *China's Insurance Agent Market Report 2011*, China Insurance Regulatory Commission, issued on July 18, 2012. (《中国保险中介市场报告(2011)》保监会 2012 年 7 月 18 日发布. http://www.chinairn.com/news/20120719/412256.html, accessed on July 8, 2013)

② In most China's rural areas, the insurance agents try to sell insurance policies through their relationship networks (*Guanxi*, or the familiar people, relatives, friends, etc.). It has been observed that most of the clients have little or even no clear understanding about insurance conditions and clauses. Due to their trust in the agents, they sometimes follow blindly the recommendations of the agents, which may create problems when it comes to disputes for later payment or even claims.

from various disciplines, from economics to political science, from sociology to cultural studies, have utilized their expertise in their own respective areas to capture and describe such a transformation over the past several decades. The economists generally agree that China has shifted from a planned, centralized economy to a more market-oriented economy, with the privatization of public ownerships (the state-ownership and the collective ownership) shifted into privately owned or family contractual relationships (Wang, 2013; Pei, 2014). Meanwhile, Chinese sociologists, based on their empirical social investigation, describe, summarize and classify Chinese society into different social strata (Lu, 2002; Sun, 2001). As observed by a few sociologists (Cao and Chen, 1997; Gong, 2001; Lu, 2002), the general tendency of the Chinese society is the transformation from a *Danwei*① society to a society which centers more on individual interest.

Moreover, such political scientists as Liu (1999) and Sun (2001) argued about the socio-political changes in China as a transformation from power centralization to democracy, manifested by a decentralization of power from the central government to the local governments and to the individual enterprises, and by an enforcement of rule of law.

Despite the extensive research efforts into the macro-level to unveil the changing socio-political structures in economics, sociology and political sciences, very few studies (except for Gu, 2001; Ouyang, 2004) have attempted to address this issue from the micro-level and from the discourse analysis perspective. Discourse analysis upholds a strong constructivist epistemology and the world cannot be known separately from discourse (Philips and Hardy, 2002: 6; Wang, 2000: 10). Discourse analysis provides hard and empirical evidences of

---

① *Danwei*: Work unit or *Danwei* (in Chinese: 单位) is the name given to a place of employment in the People's Republic of China (PRC). Prior to the economic reform in the 1980s, a work unit acted as the first step of a multi-tiered hierarchy linking each individual with the central Communist Party infrastructure. Work units were the principal method of implementing party policy. Besides, workers were bound to their work units for life. Each *Danwei* created its own housing, kindergarten, school, clinic, shop, services, etc.

witnessing social and ideological changes. As Fairclough (1995) pointed out: "texts are sensitive indicators of socio-cultural processes and changes and it is important to highlight the role of texts in making history"; such a view was echoed by Watson (2008), who held that even the smallest utterance or mundane piece of dialogue can be linked back to the wider culture, social structure and processes of the society in which it takes place. Therefore, discourse analysis can serve as an important complement to the existing macro-sociological studies and make contributions to social research. Meanwhile, Atkinson and Delamont (2006: 169) held that "'truth' is not a property to be treated as an issue in the quality-control of information".

1.2 From Linguistic Manifestation to Social Transformation

It is within this background that the present study is conducted, and is expected to make contributions to the research of linguistic manifestation to social transformation from a novel perspective. China's changing ideologies underpin its socio-cultural transformations, especially the commercial sales sector ever since Deng Xiaoping's introduction and initiation of reform and opening-up policy that sets economic development at the top priority. In this tide of rapid development, the process of industrial advancement demands a large workforce for construction and service sectors, which in turn makes possible the emergence of a new group of people—migrant workers, who consequently drive social changes in the rural areas. All these changing dynamics are the top-down driving forces for and reflected in the changes at the immediate institutional level of social practices of commercial organizations (e.g., the insurance companies) and further at the micro-level of discursive practices of the sales agents and the prospective clients (e.g., the sales interactions).

Multiple discourses co-exist in present transformational China, where old value systems are at interplay with new ones (from the 1980s to the 2010s). Chinese insurance sales agents and clients are making their own ways of being socialized into members of these discourse communities. By adopting R. Scollon and S. W. Scollon's (2000) broad concept of discourse system as the general theoretical framework and using Goffman's (1981) concept of "footing" as the analytical tool, this study will be an empirical attempt at a better understanding of how these competing discourses are discursively constructed and mediated in the communication between the agents and prospective clients. In other words, the study attempts to address the actual dialogues between the insurance sales agents and their (prospective) clients in the rural areas in China from the perspective of discourse analysis. By doing so, the underlying conflicting and ambiguous identities that insurance sales agents display in their interaction with their (prospective) clients can be surfaced and generalized; furthermore, how their multiple identities are employed or even manipulated to achieve their economic goals can be presented. A particular focus has been placed on the trust building practices employed by insurance sales agents in order to realize the conclusion of business, i.e., successful sales. The interview data of both the insurance sales agents and the (prospective) clients will be used for the purpose of triangulation. Moreover, by detailed description and analysis of the sales interactions between the agents and the (prospective) clients, follow-up interviews and the socio-cultural contexts, it is hopeful that we can uncover the patterns of the interactions, clients' attitudes towards such ways of insurance sales in rural areas, and the features of such sales interactions. Thus the underlying ideological changes along with the general social transformation can be found and unveiled. The post-modernist concern of commodification of self and penetration of commercial life into our personal and private life will be addressed as well.

1.2.1 Introducing Insurance Sales Discourse

Insurance sales discourse is an interesting and important arena for the analysis.

First of all, sales interactions are initiated and produced by the insurance sales agents and their prospective clients in authentic settings. Their interactions can reflect the patterns of interaction and the underlying ideologies in China's rural areas, as already argued above in the introduction. Therefore, it is highly necessary to analyze the authentic data within the framework from a new perspective. Meanwhile, most of the existing literature is found to be limited to either the macro-level discussion on ideological transformations or social strata, or to the micro-level of improving sales effectiveness, practices, policies, and ethics. There are very few linguists who have conducted their studies on audio-recorded data of agent-client interactions. To the best of my knowledge, the attempt to unify micro- and macro-approaches to sales interactions is still scarce.

Secondly, since the introduction of the insurance sales agent system, the business scope and revenue have been greatly expanded and the sales of insurance policies have reached even the most remote rural areas. Moreover, the Chinese insurance industry has developed itself from almost non-existence to a multi-billion dollar business in the past decades, and insurance sales discourse can be taken as a new platform in China, through which the dynamic changes in the rural areas of Chinese society can be examined.

Thirdly, insurance discourse is chosen for a practical concern. The accessibility of data can be guaranteed. I was born and raised in the rural area, which enabled me to have more in-depth understanding of the local context and provide interpretation and explanation from an insider's point of view. What's more, since my elder sister is an insurance sales agent, it also makes possible not only the accessibility to the recordings of real sales interactions, but also the reliability and convenience of the follow-up interviews.

1.2.2 Discourse System as the Overarching Framework

Before establishing their argument of the concept of discourse system, R. Scollon and S. W. Scollon (2001) first discussed the lack of uniformity in the use of the word *discourse* among those who study discourse. They identified four groups of discourse analysts. The first group of analysts (Drew and Heritage, 1992a; Schiffrin, Tannen and Hamilton, 2001) were traditional conversation analysts, who took the logical relations among sentences in texts or conversations as their main focus. The second group of analysts (van Dijk, 2006) took a more cognitive perspective by focusing more on the process of interpretation people use in understanding discourses. The third group (Martin, 1999) took a historical approach with their focus on discourses which took place over many years or across many societies, such as the discourse of mass media (e.g. newspapers) or the discourse of law. The fourth group (Fairclough, 2001; Wodak, 2001) more focused on the socio-political domination; they set the trend to study the issues of social change, power abuse, ideological imposition, and social injustice by critically analyzing language as social action. The current study basically follows the fourth group of analysts, but adopts a less radical approach, attempting to strike a balance between the macro- and micro-perspective.

Since R. Scollon and S. W. Scollon's interest is on intercultural communication among members of different groups (or, discourse systems, as so conceptualized), they indigenously bring in ideas, terms, and methods from different schools of discourse analysis to try to create a broader framework for the analysis of intercultural communication. Grounded in years' ethnographic studies on professional communication, their framework can be widely and handily applied beyond intercultural contexts to various sites where communication is the core of social actions and practices. R. Scollon and S. W. Scollon's overarching framework of discourse system with four interdependent components (namely ideology, socialization, face system and forms of discourse), opens up possibilities for an integrated macro- and micro-analysis of the agent-(prospective) client communication in insurance sales discourse.

Chapter 2

Mechanism of the Chinese Insurance Sales, Data Collection and Analysis

The overall objective of the present study, qualitative in nature, is to explore the dynamic nature of insurance sales agent-client communication in transformational China's rural areas. This is to be done within the broad, overarching discourse system conceptual framework. This study draws on two research orientations—empirical orientation and discourse analytic orientation, based on qualitative studies and numerical evidence. It is discourse analytic because it adopts a discourse analytic approach. This chapter will raise the key questions and explicate the way how I am going to address the key questions to unveil the dynamic nature of insurance sales agent-client interactions.

2.1 Language, Friendship and Persuasion in Insurance Studies

Insurance is a core institution of a society increasingly organized around managing risk. As Beck (1992) argued, risk society was also an individual society. The utilization of insurance sales agents' identity to achieve economic goals interacts with key contemporary social tendencies: the responsibilization of the individual consumers, the erosion of the social safety net, fragmentation, individualism, the attenuation of family ties, the growth of a "flexible" labor force, and the downloading of regulatory responsibility from the government.

Chapter 2 Mechanism of the Chinese Insurance Sales, Data Collection and Analysis

Until recently, the hidden world of insurance has received surprisingly little attention from social scientists (Strange, 1996: 122). Most academic research on insurance has been done by economists and researchers in business and finance. However, driven in part by broader theoretical interest in risk, insurance studies have recently emerged as a blossoming field for other researchers, especially in sociology, socio-legal studies and criminology (Baker and Simon, 2002; Ericson and Doyle, 2003, 2004a, 2004b, 2004c).

In China, researches on insurance are mostly done by economists and researchers in business and finance, their primary interest is to investigate the current situations in China's insurance industry and offer certain suggestions to improve the efficiency and profitability of the insurance institutions from political, economic and marketing perspectives (Shen, 2009; Zhu, 2009; Hu and Wang, 2009; Shu and Li, 2006; Yuan, 2008; Guo, 2009; Li, 2008; Ding, 2008; Cao, 2009; Xu, 2009; Wang and Li, 2009; Liu and Xie, 2009). For example, such similar interests in this area also emerge as Hu and Wang (2009) adopt a sociological perspective, put insurance into social, economic and cultural contexts, and then study the inter-relationship among insurance and the social, economic and cultural contexts, such as the interaction between the insurance and many other social, economic and cultural factors. However, such studies are still rather on the macro-aspect and lack of empirical evidence, which gives rise to the present study to investigate the micro-aspect of insurance sales interactions between the insurance sales agents and the (prospective) clients with empirical data. Moreover, there are several problems. Firstly, their researches seem rather general and adopt a top-down approach. Secondly, most of their researches are based on academic reasoning and previous literature, and very few offer empirical evidence, which might create a problem in its convincing effect. Thirdly, the stance they take is mostly on behalf of the organizations. Thus they neglect the other side, that is, the agents in action and their clients. They take them as strictly passive recipients of the actions, which might not be exactly the case in reality. Due to the lack of data or difficulty in accessibility to the interactions between the agents and their (prospective) clients, there have not been any research concerning insurance sales based on empirical recorded data from the perspective of discourse study, and the present research intends to fill this gap.

As already argued in Chapter 1, modern insurance sales through agents in rural areas can offer an excellent platform for investigating the above phenomenon, since it is exactly where interpersonal and economic interests collide with each other.

In order to better understand this relatively new platform, a general introduction of the history, current situation, and background of insurance system is quite necessary. Insurance sales agent system was first introduced into China's insurance market in 1986, since then, the insurance sales agent system has been undergoing rapid development, especially after the introduction of AIA's (American Insurance Association's) marketing system in 1992. Then the insurance agent system has permeated almost every walk of life in China. Under the insurance marketing system, the insurance sales agents act as the chain that bridges the insurance company and the insured, they play very important roles in bridging the gap between supply and demand and expanding insurance business, and meanwhile, they become the major force in the insurance sales volume, especially in the sales of life insurance. According to statistics, in 2006, the insurance revenue amounted to RMB 564.144 billion yuan, increased by 14.4% than that of the previous year, while in 2007, 45.4% of the premium income of the Chinese insurance industry was realized through the sales of these agents. The total number of agents increased from 1.468 million in the end of 2006 to 2.015 million in the end of 2007 (Cao, 2009).

Of course, many other relative factors contribute to the rapid growth of insurance business in China. Nevertheless, the introduction of the insurance sales agent system must have played an important role during this process, especially in the rural areas. Due to the fact that in China's rural areas, the (prospective) clients usually live away from cities or counties, and the physical distance and accessibility of information make it virtually impossible or too costly for insurance companies to reach the (prospective) clients in the remote areas such as villages. However, with the insurance sales agents (mostly part-time agents) working as intermediary between the insurance companies and the clients, the gap can be bridged, and vast potential market can be explored into.

Insurance sales through agents are different from traditional marketing strategies in that insurance policies are sold not directly from the insurance companies but via the agents, and this may create one more intermediary during the selling process. However, it greatly expanded the coverage, possibility and credibility of insurance sales due to the fact that it is in the Chinese business context. Most of the time business is built on trust but not on law (Fang, 1999). Good interpersonal relationship is the foundation of trust. Generally speaking, in China's rural insurance sales practice, the agents promote the policies to their social network, which includes friends, relatives, colleagues, acquaintances, and virtually anyone they know. The agents live on commission based on their sales performance (volume), and usually the agents are locally respected people or who have extensive connections among the local residents or enjoy social resources in the local settings. As in the current study, the participant agents are in the following lines of work: kindergarten teacher, former bank clerk of a state-owned bank in the local area, wife to the vice president of a local middle school, wife to the local village head, or a locally respected figure due to his kindness to his fellow peasants in the village. Nonetheless, they share one thing in common: They either have or have access to positions that are considered prestigious and respected, or are simply trusted or respected in the local area. As Drew and Heritage (1992a: 1-65) claimed, interaction was a dynamic process and language was a crucial resource in managing social relations at work. Thus two interesting questions emerge: How does the interaction between an agent and a client serve to the realization of sales? How is language employed to achieve this goal?

2.1.1 Language and Friendship in Insurance Studies

Language is an inherently social phenomenon. Language is for communication, and meaning is jointly constructed by the participants. Sociological approaches to studying discourse, such as ethnography of speaking (Gumperz and Hymes, 1972; Hymes, 1972; Turner 1974; Sacks, 1972; Saville-Troike, 1982; Schegloff, 1972; Gumperz, 1982), are concerned with understanding the use of language in the social contexts of everyday life, "Communities differ significantly in ways of speaking, in patterns of repertoire and switching, in the roles and meanings of speech. They indicate differences with regard to beliefs, values, reference groups, norms and the like, as these enter into the ongoing system of language use." (Hymes, 1972: 42)

The closeness of friendship is linguistically expressed in various ways, of which the most notable is the address forms, which have been extensively studied, for example, when studying children conflicts, and when analyzing the skills and complexity of young children's talk, Church (2009) identified that using address forms (stating another child's name in the utterance) serves to align or dis-align with other speakers. Tannen (2005: 40-41) made a study of the ways of how language can be used as an indicator of mature friendship. According to her, in terms of topic management, pacing, narrative strategies and expressive para-linguistics, they all function as important indicators of friendship, as illustrated in Table 2.1.

Table 2.1 Language as Indicators of Mature Friendship

Linguistic device	Feature
Topic	A: prefer personal topics B: shift topics abruptly C: introduce topics without hesitation D: persist (If a new topic is not immediately picked up, reintroduce it, repeatedly if necessary.)
Pacing	A: faster rate of speech B: faster turn taking C: avoiding inter-turn pauses (Silence shows lack of rapport.) D: cooperative overlap E: participatory listenership
Narrative strategies	A: tell more stories B: tell stories in rounds C: prefer internal evaluation (i.e., the point of a story is dramatized rather than lexicalized)

Chapter 2 Mechanism of the Chinese Insurance Sales, Data Collection and Analysis

Continued

Linguistic device	Feature
Expressive paralinguistics	A: expressive phonology B: marked pitch and amplitude shifts C: marked voice quality D: strategic within-turn pauses

All the above features can be understood as expressing involvement, or rapport. Therefore, on the one hand, Tannen referred to the speakers who use them as exhibiting a high-involvement style. On the other hand, other speakers who use strategies that expressed (or put the signaling load on) the need not to impose. Thus, she refers to these speakers as using a high-considerateness style.

To be more specific, in a mature friendship, in terms of topic, there is a preference for personal topics, more abrupt topic shifts, ability to introduce topics without hesitation, and persistence or freedom to reintroduce new topics if not picked up immediately; in terms of pacing, there is faster rate of speech, faster turn-taking, pause avoidance, cooperative overlap, and participatory listenership; in terms of narrative strategies, there are more stories told in rounds and dramatizing the point of stories; in terms of expressive paralinguistics, there are more expressive phonology, marked pitch and amplitude shifts, marked voice quality, and strategic within-turn pauses. Besides identifying the "personal content" of the talk, the above conversational features help identify what can be classified as the "personal talk". However, ever since her study was completed, very little had been done to prove or refute her claims. Another thing that should be noted is that her study was conducted in the American middle-class context; different linguistic patterns of signaling friendship may be employed across different cultures such as that among friends in China's rural areas. This also gives rise to the present research to investigate the patterns of insurance sales interactions in the present transformational China's rural areas in terms of topic management and discourse identities.

2.1.2 Persuasion in Insurance Studies

The insurance sales interaction is the process of the realization of persuasion process, in other words, to make the sales through discourse. The following will review and relocate previous studies on persuasion and attempt to integrate them into the current study.

1. Classical view on persuasion and its current definition

Persuasion has attracted persistent attention over the years, and with great philosophers in ancient Greece such as Aristotle as the forerunners it had profound influence over the studies that followed.

In his remarkable book *Rhetoric*, Aristotle claimed that rhetoric was the art of discovering the available means of persuasion. He outlined three basic means of persuasion, namely, ethos (ethical appeal), pathos (emotional appeal) and logos (logical appeal) (Braet, 1992). He also claimed that common ground existing between persuader and persuadee made persuasion more effective. Similarly, the Roman orator Cicero identified five elements of persuasive speaking. Another Roman theorist, Quintilian, added that a good persuader had to be a "good man" as well as a good speaker (Russell, 2001).

Aristotle's three means contributing to persuasion have laid solid foundation for further research on persuasion. Even the latest models concerning persuasion, for example, the elaboration likelihood model (hereinafter as ELM), still takes in Aristotle's insights on ethos and develops it into source credibility, an important variable in persuasion. Nevertheless, Aristotle's persuasion means mainly focus on the source of the message and persuaders' skills, while leaving the other side, the persuadees, unattended. Following Aristotle, numerous studies have been conducted concerning persuasion and consequently, there emerge a variety of definitions for persuasion. Some (Aristotle, Cicero and Qunitilian, see Borchers, 2002: 29-34) focused on the speaker and persuasion skills, some others (Simons, 1986; Bettinghaus and Cody, 1987; Larson, 2001) came to realize the importance of the interaction between the speaker and the recipient, and still others (Gass and Seiter, 2007; Du, 2008) paid attention to the role of context in persuasion. Thus a working definition will be proposed on the basis of previous researches, especially that of Gass and Seiter (2007) as follows.

> *Persuasion is a reciprocal and interactive communicative activity where beliefs, attitudes, intentions, motivations, and/or behaviors are intended to be created, reinforced, modified, or extinguished through interaction within the constraints of the persuasion context.*

There are some important features of this working definition. First of all, it holds that persuasion is a two-way, reciprocal and interactive communicative activity, where participants can influence each other, not limited as a one-way communication. Secondly, it accounts intention to influence others as persuasion, instead of the final result or realization of persuasion, this is different from previous definitions in that they take the successful change of attitudes as the ultimate defining feature. To put it bluntly, as long as there is a persuasive intention which has been revealed through interaction, it can be counted as persuasion. In other words, the emphasis is on the act and the process of persuasion instead of the final result. Thirdly, the persuasion context is dynamic, ongoing and many aspects are subject to negotiation, and the context is composed of various factors.

In modern insurance sales encounters, process is manifested in the interactions between the agent and the prospective clients. In such encounters, the agent's credibility is closely related to his/her social identities, while such identities are subject to the negotiation between the agent and the prospective clients.

2. Cognitive perspective

van Dijk (2006), from the cognitive perspective, deemed persuasion as a short-term memory behavior, which made people's behavior more impulsive instead of evaluating more carefully. This can be achieved through multiple means such as the complexity of terms and expressions, the difficulty in understanding the terms and conditions involved and contract language and detailed elaboration of the benefits while downplaying or even ignoring the problems. The overall strategy of positive self-representation is found typical in various persuasion situations. He further proposed the application of the strategy to the structure of many discourse levels.

At the level of the overall interaction strategies, there are such two aspects as positive self-presentation and negative other-presentation. In other words, macro speech act implying our "good" acts and their "bad" acts, e.g., accusation, defence. At the level of semantic macro-structures, it is topic selection, to be more specific, (de-)emphasize negative/positive topics about us/them. Moreover, at the level of discourse structure, van Dijk (2006: 376) generalized the following aspects.

(1) Emphasize the position, power, authority or moral superiority of the speaker(s) or their sources, and, where relevant, the inferior position, lack of knowledge, etc. of the recipients.

(2) Focus on the (new) beliefs that the manipulator wants the recipients to accept as knowledge, as well as on the arguments, proofs, etc. that make such beliefs more acceptable.

(3) Discredit alternative (dissident, etc.) sources and beliefs.

(4) Appeal to the relevant ideologies, attitudes and emotions of the recipients.

van Dijk concluded that the overall strategy of manipulative discourse was to discursively focus on those cognitive and social characteristics of the recipients that made them more vulnerable and less resistant to manipulation or persuasion, and that made them credulous or willing victims to accept beliefs and do things they otherwise would not do.

In the sample textual analysis followed, van Dijk analyzed the UK's former Prime Minister Tony Blair's speech in March 2003 which legitimated his government's decision. Although the results were convincing, the analysis seemed to be rather general, even though van Dijk himself admitted that many more detailed analyses at discursive, cognitive and social aspects were expected. The present study attempts to carry out a more detailed analysis from several different perspectives to address the same interaction in an attempt to unveil and generalize the patterns of insurance sales interactions in the transformational China's rural areas. However, in order to make the analysis more localized and closer or truer to the local context, it is imperative to consider some distinctive features or contexts specifically in China, that is, face, rapport and *Guanxi*.

2.2　Theoretical Approaches

The following reviews the critical discourse analysis (CDA) approach to language and the identity construction.

2.2.1　Critical Discourse Analysis

CDA is an interdisciplinary approach to the study of discourse that views language as a form of social practice and focuses on the ways social and political domination are reproduced in text and talk (Fairclough, 1995). CDA also refers to the critical study of language developed within "Western Marxism". Western Marxism attaches great importance to cultural dimensions of a society, and argues that capitalist social relations are established and maintained or reproduced by and large in culture (and ideology), not just the economic foundation.

　　CDA views discourse as a form of "social practice" (Fairclough, 1989; Fairclough and Wodak, 1997; Wodak, 2001), which implies a dialectical relationship between a discursive event and the institutions/social structures at large which frame the discursive event. To put it another way, discourse is socially constructed as well as socially shaped. The primary aim of CDA is to decipher the naturalized ideologies underlying discourses and uncover power and inequality. It centers around such key concepts as "critical", "power" and "ideology". However, there are also inadequacies in CDA. First of all, most of the CDA research focuses on institutional discourses (e.g., hospital, media, reports, etc.) instead of more open, interactive and mediated ones; moreover, their research relies too heavily on text for understanding social changes, which might pose a threat of neglecting many other important contextual factors. As Chouliaraki and Fairclough (1999: 16) put it, "We see CDA as bringing a variety of theories into dialogue, especially social theories on the one hand and linguistic theories on the other, so that its theory is a shifting synthesis of other theories, though what it itself theorizes in particular is the mediation between the social and the linguistic…"

Similarly, Shi (2005) viewed discourse as "linguistic communication in social, cultural, historical and political contexts" (Shi, 2005: 1). He held that discourse was considered as neither merely text and talk reducible to linguistic forms, nor just a unit of meaning independent of the forms of realization. Rather, it is conceived as construction of meaning—representing and acting upon reality—through linguistic means in concrete situations. Thus, discourse is a unity of both form and meaning. In such a vein, linguistic representation (linguistic forms), meaning, reality (social practice) are closely related to act as a whole: social reality is reflected by linguistic representation and by construction of meaning. Therefore, by analyzing linguistic forms and other forms of representation, the particular socio-cultural context can be revealed as well.

Fairclough (1989) took up the concepts of commodification and promotionalization and applied them to discursive practices in a variety of contexts. He found that British universities' use of pamphlets and prospectus had come to resemble those of purely commercial activities. According to Fairclough, such practices had serious consequences. First of all, with the decline of meaning, there comes a loss of instrumental value; secondly, personal interaction and promotional communication are easily confused (Fairclough, 1995). People tend to imitate the promotional materials they have been exposed to in their interactions with friends, relatives, and even their families. Such view is also echoed by Bhatia, from genre analysis perspective, who argued there was a tendency of "invasion of territorial integrity" or "mixing and embedding genres" or "colonization", which resulted in the colonization of academic, professional and institutionalized genres (Bhatia, 1995, 1997b, 2005).

Such a view was echoed by other scholars. Urry (1987) found that in many countries there had been an upsurge in the extension of the market to new areas of social life: sectors such as education, health care and the arts had been required to restructure and re-conceptualize their activities as the production and marketing of commodities for consumers. Based on that, Fairclough argued that these changes had profoundly affected the activities, social relations, and social and professional identities of people working in such sectors. A major part of their impact comprises changes in discourse practices, that is, changes in language (Fairclough, 1992).

In insurance sales agents' sales interactions, it seems the activities of the agents are commodifying and commercializing personal relationships since they are utilizing their connections for commercial purposes, which makes it even more confusing to distinguish what is private and what is commercial, what is personal and what is promotional. It seems they are intertwined to achieve the purpose of insurance sales.

The second problem with CDA is that it overlooks the ability of individuals to extricate themselves from the commercial activities. In most CDA studies, individuals tend to be treated as passive recipients of what they are exposed to, and thus they ignore the other side of the interaction, reception or resistance. Even though Martin (1999) argued for a positive discourse, focusing on emancipatory discourses, the individuals or general public were still treated as passive recipients. In this way, the dynamic nature of discourse was overlooked, which left a gap for further future research in this regard.

The third problem with CDA is that CDA not only takes texts as the focal point of analysis for criticism of modern society, but also it doesn't offer productive or constructive solutions for alternative forms of social organizations or social subjects. Even Fairclough (2003: 14-15) himself admitted: "… we should not assume that no analysis of a text can tell us all there is to be said about it—there is no such thing as a complete and definitive analysis of a text... Textual analysis is also inevitably selective: In any analysis, we choose to ask certain questions about social events and texts, and no other possible questions... There is no such thing as an 'objective' analysis of a text, if by that we mean an analysis which simply describes what is 'there' in the text without being 'biased' by the 'subjectivity' of the analyst." It is noticed that social studies focus mostly on social problems by adopting social investigation or ethnographic study, while linguistic study is obsessed with its micro fine analysis of each segment of the speech. Given the inevitable trend in interdisciplinary study, it is imperative to utilize the advantages of each discipline while try to better unleash their advantages by using social concepts to investigate various discourses.

2.2.2 Identity Construction

Identity has been a central concept in various intellectual disciplines, such as sociolinguistics, social psychology and communication studies. The essentialists' view of identity has initially dominated the research circle. They held that social reality and identities were pre-determined and static entities which were like overcoats people wear and change. This view prevailed in traditional works in sociolinguistics, such as Labov (1966, 1969) who focused on the language variations across different identities, such as race and gender. Realism is another influential perspective, which considers identity as a direct perception of reality and objectivity. For example, Putnam (1981) saw the self as an actor in the world and sought to explain the self as a functional being who is present to self, the world and the others. However, both essentialism and realism's views of identity have been heavily criticized for their ignoring the dynamic and interactional nature of identities which are far from being static and stable. Thus it gives rise to the social constructionist view, in which identities are not the direct perceptions of the reality out there, nor the reflections of the environment, but the dynamic products of social interactions. "It is by now a truism... that identities are neither fixed nor categorical properties residing in people's minds" (Androutsopoulos and Georgakopoulou, 2003: 1). This has led to viewing identity as "a process" (de Fina, Schiffrin & Bamberg, 2006: 2) that is discursively constructed over and over again in particular interactions, which implies that one cannot at all view an identity as typical of a person, but instead "individuals have multiple identities" (Verschueren, 2008: 26) because of their evolving and contextually bound nature. In this study, identity is viewed as discursively constructed and negotiated by the interactants (agent and prospect). Identity is considered rather from a social constructionist perspective in which it is locally and discursively constructed within a particular social practice. Consequently, identity is not only considered to be fluid, but it is also resolutely social and this results in the construction of "a number of contextual selves" (Wetherell and Maybin, 1996: 223).

The phenomenon of multiple and overlapping identities has been one of the most important concerns in the social constructionist paradigm (Hage and Powers, 1992). The interactions and conflicts between them have aroused concern for researchers across different fields. Among which, class, race and gender are the most thoroughly researched. This still leaves a gap of research to be filled in order to better understand the social identities we construct in our daily lives. To be more specific, the conflict of our *Guanxi* and professional/ institutional identities. As argued by Drew and Heritage (1992a), institutionality of an interaction was not determined by its setting, but by the work activities in which the participants were engaged, which supports the idea that conflict exists in our professional/institutional identities and interpersonal identities with our relatives, friends and acquaintances at any time and at any place.

We, as social beings, need friends or people who are close to us and can share feelings of trust and goodwill for one another. One important feature of such interactions is that it is generally economic interest-free and goal-free; however, this goal may come into conflict with another situation: that we want to maximize our economic benefits and minimize costs. Therefore, achieving a better understanding of our interpersonal and institutional/economic conflicts will prove quite useful, and insurance sales communication in China's rural areas offers an excellent arena for such an enquiry. More specifically, it is my hope to ascertain the underlying operation mechanism among rural residents in transformational China's rural areas. Since insurance is a relatively new form of business in China and conveys a strong Western ideology, while it has been introduced to China's rural areas, it definitely will have conflicts with local Chinese ideology (being oral agreement, trust of the familiars, word of mouth, respect for hierarchies, family, etc.). Simply put, insurance as a form of business brings changes to China's rural areas, has impact on the local society and transforms the local society. In 1998, the State Council established the Ministry of Labour and Social Security to centralize the management of the social security fund. The management of pension also changed from a pay-as-you-go program under the planned economy to a partially funded scheme under the socialist market economy. The Sixth Plenum of the 16th CPC Central Committee in 2006 and the 17th CPC Central Committee in 2007 suggested building a comprehensive social security system covering both urban and rural residents which provides basic pension insurance, basic health care, and minimum living standard. First, the state promoted enterprises, administrative organs, and service organizations to experiment with basic old-age pension reform, while the state attempted to build a rural old-age pension system. 218 million Chinese, only 29% of the total 764 million employed workers, were covered by the existing pension system (Li, 2010: 467). Thus, it leaves a rather large uncovered population, who, nonetheless, would seek for other forms of coverage to ensure their well-being while they are still capable of earning, which gives rise to the booming development of commercial insurance in China's rural areas. Second, the state attempted to build three national health insurance programs for workers, urban residents, and rural residents respectively. To be more specific, China introduced a national basic health insurance program for workers in 1998, a new type of rural cooperative medical scheme① in 2003, and basic health care insurance for urban residents in 2007. The goal of the three programs is to cover all of the Chinese population by 2010. Third, the state will improve the Minimum Living Standard Guarantee System (MLSGS) and raise standards of program benefits. MLSGS have already been established in most urban areas, and in 2007 MLSGS were built in some rural areas (Li, 2010: 467).

The participants of the basic pension insurance, basic health care insurance, unemployment insurance, occupational accident insurance, and childbirth insurance were RMB 196.76 million, RMB 188.96 million, RMB 114.73 million, RMB 115.3 million and RMB 73.27 million in September 2007, respectively. Compared to December 2006, these numbers increased by 4.6%, 16.7%, 2.5%, 10.9% and 11.8%, respectively. Meanwhile, local governments actively experimented with social security programs exclusive to migrant workers, who are major force in urban construction and various service areas. Ru, Lu and Li (2008: 5) found that at the end of September 2007, 34.47 million and 29.03 million migrant workers were covered by occupational accident insurance and basic health care insurance, with 26.4% and 18.5% increases from 2006 correspondingly. The coverage of MLSGS extended steadily in both rural and urban areas. The MLSGS covered 22.377 million of urban residents, one million more than the number in the previous year, while MLSGS covered 27.813 million of rural residents, 155.92 million more than the number in the previous year.

It is a crucial decision in the development of social policy that a social security system covering both rural and urban areas is created. This reform will end the century's long historic pattern of Chinese peasants living without social security.

---

① New Rural Cooperative Medical Scheme（NRCMS, 新型农村合作医疗制度）: It was established to overhaul the healthcare system, particularly intended to make it more affordable for the rural poor. It was initially outlined in *Decisions on the Strengthening of the Rural Health System* issued in 2002 by the CPC Central Committee, the highest decision-making authority in China. Pilots started in 2003, followed by fast expansion. By 2008, more than 90% of the total population was enrolled in the scheme. In 2016, China's government decided to merge NRCMS with Urban Residents Basic Medical Scheme (URBMS) to create a universal basic medical scheme.

However, so far, such coverage in rural areas is far from being comprehensive, the absolute majority of the rural population still have to resolve to independence and rely on their accumulation in their early ages to support their living or resolve to other forms of assurance like commercial insurance burgeoning in the rural areas.

2.3　Three Key Questions

The overall objective is to examine the dynamic persuasion process of insurance sales by the agents' employment of their conflicting and ambiguous identities in the interactions between the agents and the (prospective) clients in transformational China's rural areas. By adopting the broad discourse system as an overarching framework and analytical concepts such as frames, footing and contextualization cues, it is to enhance our understanding of such interactions between insurance sales agents and their prospective clients in transformational China's rural areas. To be more specific, it aims to address the following questions.

(1) How do moves and steps constitute the insurance sales discourse in today's China's rural areas?

(2) How is the topic management strategically employed by both the insurance sales agents and the (prospective) clients?

(3) How is discourse identity inter-subjectively negotiated between the insurance sales agents and the (prospective) clients?

The first question attempts to discover the discursive patterns in the agent-(prospective) client interactions and discursive strategies employed by both the agents and their (prospective) clients. Moves and steps are treated as analytical units to analyze the recorded data in order to generalize the overall discursive pattern of insurance sales interactions between the agents and the clients. This question locates the analysis in the actual conversation between the two parties by using such concepts as communicative purposes, moves and steps.

In other words, this is the fine linguistic analysis part. By analyzing audio-recorded conversational data, our primary purpose is to generalize from empirical linguistic resources and the overall discursive pattern formed by both parties employed to achieve their respective interactional goals.

The second question intends to locate the agents and their prospective clients in more detail from the perspective of topic management in the context of two discourse systems in which there are inherent conflicting ideologies in transformational China's rural areas. In the friendship discourse system, it is generally goal-free and intimate. Meanwhile in the buying and selling discourse system, it is more profit-driven and contractual. For most of the time, insurance sales agents and clients have different hidden agendas, while they need to maintain the friendly atmosphere of communication. Therefore, the strategic shifts from different topics for achieving their respective interactional goals are worthy of our attention. It further discusses how they identify themselves with the two conflicting discourse systems and how the interplay of the two different frames work to achieve the goal of persuasion, i.e., the conclusion of insurance sales.

The third question probes into the process of the negotiation of discourse identities between the insurance sales agents and the clients. Such concepts as interactive frames, footing and contextualization cues are employed to carry out the analysis. Furthermore, it extends the analysis to the broader social phenomenon of transformation from traditional society to modern society manifested by the agent's strategic use of his/her identities in realizing his/her goal of sales. It addresses the post-modern concern of penetration of economy into personal or private lives and commodification of self as well.

2.4 Discourse System and Maxims of Friendship Engagement

In order to operationalize the research, it is imperative to propose an analytical framework appropriate to the analysis of the collected data by treating the data with analytical units. The study is broadly divided into two parts — macro-analysis and micro-analysis, detailed as follows. Figure 2.1 illustrates the proposed framework guiding the present study.

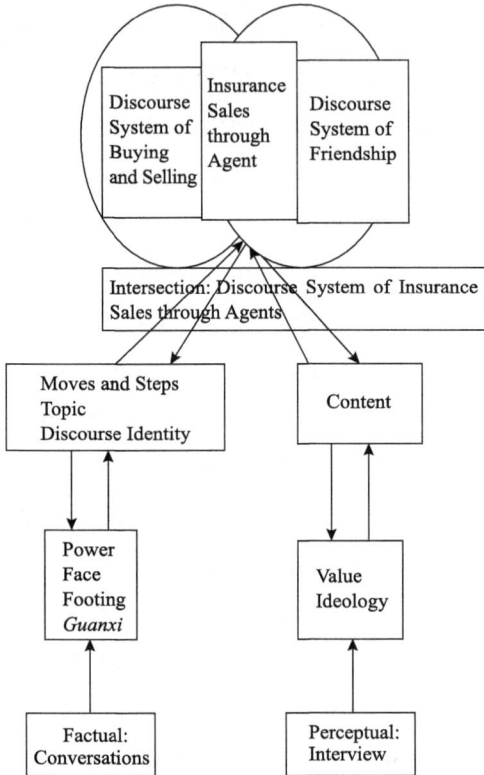

Figure 2.1　The Analytical Framework

Insurance sales through agents intermingles business and friendship, due to the fact that almost all sales are achieved between friends or at least the familiar ones, especially in rural areas. In fact it operates between friendship and business and blurs the boundary of friendship and business. It is in this intersection that I locate my analysis to investigate the dynamics in the process of insurance sales.

First of all, I set out from collecting authentic recorded data, i.e., the actual conversations conducted between the agents and their clients and interviews with both the agents and the clients. After transcribing the data, I analyze the conversations from the perspective of moves and steps to generalize the overall discursive patterns, and then relate them to such concepts as power, face, footing and *Guanxi*. Interview data will be used not only for analyzing value and ideology, but also for the triangulation purpose. Therefore, the first research question, how do moves and steps construe the insurance sales discourse in today's China's rural areas, can be addressed.

Secondly, in order to capture the dynamics of insurance sales, I analyze the data from the perspective of topic management, in an attempt to reveal the features of different discourse systems. It shows the negotiation, mediation and interplay of different frames, and thus different discourse systems at large. Thus the intricacies of power, face and *Guanxi* can be revealed. Furthermore, the perceptual data, i.e., interviews are used for the triangulation purpose. In all, this part addresses the second research question—How is the topic management strategically employed by both the insurance sales agents and the clients?

Thirdly, in order to analyze the process of how the agents and the clients mobilize such interactional devices as footings and discourse identity, I analyze the data from the perspectives of discourse identity to present how different frames are activated to their respective advantages, and thus the dynamics of agent-client interaction can be captured and described. Meanwhile, the interviews again are used to show the values and ideology of the agents and the clients, and for triangulation purpose as well. It addresses the third research question—how is discourse identity inter-subjectively negotiated between the insurance sales agents and the clients?

In summary, I analyze the data from three perspectives, namely, moves and steps, topic management and discourse identity in a hope to demonstrate and analyze the shift of identities in the process of insurance sales in China's rural areas.

2.4.1 Discourse System

Using R. Scollon and S. W. Scollon's (2001) framework of the discourse system, the macro-analyses are to achieve two objectives. Firstly, to investigate the broader social context of insurance sales for a better understanding of the interactions taking place within it. Secondly, to show how insurance sales are operated as a discourse system. By investigating the socialization process of a sales agent and the ways that the insurance company employed, the guiding ideology can be revealed.

In studying the social context of insurance sales, R. Scollon and S. W. Scollon's framework of the discourse system was proposed. In the following, the notion of discourse and discourse system are discussed. This approach does not confine itself in the realm of intercultural communication, and as Duszak (1997) mentioned, R. Scollon and S. W. Scollon's approach "has the capacity to provide a more complete and integrated description of the phenomena that contribute to the formation of social structures in response to the specific interactional communicative and practical needs (e.g., exchange of information) of individual".

As having been argued so far, social reality and relationship are constructed discursively and interactively. The discursive dimension of social construction is broader than the concept of language in use. What discourse means here is similar to the notion of discursive practice, as put forward by Fairclough (1992), who argued that discursive practice was a kind of social practice in which "texts" were the manifestations and constructions of social reality, relationship and change. R. Scollon and S. W. Scollon's framework of discourse system, which consists of ideology, socialization, face system, and forms of discourse which are interrelated to one another, is a system of thinking, social practice, and communication. The relationship between the two similar concepts of discourse can be outlined as follows:

Social practice	ideology and socialization
Discursive practice	face systems
Texts	forms of discourse

It can be drawn that Fairclough and R. Scollon and S. W. Scollon shared the basic idea of discourse, the interrelationship between components, and especially how society mediates discursive practices and vice versa. In the meantime, they also differed in different emphases. Fairclough emphasized discursive practices such as intertextuality, and textual practices such as positions of subjects and themes reflect the social practice and change. Therefore, Fairclough basically treated texts as the focal point of analysis in understanding the social construction, to put it another way, by examining discursive and textual patterns to generalize the relationship between texts and society.

R. Scollon and S. W. Scollon (2001) defined a discourse system as the broad, functional uses of language in social contexts or to a whole system of communication with particular ideological positions, specific forms of discourse, interpersonal relationships and socialization practice. Then they further elaborated the four components involved:

(1) Members hold a common ideological position and recognize a set of extra-discourse features which define them as a group (ideology).

(2) Socialization is accomplished primarily through these preferred forms of discourse (socialization).

(3) A set of preferred forms of discourse serves as banners or symbols of membership and identity (forms of discourse).

(4) Face relationships are prescribed for discourse among members or between members and outsiders (face systems).

These four components are mutually dependent and combined to form a particular discourse system.

Compared with Fairclough's notion of discourse, R. Scollon and S. W. Scollon gave a more comprehensive and balanced view of discourse, which was analyzed as a cycle in which the four elements of discourse were influenced and related to one another. In order to illustrate the concept of discourse system, they offered an example of the discourse system of a company. Through socialization (training), the staffs of the company learned and practiced those ideologies which were reflected by the face system and forms of discourse. They in turn reinforced the set of ideologies already established by the company. The cyclic development of discourse in fact reflects the dynamic nature of social construction, which is not one-sided in terms of only the society or individuals. In order to exemplify their notion, R. Scollon and S. W. Scollon classified discourse systems into two general categories, involuntary (those to which members have no choice in belonging, such as age, gender, or ethnicity) and voluntary (goal-oriented discourse systems, usually referring to the institutional structures which have been formed for specific purposes, such as corporations or governments).

Thus it can be concluded that both concepts of discourse are constructive ones, complementing the weaknesses of each other. Fairclough's model offered more detailed analysis of the mediation of text through discursive practice, while R. Scollon and S. W. Scollon's framework was more comprehensive and complete in understanding the dynamics of discourse. In the present study, R. Scollon and S. W. Scollon's model will be employed as the general framework for analysis while some of Fairclough's concepts such as intertextuality will be integrated as well.

With this general understanding of the discursive dimension of social construction as outlined above, it can be concluded that in order to understand textual practices or discourse forms, it is imperative for us to treat them as they are instead of isolating them. In other words, a broader view of discourse has to be taken to examine the inter-relationship between texts and the broader context in order to more fully understand the negotiation process between the agents and the prospective clients. To illustrate this view, I use the example of experience sharing seminars of insurance agents, which is a very frequent and popular genre of insurance sales. In order to train and boost the morale of the agents, the insurance company frequently organizes such seminars, not only for the purpose of explaining in detail the insurance policies in promotion, but also a series of invitational talks by some successful agents who share their successful experiences. After the seminar, the agents will talk with their friends and start their own practice.

In R. Scollon and S. W. Scollon's framework, the seminars are the settings in which insurance agents are socialized, instilling their beliefs in the advantages of the products they are selling. Then the agents in turn enhance such ideologies; these materials will be used in the analysis process. In all, what I am illustrating here is the importance of looking at the broader context in which a conversation takes place. It is insufficient to examine discourse forms alone and be independent of context. Without the background knowledge, analysis of the interactions cannot be complete.

By adopting Fairclough's and R. Scollon and S. W. Scollon's concepts of discourse, I will first examine the broader context in which the conflicting identities are constructed, and then how significant that context is to understanding the interactions in the insurance sales. It is also a good arena to see how our social relationships are constructed through discursive practices nowadays. Nonetheless, our social relationship is constructed both discursively and interactively. Moreover, the management of conflicting identities as a discourse event can only be analyzed by examining the event itself. Therefore, the interactions will form the most important focus of analysis.

2.4.2 Maxims of Friendship Engagement

In order to understand better how friends draw inferences among themselves, a synthesis of two theoretical works in the role of communication in relationship development is proposed. Rogers and Millar's (1988) and Montgomery's (1988) works gave a clear picture of the ideological ideals of what is expected of being a friend to other people. However, it must be noted that ideological ideals are only idealistic elements of friendship, and they are subject to negotiation among members of a society. Simply put, they are not the rules of friendship behavior in the real world. As Montgomery put it, "not only do societies develop communication standards for personal relationships, but also do relationship members" (Montgomery, 1988: 353). There are three dimensions of any kind of relationship in Rogers and Millar's (1988) model: trust, control and intimacy. While Montgomery's model of "Ideals of Relationship" includes only the latter two of these, but with an additional dimension of positiveness. With expansion and modifications, the two models can be synthesized as follows.

Maxim of Trust:

    Be sincere.

    Be empirically veracious.

Temporal Relevance: Future.

Functional Significance: Regulation of commitments and uncertainties.

Maxim of Intimacy:

    Be affectionate.

    Be understanding.

Temporal Relevance: Past.

Functional Significance: Regulation of personal identities and enmeshment, as Rogers and Millar (1988) put it, "intimacy centers on the strength of members' attachments", on the extent to which specific others are built into one's identity and thereby become "crucial to the legitimization and enactment of those identities" (Mccall and Simmons, 1966: 295)

Maxim of Control:

    Do not dominate.

    Be equal.

Temporal Relevance: Present.

Functional Significance: Regulation of definitional rights and constructive efficacy.

Maxim of Positiveness:

    Be positive.

    Do not say or do anything if you cannot say or do anything nice.

    Be polite.

Temporal Relevance: No time boundaries.

Functional Significance: Regulation of confirmation, agreement, and conflict.

The above four synthesized maxims are not rules governing how a person should act accordingly in a personal relationship, and I do not attempt to argue for their universality since friendship can be interpreted differently across various societies and cultures. However, it is safe to say they represent the core values or assumptions of most societies, including Central China's rural areas, where my data are collected.

The four maxims of friendship engagement (trust, intimacy, control and positiveness) can be exploited, or sometimes suspended at the expense of others. Friends may draw inferences of what has been said in their conversations. They are not only assumptions shared by friends in their interactions, but also the important criteria of friendship by which our relationships are subject to negotiation and re-negotiation in our conversations.

In all, the specific and context-bound maxims of friendship engagement by which friends can negotiate meanings in their conversations can help us better understand the interactions between the insurance sales agents and their prospective clients.

2.4.3 Confucianism and Utilitarianism

There are two well-established discourse systems in competition, namely Confucianism and utilitarianism. The following will briefly illustrate the features of the two discourse systems and how they are applied in the study of business communication.

1. Confucianism

In studying intercultural communication, there are many dichotomies in terms of communication style and strategy, such as high- and low-context (Hall, 1989), individualism and collectivism (Hofstede, 1991), affectional and instrumental (Bond, 1986). More recently, the most prominent dichotomy in intercultural communication is the discourse systems of Confucianism and utilitarianism (Flowerdew, 1997; Ouyang, 2004; Gu, 2001; Wu, 2008).

R. Scollon and S. W. Scollon (2001) also argued discourse system as work at different levels, from macro- to micro-levels. The Confucianism and utilitarianism discourse systems will be working at the macro-level to conduct study on social research, while buying and selling discourse system working at the micro-level to evaluate the agent-client interactions. To a certain extent, we can correspond Confucianism discourse system to friendship discourse system and utilitarianism to buying and selling due to the similarities in patterns and features.

For Confucianism discourse system, there are such features as hierarchical, indirect, autocratic and authoritarian identified and heavily discussed by a number of well-established scholars (Flowerdew, 1997; Wu, 2008). However, utilitarianism discourse system embodies such features as openness, directness, truthfulness and clarity (Flowerdew, 1997). R. Scollon and S. W. Scollon (2001) highlighted some of the key concepts characteristic of the Confucianism discourse system. In regard to the hierarchical relationships that govern Confucianism discourse, they acknowledged that, in general, "most Asians are quite conscious in an interaction who is older and who is younger, who has a higher level of education, who has a lower level, who is in higher institutional or economic position and who is lower or who is teacher and who is student" (R. Scollon and S. W. Scollon, 2001: 82).

In addition to the hierarchical relationship among interactants, indirectness is also found in Confucianism discourse. Hara and Kim (2004) provided research support for the claim that indirectness was motivated by "concern for the other's face" which was generally associated with Eastern cultures.

In summary, Confucianism represents a discourse system that values collectivism, hierarchical relationships, high-context and indirectness. The Chinese culture is primarily collectivistic in nature. For example in China, people tend to exhibit the values of "harmony, solidarity", and members view themselves "as inter-connected with others" (Gudykunst, 1998). Trust, reciprocity, face, time, harmony, hierarchy, power distance, and long-term orientation have been identified as the key Chinese cultural values (Bond, 1992). These Chinese cultural values are the main representations of the core rituals of Confucianism.

2. Utilitarianism

Flowerdew (1997) highlighted utilitarianism through his study of transformational Hong Kong public discourse, as more characteristics of democratic societies, such as the United States and the United Kingdom, with its openness, directness, truthfulness, rationality and clarity. Given that he acknowledged that in making his dichotomy he might be guilty of "over-generalizing", it was his intention to demonstrate "how discourses are inherently unstable constructs and that an element of idealization is necessary if the concept of discourse is to have any value" (Flowerdew, 1997).

R. Scollon and S. W. Scollon (2001) argued that the utilitarian discourse system had its origin in the 18th century Enlightenment and the writing of Kant, Locke, Bentham and Mill where the central concepts were "the greatest happiness for the greatest number" and "free individual expression" as "the basis for society". It is the discourse system that develops in democratic societies, which contributes to the characteristics of openness, directness, rationality, truthfulness, and clarity. In fact, Scollon (1998) used strong language to say that in the utilitarianism system there was an "obligation on the individual to express himself or herself as an individual who is motivated from internal motives".

3. Two discourse systems in interplay: Confucianism and utilitarianism

China is a unique community in terms of its cultural complexity, with its pre-dominantly Chinese cultural values but being widely open to Western cultural influence since the initiation of its reform and opening-up policy. Insurance sales in China seem to be a complex blend of Western ideology, although traditional Chinese has already developed similar mechanism to share the risks. In this sense, insurance sales in China offers a particularly interesting arena for analysis due to the fact that insurance, typical of Western ideology and values, is sold in a Chinese population that practices many Chinese cultural traditions.

The conceptual framework of contemporary Western insurance practices and ethics has focused on individual rights, with particular emphasis on autonomy and self-determination in decisions regarding one's insurance policies. This fundamental ethical principle of client autonomy has its roots in Western philosophy, as well as in American, more generally, the Western, cultural values, which emphasize liberty, privacy and individual rights. In contrast, in traditional Chinese society, there is less emphasis on individual rights, self-expression, and self-determination. In the specific community, qualities such as harmony, function, and responsibility are stressed more than individual rights, and collective relationships assume primary importance.

In arguing such Western and traditional Chinese differences, Ip and her colleagues (1998) made an interesting study on ethical decision-making in critical care in Hong Kong, and they reviewed the nature and sources of cross-cultural conflicts in the intensive care unit settings that often arise between physicians trained in Western medicine and patients from a Chinese cultural background. They found that paternal role of the physician had persisted in Hong Kong. Generally speaking, patients perceive the physician as an authoritative figure, and deference of medical decision-making to the doctor is the norm. While in Western medical ethics, health care decision-making by physicians without input from the patient is regarded negatively as paternalism. Nonetheless, partly due to the strong influence of Confucianism and rampant practice of the traditional values, the Chinese culture places great emphasis on maintaining harmony in interpersonal relations through respect for hierarchy. Therefore, while many Americans question paternalism as an affront to the individual, to a Chinese client, deference may preserve the positive goodwill of harmony and prevent an affront to the social order of the community.

With years of training and practice in insurance sales for agents on the one hand, and with almost no knowledge or awareness of insurance for the clients on the other hand, the clients seem to be easy victims of agents' manipulation in their communication. However, there are several points worthy of our attention here.

First, relationships between the agents and the clients in China are not static and mutate in different ways over time. The relationships are not only one-time transaction, but rather long-term oriented. Unlike most Western insurance sales practice, where both parties strictly adhere to the clauses and legal aspects of the insurance policies, Chinese insurance sales practice, especially rural insurance sales practice seems to be more flexible and in an all-round way. In the meantime, the transformation of a state-planned economy into a market economy in China necessitates changes in cultural values and social structures. As Habermas (1973) argued, a market economy had its foundation on "the bourgeois value orientation of possessive individualism and Benthamite utilitarianism". As we have entered the 21st century, the agent-client communication has moved more or less towards the trend of a "fleeting relationship", while "agent" and "client" for "friends", "relatives" or even "family" reflect the increased impersonality of the communication and the commercialization of relationships (Potter and McKinlay, 2005).

This changing ideology leads to a second point that relationships between insurance sales agents and (prospective) clients in China are not defined by one single discourse system. Through formal education and informal family and social immersion into traditional Chinese cultures and value systems, and mostly with years' of frequent training and practice in the insurance sales, insurance sales agents are socialized into the insurance sales discourse system by learning how to act in particular ways. Their way of socialization through training and practice grants them with established professionalism in routine insurance sales practice, which are characterized as a goal-oriented community. The changing ideology from a state-planned economy into a market economy in China has also driven Chinese clients to seek for individual voices and secure personal interests. Traditional Chinese values can co-exist with modern Western values. Chinese insurance sales agents and clients are perceived as those who embrace modern values but at the same time retain traditional Chinese values. A modern Chinese is believed to be different from a traditional Chinese who also values thrift, social harmony and authoritarianism (Bond, 1992). To put it another way, hybridization is an alternative to the sole endorsement of either traditional Chinese or Western values.

In a more recent reflection of intercultural communication, Pan, S. W. Scollon and R. Scollon (2009) discerningly pointed out that the set of principles outlined in the Scollons' framework can not only be a practical guide to analyze intercultural communication by "bridging cultural differences in the use of language", but also "be applied to studying communication in any community of practice or in any language and culture". This is what makes their discourse approach "valuable and timeless".

Such dichotomies as directness-indirectness, individualism-collectivism, high- and low-context and other cultural characteristics may appear to be arbitrary and sometimes simplistic. As mentioned earlier, in characterizing the two competing discourses of transformational Hong Kong in such dichotomous terms as utilitarianism and Confucianism, Flowerdew (1997: 534) himself was fully aware that "there is a danger of over-generalizing". Nonetheless, as the accepted concepts in the research literature, they can be used as sub-categories of analysis. Since they do capture the more comprehensive perspective, it is my belief that they are more inclusive cultural categories as they are broader in scope and suggest more historical dimensions in their meaning.

All in all, it would be appropriate to adopt R. Scollon and S. W. Scollon's discourse systems as the overarching conceptual framework. Such a "de-politicalizing" approach is employed with special consideration of the present societal transformation from the "Cultural Revolution" to a Deng Xiaoping's socialist market economy, which has been the central theme for the present China, as most Chinese citizens are reluctant to go back to those "fighting among themselves" movements but focus themselves more on economic development of the country, contrary to the critical discourse movements witnessed in the West during the same period of time (Ouyang, 2004).

The relationships between Chinese insurance sales agents and their clients have received harsh criticisms, and the communication between them often fails to produce favorable outcomes for both parties. However, against this troubled reality, there is an ever growing appeal to reforms and changes for an enhanced, harmonious and trust-based relationship. Within this overarching discourse systems framework, Chinese insurance agents and clients will be identified with shared memberships of the two competing discourse systems.

2.5 Business Communication and Culture

No one doubts that business communication is greatly associated with cultures although there is very little agreement on what people mean by the idea of culture in the first place. Culture can be viewed as everything that people have, think and do as members of their society (Ferraro, 1990): communication (Hall, 1989), a system of shared meanings (Geertz, 1973), the way of life of a group of people (Barnouw, 1979), collective programming of the mind (Hofstede, 1991), a set of understandings shared among persons who have been similarly socialized (Terpstra and Baker, 1991), or a system consisting of subsystems, such as kinship, education, economy, politics, religion, association, health and recreation systems (Harris and Moran, 1996).

Cultural factors are important for the understanding of communication system of discourse. As Hall (1989) pointed out, culture was communication and communication was culture. According to R. Scollon and S. W. Scollon (2001), ideology, socialization, forms of discourse and face system are the major cultural factors that people need to consider in communication. Communication is the process through which individuals—in relationships, groups, organizations, and societies—respond to and create messages and adapt to the environment and one another. In the following, I will mainly review relative studies in Chinese business culture, socialization process (*Guanxi*), face value and politeness.

2.5.1 The Chinese Business Culture

Chinese business culture is the key to the Chinese way of doing business and their style of communication or negotiation (Fang, 1999). As Fang (1999) held, there were three key components of Chinese business culture: the PRC condition, Confucianism and Chinese Stratagems which all contain various complex factors. The conditions of the PRC can be understood as "China's situation", "Chinese characteristics", "the special situation in China", and "Chinese tradition" which may involve politics, economic planning, legal framework, technology, country size, backwardness, rapid social changes, and Chinese bureaucracy. These factors have been constantly changed after the 1980s and form a very unstable and complex situation for business interactions.

As for Confucianism, it is a Chinese philosophical tradition that has fundamentally shaped Chinese mentality for over 2,500 years. Many contributions to the area of Chinese business negotiating styles belong to the Confucian school (Kindel, 1990). Most of the studies are conducted from the perspectives of sociology (Fang, 1999), economics (Seligman, 1990) and marketing (Gao, 1993). As Fang (1999) pointed out, to generate a theoretically sound Confucian explanation of Chinese business interaction style, we need to start with a knowledge of six key Confucian values: moral cultivation, importance of interpersonal relationships, family orientation, respect for age and hierarchy, avoidance of conflict and need for harmony, and concept of face. Few, however, adopted a clear orientation to identify how these key elements or values of Confucian traditions affect the structure and language of Chinese business interactions, let alone transformational Chinese rural business interactions. As a prevailing practice, Chinese business is built on trust but not law (Fang, 1999). Interpersonal relationship is the foundation of trust. One can negotiate a deal with the Chinese most effectively when the relationship is well established between the parties, which are closely related to *Guanxi*, *Renqing* (social exchanges) and *Li* (politeness). Fang (1999) also contributed an interesting phenomenon in Chinese business negotiation: Chinese stratagems, which are a strategic component of Chinese business culture. These stratagems form the very core of the strategic Chinese thinking and offer a cultural explanation of the strategic patterns of Chinese negotiating style—Chinese negotiating tactics. These stratagems are developed from *Sun Tzu's The Art of War*, in which 36 stratagems largely affect the negotiation styles of Chinese business people as negotiating tactics.

For the purpose of the present research, the main concern is to see how the relational positions of Chinese culture and of discourse politeness systems become factors in the business communication from a perspective of linguistics; it is not to decide which of the above-mentioned positions on the nature of "Chinese business culture" is the most important one.

2.5.2 *Guanxi*

Guanxi is one of the major dynamics of Chinese society. *Guanxi* has been a pervasive part of the Chinese business world for the last few centuries, by which millions of Chinese firms were bound into a social and business web. It has been generally recognized that *Guanxi* is a key business determinant of a firm's performance, especially its market growth. In China's new, fast-paced business environment, *Guanxi* has become more entrenched than ever, heavily influencing Chinese political landscapes, social behavior, and business practice.

Guanxi is also an important cultural feature that affects the Chinese business communication as argued by many anthropologists (Yang, 1994), historians (King, 1992; Yang, 1994), sociologists (Fang, 1999) and sociolinguists (Pan, 2000). *Guanxi* is literally translated as "relationship" or better described as "relationships which incur obligation" (Sorkhabi, 2012). To determine whether time and effort should be spent to develop a relationship with a particular individual, one must obtain information regarding to that person's background. Knowing who the other person is must be ascertained first, even if it requires more than one meeting with several people (Sorkhabi, 2012). Yang (1994) showed that *Guanxi* had not only use-value, but also exchange-value in contemporary China, and the reliance on established social relationships to get things done had had a long tradition in China. The concept of personal connections is an underlying cultural assumption shared by the Chinese everywhere in China.

Guanxi, a concept evolved in China's several thousand years' development, has been generally referred to as interpersonal relationships, also as *Renqing*, face, gift or even *Renlun* in Confucianism. Some scholars (Zhai, 2007a, 2009) held that traditional Chinese society was a "society of the familiar", which corresponded to Fei's (2007) description of Chinese society as a "differential mode of association".

Although *Guanxi* is embedded in almost every part of social life in China, most researches are situated at the institutional level, i.e., Chinese firms developing *Guanxi* as a strategic mechanism to overcome competitive and resource disadvantages by cooperating and exchanging favors with government authorities and other stakeholders (Luo, 2007).

Due to the significant influence of Confucianism, Chinese often view themselves as interdependent with the surrounding social context. The self in relation to the other becomes the focus of individual experience. This view of an interdependent self is in sharp contrast to the Western view of an independent self. The latter sees each human being as an independent, self-contained, and autonomous entity who a) comprises a unique configuration of internal attributes (e.g., traits, abilities, motives and values) and b) behaves primarily as a consequence of these internal attributes. This divergent view of self has implications for a variety of basic psychological processes (e.g., cognition, emotion and motivation) and may be one of the most fundamental differences between the East and the West in social relations.

In a relation-centered society, social relations are accorded much greater significance. Relationships are often seen as the ends in and of themselves rather than as means for realizing individual goals. As part of the emphasis on differentiated relationships, attention to others is highly selective and mostly characteristic of relationships with in-group members. Many observers of Chinese social relations (Butterfield, 1990) noted that in comparison to the West, Chinese have a much stronger tendency to divide people into categories and treat them accordingly. This tendency of treating people differently depending on one's relationship to them constitutes the basic reason why *Guanxi* is of such great importance to the Chinese society.

Yang (1994) described the three major categories of interpersonal relations in China: *Jiaren* (家人, family members), *Shengren* (生人, mere acquaintances or strangers), and *Shuren* (熟人, familiar persons such as relatives outside the family, neighbors or people in the same village, friends, colleagues, or classmates). These three categories of relationship have completely different social and psychological meanings to the parties involved and are governed by different sets of interpersonal rules.

The *Jiaren* relationship is characterized by relatively permanent, stable, expressive relationships in which the welfare of the others is part of one's duty. The general rule of exchange is that one must do his/her best to attend to the others' needs with little or no expectation of return in the future. In traditional Chinese societies, primary loyalties cluster around the family, surrounded by circles of decreasingly potent identification with the lineage group and then the regional clan. One of the most distinctive features of Chinese society is this family orientation. The in-group favoritism based on kinship *Guanxi* is due to strong family identification and role obligations. It is rendered largely without anticipation of reciprocity.

The *Shengren* category includes all those who are outside the family unit and with whom one has not established any meaningful relationship through past interactions. These can include members of one's local community, fellow employees who work in the same (large) company, or business customers. Interactions with *Shengren* are superficial and temporary and are dominated by utilitarian concerns. The focus is on personal gains and losses. The defining characteristic of this relationship is instrumentality without affection, unlike the relationship with *Jiaren*, which involves primarily affection, or *Shuren*, which has both an instrumental and an affective component.

A *Shuren*, by definition, is neither a *Jiaren* nor a *Shengren* but rather someone with whom one has a friendship that may range from superficial to extremely intimate. A co-worker or a subordinate can fall into this category. The relationship with the *Shuren* is a mixture of *Jiaren* and *Shengren* and takes both utilitarian and expressive forms. The principle of *Renqing* that underlies most friendships suggests that favoritism is often followed by a strong expectation of reciprocity. Cultivating *Renqing* is said to be a prerequisite to establishing or sustaining the relationship among friends.

In summary, depending on the bases of *Guanxi*, an interpersonal relationship can fall into any one of the above three categories. With each category, the relationship can vary in the degree of closeness or strength. To the traditional Chinese, *Guanxi* was primarily meaningful to the *Jiaren* and *Shuren* categories. However, as Chinese societies moved away from a traditional, agrarian life style to an industrialized, pluralistic one, individual freedom has risen and collective forces have ebbed. The potential for interpersonal relationships in the *Shengren* category has become increasingly important (Tsui and Farh, 1997). An interesting phenomenon in the current study is that the insurance agents take advantage of *Jiaren* and *Shuren* (turning *Shengren* into *Shuren*) in their efforts to make the sales. In later analysis and discussion part, there will be more detailed discussion on this issue.

Guanxi are delicate fibers woven into every Chinese individual's social life, and therefore, into many aspects of Chinese society (Luo, 2007). Although the cultivation of *Guanxi* has become the focus of researchers' attention only since the decentralization and privatization of the Chinese economy, its roots are deeply embedded in about 2000 years of Chinese culture. Confucian social theory is concerned with the question of how to establish a harmonious secular order in a man-centered world. According to Confucianism, the individual is never an isolated, separate entity; all humans are social or interactive beings. The word *Lun* (伦, human relations) was used to concern the differentiation of individuals and the kinds of relationships to be established among individuals. Bluntly put, Confucian social order is constructed upon the concept of *Lun*.

Ever since Confucius codified the societal rules, values, and hierarchical structures of authority during the sixth century B.C., Chinese society has been functioning within clan-like networks. Such networks can be viewed as concentric circles. Close family members are at the core and distant relatives, and classmates, friends and acquaintances are peripherally arranged in accordance to the distance of relationship and degree of trust. A purposeful investment in time and energy is frequently made to maintain and extend such networks. Concerning the Chinese communication, King (1992), argued that the Chinese made a clear distinction between in-group and out-group members, and placed great emphasis on group cohesion and interdependence between in-group members. The in-group members include family members, relatives, friends and fellow villagers, fellow schoolmates and fellow colleagues. In-group members form the basic structure for social interaction, and it is within this relationship that social etiquette is observed and practiced. As for out-group members, they are considered temporary contacts not holding any long-term value in the social relationship. Meanwhile, Yang (1994) also argued that, once there was some personal connection to introduce the outsiders to the insiders, out-group members could be easily accepted. Because the Chinese make a strict distinction between insider and outsider relations, *Guanxi* has become an important medium in all sorts of social interactions, ranging from official to business and personal activities (Pan, 2000). Nonetheless, Kong (1998b) argued that insider and outsider relationships are manipulable and negotiable variables, rather than fixed governing factors of politeness behavior in the Chinese settings.

The value of the Chinese *Guanxi* takes roots in the social practice of "distinction between the insider and outsider". The primacy of *Guanxi* and binding power of personal relationships are perpetuated in Chinese business life and consequently affect Chinese linguistic politeness. Since linguistic politeness is part of language use and social practice, there is no doubt that it encodes the insider and outsider distinction in the Chinese culture and it plays an essential role in the consideration of face strategies (Pan, 2000; R. Scollon and S. W. Scollon, 2001). In this case, I will just try to restrict his attention to this aspect of culture due to the fact that their research has shown to be of direct significance in discourse between interpersonal groups, and that their research impinge directly upon the interactional elements of a discourse system, such as interaction structure and language use and their associated forms of discourse, socialization, facework and politeness strategies.

2.5.3 The Key Values of Facework and Politeness in the Chinese Society

Cultural variations affect people's perception towards facework and politeness strategies in communication. Some researchers believe that people's thinking patterns will greatly affect their communication. Among them, R. Scollon and S. W. Scollon (1991, 2001) claimed that the Chinese differed from the Anglo-Americans since they organized their ideas, persuaded others and structured their conversations differently. The Chinese are postulated as having their own values and specific rhetorical patterns in discourse and different interpretive frameworks. To be more specific, they are often favoring many such linguistic strategies as being indirect (R. Scollon and S. W. Scollon, 2001; Oetzel, Garcia and Ting-Toomey, 2008, etc.), ambiguous (Chang, 1999; Zhang, 1998), modest (Gu, 1990) in their daily communication, and being cautious in business communication (Bilbow, 1997). When the Chinese speak, they provide information about their subject matters, and simultaneously reveal such things as their sense of "self", the roles they are adopting or expecting others to adopt (the age, rank and social differences). They also provide information about the values they want to express, their perceptions of the relevant interactions, their expectations of other negotiators' behaviors, and their anticipation of the outcome of communication. In this sense, the Chinese language use has

Chapter 2 Mechanism of the Chinese Insurance Sales, Data Collection and Analysis

potentially serious social consequences and effects on communication.

To understand the Chinese linguistic politeness and facework, it is imperative to understand first its unique concept of "face", which was first introduced to the outside world by a Chinese anthropologist, Hu, in 1944, though this term had existed in the Chinese culture for thousands of years in Confucian thoughts. Gu (1990: 238-239) argued that the Chinese word for "politeness" (*Limao* in Chinese pinyin) was literally translated into "politeness appearance". *Limao* was formulated by Confucius and was derived from the Chinese word *Li*, which refers to the social hierarchy and order of the slavery system of the Zhou Dynasty (dating back to 1100 B.C.). Neustupny (1968) defined this sort of *Li* as the function of which (politeness behavior) was a primary communication about vertical relations. But in modern China, social structure and social relationships have changed dramatically after the 1980s. The Confucian meaning of *Limao* entails a much broader meaning. Gu (1990) stated that there were four notions underlying the Chinese perception of *Limao*: respectfulness, modesty, attitudinal warmth, and refinement. Respectfulness is self's positive appreciation or admiration of others, concerning the latter's face and social status. Modesty is a way of denigrating self. Attitudinal warmth is the expression of consideration, kindness and hospitality to others. Refinement is the proper behavior to others. Besides the above four notions, sincerity and balance are very important values as well. Yet in different cultures, and in different speech contexts within the same culture, different opinions or points on the continuum could be favored, which point on the scale is "optimum", depending partly on pragmatic contextual variables and partly on culturally-based socio-pragmatic preference (Spencer-Oatey, 2002).

Chinese politeness and facework in communication have been studied mainly from a social perspective. In many cases, Chinese politeness is closely related to Chinese facework (Lim, 1994). Ghauri and Fang (2001) argued that Chinese facework is linked to the Confucian notion of shame. Confucius preached a kind of statesmanship that governed people's communication behavior by instilling "a sense of shame" into their minds. Face as a self-regulating moral mechanism has a fundamental impact on the Chinese way of life, because every person is entitled to respect, which is spoken of in English as "having face". Showing respect for someone causes him/her to gain face. Embarrassing someone in public causes him/her to lose face—a very serious breach of the Chinese etiquette (Bond, 1994).

To maintain harmony, the Chinese are preoccupied with the concept of face and are very sensitive to having face in all aspects of social and business life. The Chinese perception of "face" reflects "the approval of the community" (Brunner and Wang, 1988), and "favor exchange" (Hwang, 1987), therefore, is of far greater value than material wealth. In a relative way, the social orientation and public self-image of the Chinese face comply more with the face notion of Goffman's (1967), who claimed that face is a public image. Mao (1994: 19) argued that "to be polite" in the Chinese discourse was "to know how to respond to each other's *Lian* (*Mianzi* or face) as well as to perform speech acts appropriate to and be worthy of such an image". "The interactional dynamic of facework…is positively reciprocal with both parties engaged in mutually shared orientation to negotiate, elevate, and attend to each other's face as well as one's own face. The Chinese facework is actually 'face-balance', which means giving face to others simultaneously enhances one's own face and depriving of other's face simultaneously damages one's face" (W. Zhang, 1995: 85). Both self face and group face (sometimes the community face or the public face the speaker representing for his or her affiliation) should be considered in communication.

At the linguistic level, Lee-Wong (2000: 310) argued that "face threat and face maintenance (in the Chinese contexts) do not pose a major issue in situations, involving interactants who have clearly defined role relationships". In an asymmetrical role relationship, the issue of face threat is quite often irrelevant as there is little room for negotiability of social position or power. The speaker with high power does not need to maintain or enhance hearer's face beyond the normal observation of normative politeness. The hearer otherwise does not

Chapter 2 Mechanism of the Chinese Insurance Sales, Data Collection and Analysis

expect speaker to resort to countless linguistic devices of mitigation to reduce face threatening acts. However, it might be true that the speaker with low power threatens a high-power hearer by not taking accordance to deference, which is a face threat to the hearer. She further argued that politeness was "culturally colored". Each culture has its own linguistic devices for expressing politeness (by studying the request situation): a) propositional content: being clear and explicit; b) attitude: being sincere, reasonable and considerate; and c) linguistic etiquette: being polite (e.g., use polite marker). Her findings represent the interactional features from hierarchically structured relationships and proves to be fruitful and interesting. Meanwhile, the field of insurance agent-(prospective) client interactions in transformational China's rural areas had not been touched. Therefore, a study of the interactions of egalitarian relationships at various interpersonal levels is needed not only to illustrate the face applications in the speech by interlocutors but also to understand how interlocutors make sense of themselves in the speech in various situations.

Despite the pervasive discussions on social factors, the Chinese politeness still needs to be read in the context of conventional rituals not only socially but also historically, ethnically, emotionally and professionally, which are encoded as proper and contextual linguistic expressions. To understand it and its related framework, one has to reach its tradition, its historical truth, its context and their changes. Concerning the integration of politeness principle and conversation analysis on Chinese data, Kong (2003) provided an inspiring example by demonstrating how conversation-analytic work could be brought to bear on the Chinese and Chinese politeness perceptions. In the area of Mandarin Chinese, in particular, there have been very few investigations following a conversation analysis approach on business language and interpersonal communication studies. Most current studies of Chinese communication do not provide sufficient evidence to grasp the complexities of the negotiation styles and socio-pragmatic preferences under different interpersonal relationships, which may reflect different social norms, cultural and linguistic conventions, politeness strategies and faceworks.

Largely as a result of the proliferation of traditionally experimental and empirical studies of the negotiation patterns and language use, linguistic findings from one culture might not satisfactorily explain the communication, linguistic and politeness phenomena occurring in another culture. In view of this, society-based and language-based approaches to business negotiating activities are essential to provide insights into how to identify, interpret and understand the structure or discursive patterns of business negotiations, socio-pragmatic preferences and their interrelationship with interpersonal relationships and politeness. This part offers an overview of the scholars' relative findings and their propositions, and it also lays out the most related interpreting framework and assumptions and the possible orientations of this research. To sum up, research is needed to develop a new coherent model through not only systematically analyzing but also interpreting the complexities of Chinese insurance sales in rural areas.

2.6 Genre Analysis, Participation Framework and *Guanxi*

Discourse system offers an overarching framework for analysis. However, in order to operationalize the study and capture the micro-aspect of agent-client communication, it is imperative that we break the analysis into more detailed analytical concepts and units. The following offers an account of the analytical concepts and units, more specifically, genre analysis by communicative purposes, moves and steps, participation framework, frames, footing and contextualization cues, topic and discourse identity. Generally speaking, the micro-analysis will focus on the interactional mechanisms through which the agents employ for various interactional goals.

In order to get to the fine analysis of the conversations between the sales agents and their (prospective) clients, even though the broad conceptual framework of discourse system can serve as a general guideline for the present study, it is still quite necessary to employ several analytical concepts such as participation framework, frame, footing and contextualization cues.

2.6.1 Genre Analysis: Communicative Purpose, Moves and Steps

Swales' (1990) and Bhatia's (1993) concepts of genre, communicative purposes, moves and steps can serve as appropriate analytical tools since they offered a good fusion of linguistic and sociological factors in their definition of genre, which set up a relationship between the purpose accomplished by a genre and the structure of the genre by suggesting that the communicative purpose of a genre shaped the genre and provided it with a schematic structure. Moreover, Bhatia's (1993) works are mostly situated in the areas of promotion letters, research articles, legislative provisions, etc., which are mostly institutional in nature, and can offer an established framework for the analysis of the communication between the insurance sales agents and their clients. By applying this model of analysis, the discursive pattern of the communication between the insurance sales agents and their clients in transformational China's rural areas can be revealed and summarized, since this model shows a genuine interest in the use of language to achieve communicative goals. By examining the generic features of insurance sales agent-client interactions, insights into the overall functions of such features may be further delineated, and thus broaden the focus of previous research by examining the discourse of speakers in transformational China's rural areas.

As argued by Swales, "A genre comprises a class of communicative events, the members of which share some set of communicative purposes. These purposes are recognized by the expert members of the parent discourses community and thereby constitute the rationale for the genre. This rationale shapes the schematic structure of the discourse and influences and constrains the choice of content and style." (Swales, 1990: 58)

Swales offered a good fusion of linguistic and sociological factors in this definition, and it set up a relationship between the purpose accomplished by a genre and the structure of the genre by suggesting that the communicative purpose of a genre shapes the genre and provides it with a schematic structure.

Bhatia further developed Swales' understanding of genre, "It is a recognizable communicative event characterized by a set of communicative purpose(s) identified and mutually understood by the members of the professional or academic community in which it regularly occurs. Most often it is highly structured and conventionalized with constraints on allowable contributions in terms of their intent, positioning, form and functional value. These constraints, however, are often exploited by the expert members of the discourse community to achieve private intentions within the framework of socially recognized purpose(s)." (Bhatia, 1993: 13)

In this definition, Bhatia combined psychological factors and consider genre as a dynamic social process. Just as Bhatia (1993: 16) commented: Swales underplayed psychological factors, thus undermining the importance of tactical aspects of genre construction, which plays a significant role in the concept of genre as a dynamic social process, as against a static one.

Swalesian genre analysis takes genre as "an instance of successful achievement of specific communicative purpose using conventionalized knowledge of linguistic and discoursal resources". And such "linguistic and discoursal resources are revealed by such schematic structure as specific moves and steps, governed by communicative purposes in question" (Bhatia, 1993: 3).

Although it is crucial to define a term before applying detailed analysis into it, the term "move" has been used extensively by genre analysts in the past. Swalesian analysts note that there is a regular pattern of "moves" and "steps" appear in certain order in the majority of the texts they investigate. A "move" is thus a unit that relates the writer's purpose to the content that he/she wishes to communicate. A "step" is a lower text unit than the move that provides more detailed perspective on the options open to the writer in setting out the moves

(Swales, 1990; Bhatia, 1997b, 2008). In analyzing insurance sales interactions in transformational China's rural areas, due to the complex, flexible and variable nature of spoken discourse, and with the preliminary studies of the data, it is found that certain schematic structure patterns emerge in the collected data, and the analysis of the communicative purposes, moves and steps would prove particularly useful.

Bhatia's (1993) model for sales promotion letters in several aspects. First of all, for sales promotion letters, Move 1 is establishing credentials, while for insurance sales dialogues, Move 1 is warming up, which is the most significant difference between sales promotion letters and insurance sales dialogues. Table 2.2 shows the moves and steps for sales promotion letters by Bhatia (1993).

Table 2.2 Bhatia's (1993) Moves and Steps for Sales Promotion Letters

Moves	Descriptions	Flexibility
1	Establishing credentials	Obligatory
2 (i) (ii) (iii)	Introducing the offer (i) Offering the product or service (ii) Essential detailing of the offer (iii) Indicating value of the offer	Obligatory
3	Offering incentives	Optional
4	Enclosing documents	Optional
5	Soliciting response	Obligatory
6	Using pressure tactics	Optional
7	Ending politely	Optional

With this general generic patterns in mind, we can further analyze the discoursal and linguistic resources employed in the insurance agent-client interactions, more specifically, the interaction and mediation of different frames through the analysis of topic through frame analysis to uncover the underlying dynamics of *Guanxi* in rural insurance sales.

2.6.2 Negotiation of Participation Framework through *Guanxi*

Based on the ideas of Goffman (1981), a participation framework is made up of "a set of positions which individuals within perceptual range of an utterance may take in relation to what is said" (Schiffrin, 1990: 242). Participation frameworks are negotiated during the interpersonal relationship. They are the results of actions and alignments that the individuals adopt towards themselves and others under certain circumstances. According to Goffman (1981), they are the results of the various footings used by the participants. Within such frameworks, both producer and recipient can occupy a certain position, as shown below, although the reception end of a discourse is seldom made explicit in literature (Scollon, 1995a):

Productive		Receptive
(1) Animator	mechanical	receptor
(2) Author	rhetorical	interpreter
(3) Principal	responsibl	judge
(4) Figure	narrative	any of the above roles

An animator is basically an aspect of a producer involved in the actual physical production of the talk; an author is an aspect creating the talk; a principal is an aspect responsible for the content of the talk; and lastly, a figure is portrayed through the talk. These different roles may or may not be performed by the same person even if they are all activated in an utterance. Similarly, from the receptive side, a receptor is an aspect of recipient which only technically receives what is said. An interpreter may need to interpret what is said; a judge is responsible for the quality of an utterance, in terms of truth, validity, and so on. Here again, a single person may or may not perform all these receptive roles during interaction.

The notion of participant roles (especially the productive roles) has been taken up by a number of linguists, most vigorously in the concepts of discourse role (Thomas, 1986) and discourse identity (R. Scollon and S. W. Scollon, 2001). Thomas (1986) defined the relationship between the speaker and the message by a number of specifications, such as "spokesperson" (corresponding to "principal"), "mouthpiece" (corresponding to "animator"), "reporter" (similar to "author"), "overhearer" and "bystander". Therefore, Thomas made contribution to the understanding of participation framework by adding two extra specifications, "overhearer" and "bystander". However, on the one hand, these two specifications are rather intermittent and peripheral in nature. On the other hand, Scollon's concept of discourse identity seems to offer better understanding of the dynamic nature of participation in discourse since this concept makes possible that the participation framework be extended to the receptive side of communication and the socio-interactive roles of participation. As R. Scollon and S. W. Scollon (2001) put it, discourse identity is the role/roles a person can claim with degree and range of power and comprises the productive and receptive roles demonstrated above, intersecting with the socio-interactive roles a person has power to enact. The socio-interactive roles include "framers", who have the authority to define the communication event; "players", who are participants of the event; and "observers", who are neither framers nor players but have the right to observe the event.

Nevertheless, it should be noted with caution that discourse identity does not have the same status as other social identities; discourse identities are only the ancillaries of social identities, without which they mean very little (Sarangi and Slembrouck, 1996). Or in other words, discourse identities can be the specific representation of social identities in communication. This is so because the role a person can claim—whether animator, principal, or author—depends on the social identity that a person possesses. For instance, a scholar in insurance can be an "author" and "principal" of his expert knowledge in insurance, while an insurance sales agent cannot. When selling insurance policies, an insurance agent may only borrow or quote, as a mouthpiece, the insurance knowledge to convince his prospective clients to buy the policies. Of course, one may argue that a person can falsify a particular social identity to perform certain participation roles, but it is still that "falsified" social identity that makes its discourse identities relevant. As a result, discourse identity and social identity are interrelated and inseparable.

Moreover, although a particular social identity can entitle a person to a particular discourse identity, this will not hold up in a simple one-to-one relationship. The reason is simply that we rarely play only one social identity in any interaction. In R. Scollon and S. W. Scollon's discourse system, at any one time we may belong to more than one social identity (sometimes these identities may conflict with each other) or one discourse system. The "final" discourse identity we engage will be one negotiated from all potential discourse identities defined by the discourse system to which we belong (R. Scollon and S. W. Scollon, 2001). To relate this to the context of the present research, the discourse identities of the participants involved will be a combination of those entitled by the social identities of friends and salespersons/clients. They are obviously different discourse identities defined by two different discourse systems.

Since discourse identities are a negotiated result of two, three, or even more discourse systems, they are in a dialectical relationship. As already argued above, discourse identities are only ancillaries of social identities. Subordinating social identities to discourse identities in analysis is impossible, because without social identities, discourse identities are basically empty entities. We will never be able to understand why a particular discourse identity is used instead of others without looking at the social identity itself. As a result, it is only possible to "negotiate" social identities by "adjusting" discourse identities, not "negotiate" discourse identities by "adjusting" social identities, since discourse identities are in essence a "tool" for achieving social identities.

A constructionist view will be highly relevant here. To examine the phenomenon from the constructionist paradigm, it can be argued that the identities involved, as friends, salespeople, or clients, are, to a certain extent, cooperatively constructed by the discourse identities participants claim, reject, or contest in an interaction. To put it another way, by actively engaging in an interaction, participants will cooperatively maintain and adjust their discourse identities in order to negotiate their social identities. It should be noted that a participant can adjust not only his/her own discourse identities but also those of his/her partners in an interaction.

2.6.3 Frames, Footing and Contextualization Cues

As already mentioned above, identity construction cannot possibly happen in a vacuum, the previous exposure of participants towards other interlocutors and the context where interaction takes place is indispensable to understanding how participants make sense of themselves and others in interactions. This concept can be visited under the broader concept of "frames", "footing" and "contextualization cues".

The concept of frames has been developed as a tool for analysis in various fields, including psychology and sociology (Taylor, 2000), business management (Watzlawick and Fisch, 1974), artificial intelligence (Minsky, 1975), decision-making (Kahneman and Tversky, 1979), negotiation (Neale and Bazerman, 1985), and environmental conflict management, linguistics, and education, although in each field it has different connotations (For example, in psychology and education the concept of frame is more commonly known as scripts or schema.). However, since the present research is more linguistics-oriented, the term "frame" means plans for understanding through which the world is interpreted and judged (Dechert, 1983). However, these plans are not necessarily static, stored knowledge or cognitive schemata as used in the traditional psychological sense (Fiske and Taylor, 1991). As a conceptual tool, frame analysis (Bateson, 1972; Goffman, 1975; Tannen, 1986, 1993) is particularly suited for understanding how people construct meaning from moment to moment. Interactants jointly signal their definition of a situation through framing. That is, as people speak and act, they signal to each other what they believe they are doing (e.g., what activity they are performing or what speech act they are producing) and in what way they want their words and gestures to be understood. The intricate ways in which framing is accomplished in verbal interaction is captured through Goffman's (1981) notion of footing, or the alignment that speakers and hearers take toward each other and toward the content of their talk. Interlocutors jointly construct frames by signaling their own ever-shifting footings while recognizing and ratifying those of co-participants. Nonetheless, it should be noted with special caution that footing is not the same as frame. As already mentioned, footing refers to the speakers' and listeners' adjustment of their stances or alignments towards each other during interactions, while frames are, to a certain extent, made up of alignments we bring to interactions prior to interactions, apart from their script- or content-based elements. In other words, frame refers to somewhat already existing understanding of the interactions, while footing is most suited for the analysis of moment-to-moment interactions. Still, the two concepts—frames and footing—are closely interrelated: Interactive changes in footings of speakers or listeners may lead to corresponding shifts in frames, and vice versa.

The concepts of frame and footing are closely related to the present research in the way that by "describing the form and meaning of social and interpersonal contexts that provide presuppositions for the decoding of meaning" (Schiffrin, 1994: 105), these concepts are extremely useful in revealing how participants make sense of themselves in interactions. This corresponds to the focus of the present research on how people maintain and construct various identities in a new, unfamiliar context. The frames that will be activated in an insurance sales agent's interactions include those of friendship, selling, buying, institutions, health, family responsibility, and future risks. A reconstructed example will be demonstrated in the sample analysis in Chapter 5.

However, Goffman's concept does not focus on the language, they are insufficient in the sense that the role of language is still unclear in the inferring process. This gives rise to Gumperz's (1982, 1992b) more fine-grained linguistic concept of contextualization cues, dealing with the weaknesses of the sociological notion of frames, which is more general in nature and more geared to the structure of interaction itself. The key notion of Gumperz's works is to "account for our ability to interpret what participants intend to convey in everyday communicative practice" (Gumperz, 2001: 215). That is, Gumperz develops a way that not only explicates the interpretive procedures underlying talk, but also addresses the consequences of real-life, everyday conversational misunderstandings between members of different cultural groups (Duranti and Goodwin, 1992: 229-230). To put it another way, he is interested in speakers' and listeners' interpretation of local linguistic (or metalinguistic) meanings in order to draw wider inferences about what is happening in an interaction. The constant drawing of similar inferences will in turn reinforce the perception, values, and knowledge, forming the stable social identities we have in society.

Thus contextualization cues serve as signaling frames, for Gumperz (1982: 131) defined contextualization cues as the following:

> *Constellations of surface features of message form are the means by which speakers signal and listeners interpret what the activity is, how semantic content is to be understood and how each sentence relates to what precedes or follows.*

Gumperz also remarked that "Contextualization cues, along with other indexical signs, serve to retrieve the frames (in Goffman's sense) that channel the interpretive process" (Prevignano and di Luzio, 2003: 10). In other words, using a speaker's contextualization cues as guidelines, a listener imagines himself or herself to be in a particular kind of situation; this enables a listener to assess what the speaker intends. Therefore, contextualization cues are a means of collaboratively accomplishing framing in discourse.

2.6.4 *Guanxi* and Topic

The description and analysis of the dynamic management of topics in agent-client interactions in transformational China's rural areas can reveal vividly not only the interactive patterns but also the underlying dynamics operating under the interactions.

1. *Guanxi* in communication

Guanxi has been generally referred to as interpersonal relationships and also as *Renqing*, face, gift or even *Renlun* in Confucianism. While in insurance sales discourse, there is clear evidence of the interaction and mediation between traditional Chinese society as a "society of the familiars" and a more modern society as "society of contracts". The concept of *Guanxi* has always been the focus of social studies, since it is the nature of human society (Zhai, 2007b: 118), while such other concepts as contract, democracy, power, regulation, game, trust and face are evolving around *Guanxi*. In order to make the analysis into a finer and more detailed one, it is highly necessary to divide the analysis into such micro-units as topic and discourse identity.

However, it needs to be noted that *Guanxi* is a complex concept, buyer-seller similarity could be one aspect of *Guanxi*, and it has been generalized that buyer-seller similarity positively influences sales across four dimensions: 1) similarity of expertise in product use experience, 2) similarity in attitudes, 3) similarity of physical and demographic variables, and 4) similarity of affiliation characteristics or communicator style (Jamie and Gary, 1997). Specifically, sales people generally are advised to present themselves as similar by adapting to their clients' topic preference (Micali, 1971), physical characteristics (Crosby, Evans and Cowles, 1990; Evans, 1963), or communicator style (Dion and Notarantonio, 1992; Miles, Arnold and Nash, 1990; Weitz, 1978).

It is noted that identities are indirectly indexed through language (Hamilton, 1996; Ochs, 1992). Meanwhile, direct indexing of one's identity through language is also possible, for example, someone explicitly claims his/her identity in a discourse (Mokros, 1996). In the context of sales discourse, it has been well accepted that successful sales people are competent communicators (Williams, Spiro and Fine, 1990) who have the relative knowledge, skill, and motivation to interact effectively and appropriately (Spitzberg and Cupach, 1984). Specifically in rural insurance sales, before the actual interaction between the agents and the prospective clients happens, there has already been a certain relationship between them, and such relationship tends to be built into an ongoing relationship. What is argued here is that insurance sales agents' identities are utilized to realize the conclusion of policy sales. That is to say, existing relationships are first an instrument or lubricant used to facilitate or enhance the sales, and then they are further strengthened, as will be illustrated and analyzed later.

2. Topic in communication

In everyday conversation, the participants organize their talk in an orderly, connected, coherent, meaningful and acceptable way. One of the organization ways is through the topic. Topic is defined as "what the speakers talk about" (Stenstrom, 1994: 150). Similarly, Yule (1980) defined discourse topic as "what is generally being talked about". Conversation analysis posits symmetries between speakers (Drew and Heritage, 1992b; Sacks, 1974; Schegloff, 1987, 1992a). It holds that in a conversation, topics are neither pre-planned nor predictable in their number and in the scope and development of their content by any one party, which implies there is an equality of speaker rights to initiate and develop topics. However, in insurance sales conversations, it is found that some parties are trying to maintain topic control and domination. Even in most conversations, topics are negotiated through the turn-taking process with the cooperation between speakers and hearers. Such cooperative topic management by all speakers can be motivated by the needs and priorities of conflict-avoidance, mutual and balanced interest, consideration of the participants, creation and maintenance of common ground, harmony, cooperation and agreement (Wilson, 2009; Geluykens, 1993; Bublitz, 1988).

Previous studies on topics also show cross-cultural differences in structure, lexical choice, functions, response types, distribution, and intent (Chen, 1993; Creese, 1991; Herbert 1986, 1989, 1991; Holmes, 1986, 1988; Knapp, Hooper and Bell, 1984; Manes and Wolfson, 1981; Pomerantz, 1978; Wieland, 1995; Wolfson, 1981, 1983, 1984). Other dialogical studies such as Mentis (1994), in examining topic management, suggested that successful topic management, which was a necessary prerequisite for the establishment of conversational coherence, involved an interaction among situational, social, textual, topical, interpersonal, linguistic and cognitive conditions that were specific to the context of situation. Thus, different topics, driven by the underlying conversational purposes, can reveal the features of different discourse systems. More specifically, in friendship discourse, social topic is one of the typical features; while in promotional discourse, business topics are more preferred. Nonetheless, in insurance sales interactions, for most of the time, it is hard to clearly delineate the boundary between social topics and business topics, since sometimes social topics are picked up for the preparation of business topics, or as a kind of smoothing instrument to facilitate the communication.

The data for this study will be first analyzed according to topics, categorized as social and business, which will represent the features of the two different discourse systems, after that such finer detailed analysis as footing and contextualization cues, to reveal the implicit power relations between the agents and the prospective clients.

3. The management of topic and *Guanxi*

Since the objective of the present study is to unveil the dynamics through analyzing the conversations between the insurance sales agents and their clients, one of the dynamics in such interactions is the conscious/unconscious control/manipulation of topics in the conversations. Different topics can reveal features of different discourse systems, and more specifically, the management of topics in agent-client interactions can show how the intricacies of *Guanxi* involved are working in the sales of insurance policies.

2.7 Data Collection and Data Analysis

Based on the transcribed data, the chief methodology of the present study is discourse analysis, focusing on conversation analysis (CA) at the micro-analytic level. It is a field of research that originated in the 1960s, but later collaborated by conversation analysts, such as Sacks (1974), Heritage (1984), Jefferson (1984,

1987, 2004) and many other researchers (Duranti, 1988; Heritage, 1984; Hutchby and Wooffitt, 1998; Psathas, 1995; Zimmerman, 1988). Many analysts have studied mundane social action and have achieved desired results in such areas of discourse organization as turn organization (Boden, 1983; Roger, 1989; Sacks, 1974; Schegloff, 1996, 2000a, 2001), repair organization (Schegloff, Jefferson and Sacks, 1977; Schegloff, 1979, 1987, 1992b, 1997a, 1997b, 2000b; Jefferson, 1987), preference organization (Goodwin, 1984, 1986; Pomerantz, 1984), assessment organization (Goodwin and Duranti, 1992; C. Goodwin and M. H. Goodwin, 1987; Pomerantz, 1984), and sequence organization (Schegloff, 1990, 1995; Wilson, 1991). Other scholars study the structure of social interaction (Eggins and Slade, 1997; Lin, 2004; Yang, 1994; Zimmerman and Boden, 1991), intra-cultural communication in various languages (Egbert, 1993, 1996, 1997a, 1997b; Hayashi, 1999, 2001, 2003; Hayashi, Mori and Takagi, 2002) and intercultural communication studies (Cheng, 2003; R. Scollon and S. W. Scollon, 1991, 2001; Tanaka, 1999). Regarding Chinese data used in CA approach, most of it focuses on Cantonese (Kong, 2001, 2002, 2003; Luke, 1990). Nonetheless, their findings on Chinese communication may not satisfactorily explain the interaction pattern and linguistic features specific to the Mainland Chinese for the data they collect and use for their analysis.

The CA approach can uncover and describe the organizational features of conversation, the tacit reasoning procedures and sociolinguistic competence underlying the production, the ways in which participants understand and respond to one another and the generation of their sequence of actions. In the following, I will argue for and justify data collection, subjects and research procedures.

2.7.1 Data Collection and Transcription Conventions

A qualitative approach has been chosen as the major method. In the first place, the study is by nature a sociolinguistic investigation of how the insurance sales agents and the prospective clients in insurance sales interactions mobilize such social resources as familiarity, credibility, social status and such linguistic devices as discourse identity and topic to achieve their individual communicative purposes respectively.

The data for the current study has been recorded from naturally occurring authentic conversations between the insurance sales agents and their prospective clients. In sociolinguistics or business English studies (Cameron and Taylor, 1988; Planken, 2005), and cross-cultural/intercultural pragmatic studies (Bargiela-Chiappini, 2009), data are generally gathered in a controlled and selective way and the focus is always on one or several types of speech acts. As Huo (2004: 69) noted, it is preferred that this type of data for this kind of research be collected in a natural, uncontrolled way in that we did not confine ourselves to a certain type of data but include all instances of dynamics in our corpus. Determined by the nature of the study, we hold that such a corpus tends to be more suitable for the qualitative approach although sometimes, some statistics might be conducive to its better interpretation (Huo, 2004).

The data for the present research are recorded data of authentic conversations or interviews, thus, they are naturally occurring data and can be considered as reliable. The data collected are recordings of conversations between the insurance sales agent and their clients at their homes, tea houses, meeting rooms or other places where the conversations take place from 2009 to 2013 (about 80 hours, 50 conversations). The conversations are carried out between 5 agents and 45 (prospective) clients, all of whom are located in a county in mid-China.

The selected data for the analysis of the study are 10 conversations between the 5 agents and their clients, while others are used for triangulation purpose. The data have been transcribed by myself according to the conventions of CA for discourse analysis purposes. Some of them involve two agents (the more experienced agent accompanies the less experienced one to visit their clients); some of them involve more than one client (their family members or relatives might be present). In general, some of them involve two participants; some others may involve several participants since the conversations are rather informal in nature and there could be the prospective client's relatives or friends presented during the conversations. Their names, and some specific names of their products and their prices are replaced by pseudonyms or "×"s.

Technically, since CA lays a great deal of emphasis on the use of extracts from transcriptions of recorded interactions in research, it is necessary to describe the details of the interactions. A system of symbolic notations is used in transcribing the interactions according to the standard Mandarin pronunciations and the transcription conventions developed by Jefferson (1984, 2004) with slight modifications to fit my research aims. Each transcribed Mandarin utterance normally has two lines: Chinese characters and idiomatic English translation of the whole utterance, trying to preserve the "real meaning" of the Mandarin utterances if possible. Omissions, pauses/silences, overlaps, latches and the like were preserved (detailed in Appendix 1). However, due to the differences between Chinese and English, such as differences in word order and rhetorical speech use, the specifics about the speaker's delivery of the speech and turn in the English translations were not exact, and the original Mandarin utterances should be consulted when reading the transcriptions.

Concerning the regional factors, even if linguistic and sub-cultural differences did exist geographically, they were comparatively insignificant since the data was limited to Mandarin on the mainland of PRC. The participants are the Chinese people on the mainland of PRC, who generally had learned the same or similar Chinese language courses at schools, and immersed in the local environment. The findings would only reflect the generic nature of communication pattern and language use of insurance sales agents from the perspective of linguistic analysis.

2.7.2 The Sampled Location

The location has been chosen for the following reasons, through personal connections, I had access to insurance sales agents and their clients in Nanling

County, a rural area in the middle of Anhui Province. Its economic development ranks in the middle as well. In terms of geography, it locates in the middle of China; in terms of economy, it is relatively economically better off in Anhui Province, most of the local residents working as self-employed small business owners or working in various lines of business in the major cities such as Guangzhou or Shanghai in China.

Such a phenomenon has several important implications for the present research. First of all, it enables them to be exposed to the economic, cultural and socio-political development of the metropolises. According to Skinner (1977), in terms of social mobility, cities and metropolises act as mega-centers in the regional urbanization. In other words, not only commodities, technologies and services flow from the cities to the rural areas, but ideologies and values as well. This has been echoed by Madeline Levine (Levine, 2007: 28-36), who criticized what she saw as a large change in American culture—"a shift away from values of community, spirituality, and integrity, and towards competition, materialism and disconnection". Another thing she found was that emulation was also a core component of the 21st century consumerism. As a general trend, regular consumers seek to emulate those who are above in the social hierarchy. The poor strive to imitate the wealthy and the celebrities and other icons. The celebrity endorsement of products can be seen as evidence of the desire of modern consumers to purchase products partly or solely to emulate people of higher social status. This purchasing behavior may co-exist in the mind of a consumer with an image of oneself as being an individualist. The sampled location can represent the trend of macro socio-economic transformation and demonstrate the key features of such socio-cultural changes. Since the above mentioned major cities are the relatively well-developed cities in China, the values and ideologies they uphold have been more recent, new, and modern, which represent the typical features of an utilitarian discourse as openness, directness, truthfulness, rationality and clarity (Flowerdew, 1997); while in other more remote rural areas than Nanling county, there are more salient features of a Confucianism discourse as hierarchical and indirect (Flowerdew, 1997). Since these prospective clients work and earn their living there, when they come back to their hometown, they tend to bring these values and ideologies home, which will have been in interplay with the more past, old, and traditional concepts. Moreover, since they are economically better-off, they have the purchasing capacity to buy insurance policies promoted by the agents.

The research site is also chosen for the purpose of convenience of broader and accessible personal networks, since I was born and raised there. The conversations between the agents and their (prospective) clients are all recorded in the local dialect; however, this specific dialect does not pose a problem for me, since I was born and raised there, as mentioned earlier. Nevertheless, the certain features of the local dialect are to be presented in the transcription of the data, since there are certain particles, intonation or other peculiar language features serving as contextualization cues specifically only in the local settings. Also more importantly, its current cultural, economic and socio-political status is more characteristic of China's transformation from a planned to market-oriented economy.

In a word, this research site is best suited for demonstrating the target phenomenon and convenient for collecting authentic first-hand data and follow-up interviews.

2.8 The Research Procedure

The present study chooses authentic and naturally occurring talks representing the normal use of language, instead of invented and decontextualized ones or produced by "linguist's intuition" (Tsui, 1994: 6). The authentic and naturally occurring data were collected by recording face-to-face insurance sales conversations by the insurance sales agents in Nanling County. There are totally 5 agents who agreed to help record their sales talks, all of whom are local residents who know their prospective clients. Since insurance sales usually take a long period of time and are usually multi-round, the conversations recorded are also between one agent and different clients. At the present stage, 10 sales talks are transcribed for the analysis.

As to the recording procedures, I asked the agents to put the audio recorder either on the table they are sitting at or in the agents' pockets to record the conversations. I did not present myself in most of the recorded conversations for the sake of less interference. I was allowed to observe some of the agents from the beginning to the end by following their visits to their clients. For other agents, since they were less familiar with me, it was difficult to seek their agreement for participant observation. Nonetheless, they agreed to record the conversations and participated in the follow-up interviews. Some interviews on language use and interaction structure were conducted afterwards to help and affirm my later analysis and interpretation.

As already mentioned above, the study is basically a qualitative one, but supported by empirical authentic data. As Flick (2009) argued by identifying social change as an important issue in the rise in practice and interest in qualitative research, "Rapid social change and the resulting diversification of life worlds are increasingly confronting social researchers with new social contexts and perspective... traditional deductive methodologies... are failing... thus research is increasingly forced to make use of inductive strategies instead of starting from theories and testing them... knowledge and practice are studied as local knowledge and practice." (Flick, 2009: 12)

2.9 Analysis Procedure

The analysis of the data starts from the transcriptions, followed by transcription study to identify some recurrent phenomena across the transcribed conversations. The criteria for the selection of the phenomena are that they have to be linguistically significant in terms of interactions and persuasion processes, and that they are recurrently found in the conversations. The procedures are as follows.

Chapter 2 Mechanism of the Chinese Insurance Sales, Data Collection and Analysis

Listening to the data; classifying the data; selecting the data; transcribing the selected data; studying the data for recurrent phenomena on interaction pattern and linguistic realizations; examining the discovered phenomena; in-depth discourse analysis of the excerpts by focusing on the phenomena; making cultural and linguistic interpretations of the analyzed phenomena; studying the interpersonal preferences; and generating implications from the analysis.

A qualitative approach is applied first with an aim to discover and reconstruct patterns in insurance sales discourse. The data are examined for emerging patterns and language use that reflect the most striking features of the Chinese insurance sales agents in terms of discourse conventions, cultural patterns and values and linguistic manifestations in the sales process. The qualitative findings help to provide background information on the context and subject, acting as an aid for scale construction (Punch, 1998). The quantitative findings were applied to provide the basis for qualitative study with an aim to generate and frame the preferred patterns and linguistic choice in insurance sales discourse.

2.10 Summary

This chapter attempts to integrate the macro- and micro-analysis: In macro-analysis, R. Scollon and S. W. Scollon's overarching framework of discourse system is adopted; in terms of micro-analysis, such important concepts as genre, moves, steps, participation framework, footing, contextualization cues are offered and explicated, and their application is argued. Thus, the analytical framework that guides the present research is established. We adopt an approach that conducts linguistic analysis with ethnographic interviews, and the interviews are used for triangulation purpose. The three key questions are raised and their purposes are explained; data collection methods and procedures are also explained and argued for their suitability. Undeniably, the interactions between the agents and their clients have also received harsh criticism in that agents may manipulate or even deceive the clients to achieve their economic goals. Nonetheless, against this reality, there is also an appeal to reforms and changes for a more enhanced, harmonious and trust-based relationship. In the present research, the agents and their (prospective) clients will be identified with shared memberships of two different discourse systems and the communication between them as manifested in the negotiation of these two competing discourse systems.

Chapter 3

Genre Analysis of the Insurance Sales Dialogues

This chapter analyzes the data from the perspective of genre analysis. It studies the communicative purposes, moves and steps (Swales, 1990; Bhatia, 1993) of the insurance sales interactions in transformational China's rural areas to generalize generic structures underlying such interactions.

3.1 Different Schools of Genre Analysis

Ever since the introduction of the concept of genre into linguistic study in the 1970s, its definition has been widely discussed, especially by scholars and practitioners working in Systemic Functional Linguistics (Martin, 1984), Narrative School (Bamberg, 2010) and American School (or Swalesian School) (Swales, 1990; Bhatia, 1997a, 2005). The concept of genre is considered as "a fuzzy concept" (Swales, 1990: 33) as well as a controversial one (Reid, 1987) because people employ it to mean different things in different contexts. For several decades, genre analysis has been widely employed in linguistic analysis, probing into various discourses, among which, most are extensive in political, business and academic discourses. The following reviews different schools of genre analysis and justifies the choice of Swalesian approach.

3.1.1 Australian School

Australian School holds that genre is a type of discourse and that the generic structure of a text defines a genre, so that texts of the same genre will realize the same obligatory elements of structure (Hasan, 1995). Martin (1984, 1987, 1992) defined genre as staged, goal-oriented social processes and structural forms that cultures use in certain contexts to achieve various purposes. Australian genre scholars have mainly focused their attention on genre analysis relating to primary and secondary school education and non-professional texts rather than on university and professional writing activities. They focus on both global text structure and sentence-level register features, associated with field, mode and tenor. This approach offers a useful descriptive and interpretive framework for analyzing language. Nonetheless, most of their work focus on primary and secondary educational settings. They hold that education is supposed to be a process in which students are taught patterns of knowledge, ways of behaving and ways of working, which are considered involvement in social life. One major task for schools is to socialize students into knowledge of this kind. For example, Christie (1986) argued for a strong relationship between ways of learning in schools and patterns of discourse (generic structures), which are considered in a systemic perspective as ways of meaning and ways of organizing experience.

3.1.2 Narrative School

The narrative genre has been extensively analyzed and applied. One of the most widely employed analytical models (Labov, 1972) divides the main stages of the narrative genre as follows:

> ABSTRACT—What is the story going to be about?
> ORIENTATION—Who are the participants? When and where did the action take place? In which circumstances?
> COMPLICATING ACTION—What happened? What problems occurred?
> EVALUATION—What is the point of the story? So what?
> RESOLUTION—How did events sort themselves out? What finally happened?
> CODA—What is the bridge between the events in the story and the present situation of the narration?

This model offers a clear structure for application. However, not all stories have these stages and many story-tellers dispense with a formal abstract and coda, due to the fact that it holds a story which cannot normally be considered to be a well-formed narrative if it lacks any of the other main constituents. Most of genre theorists in this line of research underline the importance of teachers knowing about such structure and staging and that such knowledge can help them support pupil's writing development by encouraging children to move from less complete narratives to more complete narratives.

3.1.3 American School

American School argues that "each genre is an instance of successful achievement of specific communicative purpose using conventionalized knowledge of linguistic and discoursal resources" (Bhatia, 1993: 3). Such a definition of genre is widely accepted and extensively quoted in the fields of ESP (English for Specific Purposes), whose main concern is that genre is used as a tool for analyzing and teaching the spoken and the written languages required of non-native speakers in academic and professional settings (Bhatia, 1993: 14; Flowerdew, 2003: 20; Hopkins and Dudley-Evans, 1988: 31; Swales, 1990: 21). Scholars in this field have framed genre as oral and written text types defined by their formal properties as well as by their communicative purposes within social contexts.

In applied linguistics, Swales (1990) systematically studied the genre of research articles in academic and research settings. His approach is closely related to the ethnographic communication (Hymes, 1972; Miller, 1984):

> *A genre comprises a class of communicative events, the members of which share some set of communicative purposes. These purposes are recognized by the expert members of the parent discourses community and thereby constitute the rationale for the genre. This rationale shapes the schematic structure of the discourse and influences and constrains the choice of content and style (Swales, 1990: 58).*

Swales offered a good fusion of linguistic and sociological factors in this definition, and it set up a relationship between the purpose accomplished by a genre and the structure of the genre by suggesting that the communicative purpose of a genre shaped the genre and provided it with a schematic structure.

Bhatia (1993) analyzed sales promotion letters, research articles, legislative provisions, etc. in more detail, and further developed Swales' definition of genre.

It is a recognizable communicative event characterized by a set of communicative purpose(s) identified and mutually understood by the members of the professional or academic community in which it regularly occurs. Most often it is highly structured and conventionalized with constraints on allowable contributions in terms of their intent, positioning, form and functional value. These constraints, however, are often exploited by the expert members of the discourse community to achieve private intentions within the framework of socially recognized purpose(s) (Bhatia, 1993: 13).

In this definition, Bhatia further developed Swales' definition, by combining psychological factors and considering genre as a dynamic social process. Just as Bhatia (1993:16) commented: Swales underplayed psychological factors, thus undermining the importance of tactical aspects of genre construction, which played a significant role in the concept of genre as a dynamic social process, as against a static one.

Later Bhatia (1997a) further explained genre analysis as the study of the situated linguistic behavior in institutionalized academic or professional settings. It has the following four characteristics.

(1) Rather than providing a detailed extension, validation or otherwise of one linguistic framework or the other, genre analysis shows a genuine interest in the use of language to achieve communicative goals. In this sense, it is not an extension of linguistic formalism.

(2) However, genre analysis does not represent a static description of language use but gives a dynamic explanation of the way expert users of language manipulate generic conventions to achieve a variety of complex goals. In this

sense, it combines the advantages of a sociolinguistics perspective, especially the use of ethnographic information, with those of a cognitive perspective, especially regarding the tactical use of language.

(3) It is primarily motivated by applied linguistic concerns, especially language teaching at various levels.

(4) It is narrow in focus but wide in vision, focusing on specific differentiation in language use at various levels of generality.

According to Bhatia, learners need to develop the understanding of code, the acquisition of genre knowledge associated with the specialist culture, sensitivity to cognitive structuring of specialist genres and then, and only then, can they hope to exploit generic knowledge of a repertoire of specialist genres by becoming informed users of the discourse of their chosen field.

Among others, Makaya and Bloor (1987) analyzed economics forecasts of schematic structures; Pilegaard (1997) analyzed politeness from a text-linguistic perspective in written business discourse; Dos Santos (2000) analyzed business letters of negotiation with a genre analysis approach.

Therefore, the following questions can be raised: Why do the writers write in the way they do instead of other ways? What are the underlying reasons? With the above definitions and explanations, the answer seems to be surfaced: Such factors as socio-cultural and linguistic ones, and marketing factors need to be taken into account when a particular genre, the communication between the insurance sales agents and their clients, is being analyzed.

Genre analysis is also a very popular subject of study by many domestic scholars and researchers. Most of the genre analyses are done in a simulated way to their foreign counterparts. Few of the studies are carried out to discover the similarities and differences between two languages, namely, Chinese and English texts. There are application of theories and methodologies in the Chinese context, application of the analyses into ESP teaching, integration of genre analysis and pragmatics or other linguistic disciplines, to name just a few. But their results are all fruitful and inspiring.

Many scholars have also done research with genre analysis or cross-cultural communication in different settings. Chen (1999) employed genre analysis in the teaching of business English writing. Xu (2004) studied the pragmatic strategies employed in business English correspondence. Hu (2004) carried out an analysis on schematic structure of letters. Zhao (2001) applied Swales' and Bhatia's definitions and ways of analyzing to the moves and steps of introduction of English TV news. Huang (2001) discussed the application of genre analysis in the teaching of ESP. Zeng (2001) explored the correlation between genre analysis and the teaching of EST writing. There are still many other scholars who have done inspiring research in this field. Lin and Chen (1998) explored the writing skills of introduction to financial products and suggested some practical tips on the writing of this particular genre, but unfortunately there was not much theoretical support for their efforts.

Several important terms need to be explained before the tentative framework is proposed. Terms such as "move" and "step" will be explained at first. Although it is crucial to define a term before conducting the detailed analysis into it, the term "move" has been used by genre analysts in the past, yet no definition has been adequately formulated for it. The term "move" was first used by Bellack to refer to the maneuver of students and teachers in the classroom discourse (Bellack, 1966).

In the meantime, Sinclair and Coulthard used the term "move" in their analysis of classroom interaction to refer to the unit constituting exchange in the interaction between teachers and students (Sinclair and Coulthard, 1977). Nunan gave the same definition for move as the basic interactional unit of classroom discourse (Nunan, 1993).

In Swales' analysis, he noted that there was a regular pattern of "moves" and "steps" that appeared in certain order in the majority of the texts he investigated. A "move" is a unit that relates the writer's purpose to the content that he/she wishes to communicate. A "step" is a lower level text unit than the move that provides a detailed perspective on the options open to the writer in setting out the moves (Swales, 1990). The present study will follow Swales' definition of move and step.

To sum up, genre analysis is the study of situated linguistic behavior in institutionalized academic or professional settings (Bhatia, 2004), which extends the analysis beyond the textual product to incorporate context in a broader sense to account for not only the way text is constructed, but also for the way it is often interpreted, used and exploited in specific institutional or professional contexts to achieve specific disciplinary goals. The present research generally follows Swales (1990) and Bhatia (1993, 2004) in first identifying the communicative purposes and the root rhetorical structures of insurance sales discourse in transformational China's rural areas in terms of its moves and steps. The advantages are obvious. Firstly, the generic structure or prototypical, recurrent features of insurance sales discourse can be surfaced and summarized, which will be of value not only for academic study, but also for insurance sales practitioners, (prospective) clients and the recruiting and training of insurance companies. Secondly, with the presentation of generic structures, we can not only have a better knowledge and understanding of the use and exploitation of genres, but also organizational intentions within the constructs of "socially recognized communicative purposes". Thirdly, as Bhatia (2004: 23) argued, "genres are reflections of disciplinary and organizational cultures, and in that sense, they focus on social actions embedded within disciplinary, professional and other institutional practices". By examining the generic features of insurance sales agent-(prospective) client interactions, insights into the overall functions of such features may be further delineated. In addition, this research broadens the focus of previous research by examining the discourse of speakers in transformational China's rural areas.

3.2 Communicative Purposes

Communicative purposes are essential in determining the genre category of any given material, as Askehave and Swales put it, it "has been used as an important and often primarily criterion for whether a particular discourse falls within a particular generic category"(Askehave and Swales, 2001).

Due to the fact that the sale of insurance policies is one of the promotional efforts, the communicative purposes should be similar to sales promotion letters, even though promotional letters are in written form, while the sale of insurance policies is mostly in oral form, thus we can summarize the communicative purposes according to Bhatia's (1993) summary of sales promotion letters as follows.

(1) Insurance policies are generally addressed to those potential customers who are known to have some need (immediate or future) for the product or service being promoted. Therefore, the most important function of the agent-(prospective) client interaction is to offer a clear, objective and attractive introduction to the products or service in terms of the perceived interests, needs or inhibitions of the potential customer.

(2) Due to the rampant advertisement present in everyday life and most interactions are unsolicited, the busy working people nowadays are not likely to bother to waste their precious time on such promotional efforts. Thus the interaction must be short and effective, mostly repetitive. However, this requirement contradicts sharply to another: There should be enough details about the promoted product or service in the introduction for those interested customers who already have some need for or intention to buy the product or service. Therefore, the interactions vary according to different prospective clients. Nonetheless, most insurance sales are done between the familiar ones in China's rural areas, trust plays a significant role, and trust building process is time-consuming. Therefore, the vast majority of the interactions are similar.

(3) Insurance agents serve as the first link or communication channel between an insurance company and a (prospective) client. In this respect, they are generally seen as initiating business relations between the two parties. Therefore, the initial interactions need to solicit further communication between the two parties. There should be some ways by which the insurance company can

be contacted. In this specific context, the agent is seen as the embodiment of the insurance company.

With the above communicative purposes identified, for most of the time, as one member of the professional community, the agents are well aware of the intent, positioning, form and functional value of the communicative purposes through their training and experience sharing meetings, simply put, their socialization. They can consciously or unconsciously exploit such constraints in their interactions with their prospective clients to achieve their intentions of concluding the sales. Next, it is important to discover the generic patterns in their sales efforts and communication with their (prospective) clients.

3.3 Moves and Steps

In analyzing sales promotion letters, Bhatia summarized the moves and steps of sales promotion letters, and Table 3.1 shows the moves and steps for sales promotion letters by Bhatia (1993). More detailed analysis are as follows.

Based on the model Bhatia (1993) offered, the moves and steps of the dialogues between the insurance sales agents and their (prospective) clients can be generalized as shown in Table 3.1.

Table 3.1 Moves and Steps of the Insurance Sales Agent-Client Dialogues

Moves and steps		Descriptions	Flexibility
1		Warming up	Obligatory
2		Introducing the offer	Obligatory
	(i)	(i) Offering the product or service	
	(ii)	(ii) Essential detailing of the offer	
	(iii)	(iii) Indicating value of the offer	
3		Offering incentives	Optional
4		Establishing credentials	Obligatory
5		Enclosing documents	Optional

		Continued
Moves and steps	Descriptions	Flexibility
6	Soliciting response	Obligatory
7	Using pressure tactics	Optional
8	Ending politely	Obligatory

Table 3.1 summarizes the moves and steps in the dialogues between the insurance sales agents and their prospective clients. The most significant difference lies in the first move, warming up and the fourth move, establishing credentials, which will be analyzed in detail later. Moreover, since trust plays a dominant role in the conclusion of sales, it has been emphasized all along.

3.3.1 A Sample Analysis of Moves and Steps

The analysis below offers an account and analysis of the dialogue between an agent and her prospective client from the perspective of moves and steps. At the very beginning, the background introduction offers a clear context of the dialogue.

(1) **Gender and age**: Both A and B are female in their thirties and forties.

(2) **Relationship between the two**: B is one of A's former clients, who has purchased insurance policies from A more than a year ago. The two are old friends. A is the director of the local county-level rural network (responsible for rural insurance), who is nice, well-respected, and hard-working with excellent work performance. B has a better-off life, whose four family members all have been insured, but she is reluctant to buy some policies for herself.

(3) **Circumstances**: The following dialogue is an excerpt from a 30-minute dialogue, the beginning part. And the latter part is mostly about the introduction and analysis of the specific terms and conditions, and in the end, the client made the purchase (Table 3.2).

Chapter 3　Genre Analysis of the Insurance Sales Dialogues

Table 3.2　Move Analysis of the Sale Dialogue

Dialogue	Analysis
1. B：来来来，坐下子哒。 (B: Come on, have a seat.)	Move 1: Warming up, Obligatory
2. A：嗯，这个鞋柜好漂亮的哦！ (A: Oh, you have a beautiful shoe cabinet.)	
3. B：唵，呵呵，那是他爸爸打的。呶，来喝点水。 (B: Hmm. He he, it's made by his father. Well, have some water.)	
4. A：哎哟！不要客气的唡。 (A: Hmm. Don't be so kind and generous.)	
5. B：哎哟！水又不是什么好东西。 (B: Well. Come on, water is nothing special.)	
6. A：哦，好。[停顿 0.5 秒]你那个怎么讲哦？ (A: Well, OK. [Pause for half a second] How about that (the insurance) we talked about last time?)	Move 2: Introducing the offer—Step 1: Offering the product or service
7. B：哦，交那个大病的那些吧？嗯，那个我不想搞——买那些年！（A）太长了咳？ (B: Oh, for serious diseases? Hmm, I don't want that—for so many years! (A) Too long?)	
8. B：对！重大疾病搞那些年干么事噢——那些年，死都死了，还要去干么事噢。 (B: Yes! What is the insurance for serious diseases for? —I will have been long gone for so many years.)	
9. A：那不是的哎，就是看中了这个噢。人健康最重要，你讲可是的噢。 (A: Well, no, not necessarily, that's exactly what's important! Health is the most important thing, don't you think?)	
10. B：那个买不买无所谓，你看我前向子生病，也报不掉。 (B: It doesn't matter for buying that or not. You see, I was sick recently and couldn't get any compensation.)	Move 2, Step 3: Indicating the value of the offer
11. A：你那个是小病呶，大病早发现，不都能治好嘛；你看也花多不了多少钱，不就一百来块钱嘛。我们这个分两块儿：一块儿是大病，一块儿是小病。 (A: What you had is a minor disease. If they were discovered early, some major diseases could be cured as well. You see, it doesn't cost you much, only about 100 yuan. We have two parts for that: One is for major diseases, and the other for minor ones.)	

-83-

Continued

Dialogue	Analysis
12. B：哎哟！我那个不是有医疗保险吗？ (B: Well. But didn't I have health insurance already?)	
13. A：我们这个不一样的。我们这个有两个功能的，又存钱又保障。我劝你哩，还是把它交了，就差这么两千块钱不得过日子啦。那点钱搞么东西噢。 (A: Ours is different from that. Ours has two major functions—both deposit and guarantee. I'd advise you buy it, It only costs you several thousand a year. What can we do with so little money?)	Move 2, Step 3: Indicating the value of the offer
14. B：我想搞社保。 (B: I'm thinking about social security plan.)	
15. A：社保也不影响嘛。你看噢，这个你交再搞社保，不影响嘛——假如健健康康的，20年后给你9万；万一有个什么事情，马上给你9万,合同终止；如果有重大疾病，医保那边照样报。这个保你100岁，就是你活多老保多老。 (A: It doesn't interfere with your social security plan. You see, you can have both social security and this—if keeping healthy, after 20 years, you'll have 90,000 yuan; in case anything bad happens, you will have 90,000 yuan right away, and the contract ends; if you have major diseases, you can get compensation from social security as well. This goes as long as your life.)	
16. B：就是太长了。你讲万一我家他不上班了怎么搞哩？ (B: It's just too long. What if my husband loses his job?)	Move 2, Step 2: Essential detailing of the offer
17. A：不上班啊？不上班哪不挣钱啊？ (A: Without a job? We can still make money if losing jobs!)	
18. B：挣屁钱，挣钱！ (B: We can't make money at all.)	
19. A：不上班你在家里歇到啊——你这房子不也是固定资产嘛。 (A: Will you stay at home still and rest?—After all you have this house as your fixed asset.)	
20. B 所说的听不清。 (What B said is inaudible.)	
21. A：[停顿2秒]反正我跟你讲，你这不多这3000块钱……你买了之后就晓得，其实那钱放在那里也就放着了，买了之后如果自己有点压力反而还是好事……	Move 2, Step 3: Indicating the value of the offer

Chapter 3　Genre Analysis of the Insurance Sales Dialogues

Continued

Dialogue	Analysis
(A: [Pause for 2 seconds] No matter what, I tell you, it's only 3000 yuan… and You will know after you have it. Actually it's of no use if you just put your money there. After all, if you have this, a little pressure will do you good as well…)	Move 2, Step 3: Indicating the value of the offer
22. B：嗯，那也是的哦。 (B: Hmm, it's true in that sense.)	
23. A：再讲我们××（公司名）你晓得呀，世界500强，中国最大的保险公司，参与了西部大开发，在世界各地都有大投资，这个东西还是有保障的，这点你放心，再讲我们在这边也不是一天两天，就是有什么问题，你到时候来找我，我肯定尽量带你帮忙解决……[停顿2秒]嗯，这样子，我来给你讲下这个保险的具体情况可好啊？ (A: And as you know our company is one of the world top 500, China's largest insurance company, taking part in Western Development and having major investment in all over the world. For this you can rest assured, and we are here not for just one or two days; if there's any problem, you can come to me anytime and I'll help you solve it… [Pause for 2 seconds] Hmm, now how about my introducing some specifics of this insurance?)	Move 4: Establishing credentials
24. B：好嘛，那你讲讲看。 (B: OK, you go ahead.)	
25. A：嗯，那你坐过来，这场子有这个文字材料，其他东西那场子不清楚我再用电脑给你讲。 (A: Hmm, come here to sit, we have some printed materials here; for other matters if you are unclear, I can show you on the computer.)	
26. B：好啊。 (B: OK.)	
（五分多钟讲解具体条款，介绍） (About five minutes introducing the specifics of the insurance) 27. A：××，你以前没办过保险吧？ (A: ××, you haven't bought any insurance, have you?)	Move 2, Step 2: Essential detailing of the offer
28. B：嗯，没办过。 (B: No, I haven't.)	
29. A：哦，那你真要办一个，现在保险都是政策行为的哎，我来给你讲一下我带你选的这一种。 (A: Oh, then you really need to have one. Nowadays, insurance is a kind of national policy. You can have a look at this one.)	

Continued

Dialogue	Analysis
30. B：那好蛮。 (B: All right.)	
31. A：我们公司最近新推出一种交 20 年的，一年 3000——将将我也讲了，交了 20 年以后，从现在开始算，20 年后给你 9 万。我们有什么东西讲什么东西，你别怪嗷，呵呵。 (A: Our company recently launched one type which lasts for 20 years, with 3,000 yuan per year, starting now; as I told you just now, after 20 years, you'll have 90,000 yuan. I'll talk straight, and don't feel be offended, he he.)	
32. B：那不要紧哦，呵呵。 (B: That's fine, he he.)	
33. A：唵，就是讲这样子，我们保险就是保一份安心，没什么事肯定最好，但是我们也晓得，天有不测风云，可是的；假如万一有个什么事情，马上给你 9 万，合同终止；如果有重大疾病，医保那边照样报。这个保你 100 岁，就是讲你活多老保多老。 (A: Hmm, this is how it goes. For insurance we buy a kind of assurance. It's of course better if there is nothing happening, but we also know there is always something expected about to happen, right? If anything happens, you'll get 90,000 right away, and the contract terminates; if there are any major diseases, you can get compensation from social security as well. It goes as long as your life.)	Move 2, Step 2: Essential detailing of the offer
34. B：这个东西我都晓得哦，你看我家里人不都买了嘛。 (B: I understand that. You see, my family all have bought it.)	
35. A：那是的，你这方面意识真是特别好，我们现在跟人讲这个东西，好多人都不理解，像你这种真是很先进的了。 (A: Yes, you are well aware of that. Many other people don't understand when I explain this to them. You are rather advanced.)	
36. B：呵呵。 (B: He he.)	
37. A：唵，你家里人都买得了了，那你更应该给你自己也买一份，你像我们现在都是四十来岁了，慢慢年纪大了，也搞不动了，可是的啊？现在要是条件允许，还是搞一个比较好，你讲呢？	Move 2, Step 3: Indicating the value of the offer

Chapter 3　Genre Analysis of the Insurance Sales Dialogues

Continued

Dialogue	Analysis
(A: Yeah, you have already bought it for your family, so now it's time for you to buy one for yourself. You see, we are already in our forties, growing old and will be unable to buy insurance, aren't we? If possible, it is wise to have one, right?)	
38. B：搞呢是好，但是我们家里人都买得了了，我觉得我自己身体啊各方面都还好，就不怎么想买…… (B: Yes, it's good. But my family have already got it and I think I'm physically good now, so I don't think it'll be necessary…)	
39. A：那你真错的，现在时代不一样啦。我们虽然是妇女，也要给自己些保障哎，完全靠人家也都是靠不住，最起码自己有一点，好些哎。 (A: You are really wrong. Now it's a different time. Though we are both women, we need to get ourselves insured as well; it's hard to rely on others. At least, we need to have something to get ourselves covered.)	
40. B 所说的听不清。 (What B said is inaudible.)	
41. A：等我们老了，干不动了，那时候我们小家伙负担也重得不得了。就讲现在，你看看这个房价多贵哦，我们县的房子都要四五千一个平方，等小孩子大了，最起码要给他们买房子搞个首期啊，现在那个首期也不是一点两点的；就讲我们到时候有多大力出多大力，但最起码还是不给他们增加负担啊，多少有个保障…… (A: When we grow old, and are not able to work, our children have got much burden already. You know how expensive the housing is. When they grow up, at least we need to prepare some down payment for them. Even in our county, it takes 4 to 5 thousand yuan per square meter for buying an apartment, and that is a lot of money. Even though we say we give whatever we have, the least we can do is to shoulder them with additional burden. At least it's an assurance…)	Move 2, Step 3: Indicating the value of the offer
42. B：是的哦，我们现在就发狠存钱嘛。 (B: Yes, that's why we work so hard to deposit.)	
43. A：你们现在的实力肯定没问题，我还是建议给你自己搞一个，他们都有，你自己也要搞一个哦。 (A: Now you have no problem financially. I'd suggest you have one. They all have it already. You need to have one for yourself as well.)	
44. B：暂时还真没考虑到这个…… (B: I really haven't thought about it…)	

Continued

Dialogue	Analysis
45. A：不要紧的嘛，现在这个保险是有个推广期，再有一个月就没有了。你看我们前段时间主推的那个××，你晓得吧？ (A: It's all right. Nowadays for each type of insurance there is a promotional period which lasts for only a month. You know the ××, the one we have been promoting recently, there is no such bargain any more.)	Move 2, Step 3: Indicating the value of the offer
46. B：嗯，晓得哦。 (B: Yes, I know.)	
47. A：那个××我们就推广了几个月，你现在想买就没得了。 (A: That ×× only lasted for several months, and it's impossible for people to buy it now.)	
48. B：现在买没得啦？ (B: Impossible to buy?)	
49. A：是的啊，所以想好得差不多了，就赶紧买。 (A: No, so once you are ready, buy it right away.)	Move 7: Pressure tactics, optional
50. B：哦，那我真要考虑下子了。 (B: Oh, then I need to think about it.)	
51. A：是的啊。 (A: Yeah.)	
52. B：这样子，等我家那个回来了，我跟他商量下子，这个我自己做主也不好，你讲可是的啊？ (B: All right, after my husband is back, I will talk to him. I can't make the decision now, right?)	
53. A：那是的哦，不要紧嘛，呐，我这场子有个建议书，我留到这场子，上面有我手机，你们到时候商量好了给我电话，我到时候过来就中了。 (A: Yes, indeed. It doesn't matter. We have a suggestion form here and I can leave it with you, and there is my contact. After you have made your decision, call me and I'll come over again.)	Move 5: Enclosing documents, optional
54. B：嗯，那好嘛，咦，××，你家小孩高三了吧？ (B: OK. Well, your son has already in his senior high school, right?)	Move 6: Soliciting response, obligatory
55. A：唵，高三喽，看那个不成器的东西高考不晓得怎么样。 (A: Yes, already senior now. He is no good and we are not sure about how it will be when it comes to the college entrance examination.)	

Chapter 3 Genre Analysis of the Insurance Sales Dialogues

Continued

Dialogue	Analysis
56. B：啊也，你家小孩子成绩好哦，上××中学不就基本大学没问题了嘛。 (B: Nah, your son have very good grades. Once he got to ×× Middle School, there should be no problem in getting into universities.)	Move 5: Enclosing documents, optional Move 6: Soliciting response, obligatory
57. A：那也不行哦，他成绩也不算好。 (A: Not at all, he is not so good.)	
……(继续家常)(Continues phatic talk)	
58. A：嗯，那好，我们就这么讲，到时候再联系噢。 (A: Well then, that's it, and let's keep in touch.)	Move 8: Ending politely, obligatory
59. B：嗯，就这么讲。 (B: OK, you have it.)	

Notes: A: Agent; B: Client

Bhatia's (1993) seven moves analysis offers an excellent exemplar to refer to in the analysis of the dialogues between the insurance agent and the prospective client. It would prove quite useful and powerful tool in generalizing the general discursive patterns in the agent-client interactions. However, owing to differences in oral and written language and the specific contextual factors, insurance sales dialogues in transformational China's rural areas do have their own particular generic structure in terms of moves and steps despite the fact that both of them are promotional in nature and their similar communicative purposes of trying to achieve the sales of the product or service in general. For example, in insurance sales dialogues, there is one obligatory move at each and every dialogue, that is warming up, which is exactly one of the most interesting parts that *Guanxi* dynamics function in the process of sales.

3.3.2 Detailed Analysis of Moves and Steps

The analyses of each move and step are as follows.

Move 1, warming up, is an obligatory move in all the recorded dialogues. Move 1 is found in all of the collected data, since the whole insurance sales is initiated on the basis of the familiarity between the agents and the clients. Though Move 1 can be in different forms, it is obligatory in nature, which serves as a starting point.

From the analysis of the dialogues and the sample dialogue in Table 3.3, the most striking finding is that in each and every dialogue, actually in each and every interaction between the agent and the (prospective) client, it is imperative to have the first obligatory move—warming up, different from Bhatia's (1993) analysis of promotion letters with the first obligatory move as establishing credentials. It may be argued that this is due to the differences between written communication and oral communication. It is quite natural and important for people to greet each other before they talk about anything else.

1. Types of warming up

Warming up serves an important function in insurance sales agent-client interactions, and it distinguishes itself from other sales encounters. For most of the time, warming up appears in the form of phatic communication, while phatic expression, first introduced by Malinowski (1923) whose only function is to perform a social talk, as opposed to conveying information. In other words, people use language to establish and maintain social contact in free and purposeless social talks. Such a view is echoed by Anthony (1964), "speech to promote human warmth". Since for good or ill, we are social creatures and cannot bear to be cut off too long from our fellows, even if we have nothing really to say to them, and "Phatic communication refers also to trivial and obvious exchanges about the weather and time, made up of ready-made sentences or foreseeable statements... Therefore this is a type of communication that establishes a contact without transmitting a precise content, where the container is more important than the content." (Casalegno and McWilliam, 2004) Nonetheless, phatic communication serves as "important social lubricant" (Diana, 2002). In the words of Goffman, "the gestures which we sometimes call empty are perhaps in fact the fullest things of all." Phatic communication can occur in three categories

Chapter 3　Genre Analysis of the Insurance Sales Dialogues

of the conversations, that is, at the beginning, at the end and at anywhere as a space filler. Phatic communication is of great significance for insurance sales communication in the sense that it is exactly where *Guanxi* dynamics perform. Now the specific types of warming up used in agent-client dialogues are summarized as follows.

(1) Greetings. Most commonly seen between agents and clients who are not familiar with each other or they meet for the first time referred to by a mutual third party. For example, "×××, Hi!" ("×××, 你好啊!") or simply such expressions used with certain time limits as "Good morning!" ("早啊!"), "Good afternoon." ("下午好。"), "Good evening." ("晚上好。"), "Hello, uncle ×." ("× 叔叔好。"), "Hello, aunt ×××." ("阿姨好。"), etc. Moreover, there are some expressions with specific Chinese distinctiveness, such as "Teacher Liu" ("刘老师"), "Aunt Li" ("李阿姨"), "Manager Qian" ("钱经理").

(2) Inquiry. For example, "Where are you going?" ("你到哪儿去哦？"), "What are you doing?" ("在干什么？"), "Are you ×××? I am…" ("你可是××× 啊？我是……").

In spite of seeming to have little useful purpose or any specific content, such phatic communication is a bonding ritual and a strategy for managing interpersonal distance. For example, in one encounter between the agent and client, the agent pays a visit to the prospective client's home, but they don't know each other before and the prospective client is introduced by a third party that both the agent and the client are familiar with. The conversation goes as follows.

  1. A：你是×××吧？（Are you ×××?）

  2. B：嗯，你是哪个？（Yes, and you are?）

  3. A：我叫×××，我是刘老师介绍过来的，他昨晚给你打了电话了吧？（I am ×××. I'm referred to by Teacher Liu. Did he call you last night?）

  4. B：哦，是的哦，他跟我大概讲了下子，你就是×××哦。（Oh, yes, he talked to me briefly about that, so you are ×××.）

  5. A：嗯，呵呵，我今天刚好过来，就想过来看看，跟你刮刮——

反正不要紧，了解下子都好啊。(Ah, yes, he he, I just come by today to have a look and talk to you—It doesn't matter, and you can have some brief ideas.)

6. B：嗯，好啊。(Yes, OK.)

7. A：我听刘老师讲你想买……(I heard from Teacher Liu that you are willing to buy…)

(继续就某一保险进行介绍、对话)(Continues the talk on a specific policy)

At the beginning, the simple inquiry "你是×××吧?" is a self-answered inquiry, since the agent has been almost certain that is the one she is going to talk to. It serves as a starting point to open a dialogue to define the relationship between the agent and the (prospective) client as new acquaintances introduced through a third party. "I am ×××. I'm referred to by Teacher Liu. Did he call you last night?" ("我叫×××，我是刘老师介绍过来的，他昨晚给你打了电话了吧？") In this way, it helps new acquaintances to explore and categorize each other's social position. In this conversation, "刘老师" plays an extremely important role, since he is the friend of both the agent and the prospective client. He serves as the bridge to introduce both parties to know each other and carry on smoothly the interaction. Such a way of operation can be best captured by Fei Xiaotong's "differential mode of association" (Fei, 2007) in the relationship network of China's rural areas.

(3) Comment/compliment. For example, "This girl's hands are little and cute."("小姑娘的手小巧巧的。"), "You have a very beautiful shoe cabinet."("鞋柜好好看。") "Wow, you look so well!"("哇，你气色真好！"), "Wow, you have such a beautiful house."("哇，你家的房子真漂亮。")

The following is another reconstructed example in which an insurance agent tries to sell insurance policies to one of her friends, who is not so interested at the very beginning of the conversation. The insurance sales agent (A) is the kindergarten teacher of the prospective client's granddaughter. The prospective client (B) is one of the peasants under A's husband's management. A and B are

Chapter 3 Genre Analysis of the Insurance Sales Dialogues

talking about the little girl, who is B's granddaughter. The following script is an excerpt from a longer conversation; the conversation is transcribed in the local dialect.

1. A: 刘阿姨在家里啊？这是你孙女儿吧？小姑娘的手小巧巧的，小得很子。(Aunt Liu, glad to see you are at home. This must be your granddaughter! The girl's hands are little and cute, really little and cute.)

2. B: 小巧巧的呵？(Little and cute?)

3. A: 小姑娘小巧巧的不要紧……她的手漂亮，你看她那小手。这小姑娘在我们班，就她手最好看。(It is great to have little and cute hands... She has beautiful hands. Look at them. In our class, her hands are the most beautiful.)

4. B: 好看有什么用啊，念书又不过劲。(It is no use. Her study is a mess.)

5. A: 小姑娘的手生得好要好些，呵呵，就决定命运了……呵呵，手有些讲法。(For little girl, little hands are good, well... and sometimes, it decides your destiny... well... it seems there is something about hands.)

6. B: 那就不晓得是什么样子喽。(For that, we have no idea.)

7. A: 她那手生得好。[停顿]你的毛毛保险办了没有？(She does have beautiful hands. [Pause] Have you got insurance covered for your child?)

8. B: 手这个东西哪个说得清楚？呵呵，你家××现在念高中了哦？(We don't know yet. Your son, ××, is in senior middle school now, right?)

9. A: 嗯，是的哦，日子过得真快。我家××也买了保险，你家毛毛怎么样啊？(Yes, how time flies. I have got him covered by insurance. What about your kid?)

10. B: 保险哪？保险她妈妈准备给她搞。去年找她爸爸，爸爸说过年讲，过年后来我又忙，忙到没有来了。今年不知搞了没有，如果要搞，他肯定要跟你讲。还有那个，那个跟她爸讲了，她爸没答应。讲了，他说要交好多年来着？要交十年吧，十年到18岁拿钱吧。听他像那样讲，我儿子讲说现在经济不活泛，不想搞。(Insurance? Her mother talked about it. Last year someone approached her father, and her father said to wait until Spring Festival. But after the festival, we've been far too busy. I'm not sure whether they have bought it. But if we do, we

-93-

will definitely come to you. About that (insurance), I have talked to her father, but he didn't take it. He thought the years to pay for the insurance are too many. It seems we have to pay for ten years until she is 18. My son said we had a rather tight budget, so we needed to think about it.)

11. A: 哦，……现在搞，很多人都是给小孩搞，等于给小孩存一笔钱啊。(Oh… now that many parents buy for their children. It is a kind of savings for their children.)

12. B: 是的啊,现在像这情况搞也好,等到小孩读书(上大学)……(Yes, it might be a good idea, until the child goes to university…)

13. A: 负担要好点。(The burden will be lessened.)

14. B: 嗯，负担要好。(Yes, right.)

15. A: 一年交两三千也无所谓，(一年……一年……)。(It'll be only several thousand for one year, so it won't pose a heavy burden, this year…the next year…)

16. B: 他前年刚好将屋搞了，前年呢，前年呢没出去。这去年才出去搞了一下，他搞点钱又买个摩托车，又置个冰箱，唵。家里置东西。(He just decorated the house the year before last, and he didn't go out to work. Last year he went out to work, and bought a motorcycle and a fridge afterwards. He bought things for the family.)

Move on talking about the girl's mother, job and others…

As introduced in the background, A is the kindergarten teacher of B's granddaughter, so it sets up a complicated scenario as the agent A mentions B's granddaughter, and she uses the privilege of being the teacher of B's granddaughter. Moreover, it is their mutual knowledge that A is the wife to the director of the local village. Such phatic communication creates a complex scenario that both parties are aware and are willing to maintain. It is not expressively communicated but impressively communicated. The sentence "小姑娘的手小巧巧的" ("The girl's hands are little and cute."), "她的手漂亮" ("She has beautiful hands."), "在我们班，就她手最好看" ("In our class, her hands are the most beautiful."). They are compliments and thus phatic communication in nature; however, they serve much more than the purpose of phatic communication, which will be argued in more detail later.

(4) Retrospect. For example, "Long time no see." ("好久不见。")

As argued all through the study, the insurance sales are achieved through *Guanxi* in transformational China's rural areas, most of the interactants are either friends, relatives, the familiar ones, or at least introduced through a third party that both the agents and the prospective clients are familiar with. Thus, initial small talks to ease the atmosphere is an essential part of the successful conclusion of business. Since the degree of trust that the agents establish is one of the deciding factors of the success of their sales, as in the above sample in Table 3.2, "这个鞋柜好漂亮的哦!" ("You have a beautiful shoe cabinet.") In this setting, the client's husband is a carpenter, praising one of his works will definitely have a favorable impression on the client, and also a hidden message is entailed in this sentence—a carpenter with good craftsmanship will of course be relatively better off. It is time for them to think about having more additional well-being besides their living standard, that is, insurance will offer them a better guarantee for their future life.

2. Functions of warming up

As Malinowski (1923: 149) observes, it is "free, aimless, social intercourse", which is manifested in exchanges characterized by "purposeless expression or preference of aversions, accounts of irrelevant happenings, comments on what is perfectly obvious". Such exchanges have the important social function of creating ties of union by mere verbal exchanges, "the ties of the moment without which unifies social action is impossible" (ibid.: 149). While in rural insurance sales, such an atmosphere of sociality and interpersonal communion is of crucial importance to the successful conclusion of business, i.e., the insurance sales. In the above reconstructed example, the little girl is the target of insurance sales (The proposed policy is for her.), it would be wise to start a conversation related to this little girl. It creates "the pleasant atmosphere of polite, social intercourse" (ibid.: 152), or establishes "rapport" between the interactants, and thus facilitates the promotion of insurance sales.

Insurance sales in transformational China's rural areas distinguishes itself from the normal sales in product or service encounters, especially in warming up. For example, the following is a short segment of a dialogue between a sales assistant and a customer in a convenience store.

Context: The sales assistant, male, does not know the customer (also male), they are strangers; both of them are in their thirties. A refers to the sales assistant, and B is the customer.

1. B: 你这里有百威啤酒吗？(Do you have Budweiser here?)
2. A: 有啊。(Yes.)
3. B: 在哪里？(Where is it?)
4. A: 冰的还是不冰的？(Iced or not?)
5. B: 冰的。(Iced.)
6. A: 在最里面的冰柜里。(In the fridge down the shelf.)
(Get the beer and come to the cashier)
7. A: 22(元)，谢谢。(22(yuan), thank you.)
8. B: 好，给你。(OK, here you are.)

From this short segment of sales encounter, both of the participants are rather direct and to the point right away in the whole process. There is no warming up at all, and they don't have any social talk or friendship talk. Both of them are very succinct and brief, but the communication is still successful in nature, in terms of the outcome—successful conclusion of business. It is a customer-initiated talk with the customer's direct inquiry of "Do you have Budweiser here?". Very little or even no facework is found in this utterance. In the meantime, the sales assistant responds only with the essential information with very brief sentence "Yes." This response and pattern of interaction can, to a certain extent, illustrate that there is no much need for further and deeper or continuous interactions between the sales assistant and the customer. The sales assistant's behavior is characterized by brief responses, lack of facework, and unwillingness to do anything beyond his routine (for instance, his only inquiry to specify the customer's need, "冰的还是不冰的？" ("Iced or not?") and his far too brief answers to the questions, "有啊。"("Yes."), "在最里面的冰柜里。" ("In the fridge down the shelf."). One reason for this pattern of politeness behavior is that both of them do not need to employ any face-redressing strategies. Even with the last short segment of "谢谢" ("Thank you.") it is considered as very routine and habitual in sales or service encounters nowadays. Another reason for the above pattern of politeness behavior could be related to their mutual expectations of relationship continuity. The fact that the sales assistant doesn't take care much of the customer's face is due to their mutual expectations of their relationship continuity. The sales assistant understands that the relationship with the customer is short-term, and it is also similar for the customer. Both of them are aware that this relationship may not continue in the future. As a result, the sales assistant does not have the adequate motivation to build up rapport with him. However, it contrasts sharply with that of insurance sales in transformational China's rural areas. If an insurance sales conversation goes like the above sample, it will be very likely that it will go wrong. It would be considered as rude, greedy, inconsiderate and impossible. Regarding this, one of my informants confesses as the following: "其实我们做保险就是做人哪，要有耐心，要跟客户慢慢刮……在这场子，做事情也不容易，大家都是抬头不见低头见的，那怎么好意思哦……" ("Actually we sell insurance by making ourselves trustworthy. We need to be very patient, and talk to the clients slowly... It's not easy to sell insurance here. We are all familiar with each other and see each other frequently, and it would be a shame if we are too direct.") It can be seen from the confession that relationship plays a vital role in successfully concluding the business. Even to a certain extent, the success or failure of the sales effort largely depends on the rapport built between the insurance sales agent and the client, and the social resources the agent possesses, especially in transformational China's rural areas. In a nutshell, *Guanxi* is not only emotional, but also instrumental in transformational China's rural areas.

Since the reform and opening-up policy being implemented, the economy has developed very quickly with the people's living standard increasing. At the same time, some of the resources are not easily accessible in people's work. Thus it would be important to establish instrumental interpersonal relationship on the basis of interest. Under the current circumstances, the number of people you know and the capability of getting things done have become one major criterion in evaluating the social resources that one possesses. In this kind of society, people tend to forge a kind of relationship which might bring some benefit to them, even though sometimes this kind of relationship realizes its role in the distant future. Insurance sales in transformational China's rural areas conforms itself to the instrumental nature of the Chinese interpersonal relationship, as clearly iterated by the agent, "做保险就是做人" ("sell insurance by making ourselves trustworthy"), "慢慢刮" ("talk to the clients slowly"), etc.

The training sessions and experience sharing meetings, or the socialization process of the insurance sales agents also attach great importance to warming up. For example, in one informal experience sharing meeting of the agents, the one who had excellent performance (in her forties with about 15 years' experience) said, "其实我们做这个东西,蛮重要一点就是要察言观色。开始的时候不能太急,你越急,你客户可能就越反感;讲真的,在农村做保险不容易,经营客户一定要用心,要真正把他们当朋友来处,交朋友了,交心了,才有交易。经常有事没事跟他们去刮刮,找一切借口跟他们交流,反正总有机会就介绍的嘛。最主要他们要相信我们,相信保险,相信公司。还有一个要细心,客户拜访资料一定要记录好;已经承保的客户资料分类组织好。比如我的客户,身高、体重、收入、家庭状况,我都有非常详细的记录,所以不管到哪里,这些资料随时都能查到。另外一个态度要真诚。反正不管怎么样,要找机会跟他们拉家常,要打动一些客户,这些细节要特别注意,拉近与客户之间距离,后面沟通就容易了。比如讲他们家里的情况,孩子啊,父母啊,反正一定要找到一个切入点。" (Actually it is very important for us to be very observant in selling insurance. In the beginning, you can not be anxious. If you display any anxiety, your client might feel disgusted. It is truly not easy to sell insurance in rural areas. We have to be whole-heartedly in managing our clients; we have to take them as real friends and show them our sincerity. If we are friends, and we can tell each other the truth, then there could be deal. We need to keep visiting them and talk to them with whatever possible; there'll always be opportunities for us to introduce insurance. The key is that they have faith in us, have faith in insurance and have faith in our company. Another thing is that we need to be careful in filing—keeping good files of the clients' data; organizing well the data of the existing clients. For instance, I have very detailed records of my clients' information such as height, weight, income and family situations. So I can retrieve the data anywhere I go. Still another thing is that we need to be sincere—sincerity is extremely important. No matter what, we need to talk to them, to have such casual talks as family, children and parents. We need to pay attention to details. Once the distance between the clients and us is narrowed down, it will be much easier for later communication.) (Interview, March 8, 2014) In this segment of experience sharing, such units as "sincerity", "faith", "friends", "observant", "keep visiting", "whole-heartedly" are clearly highlighted. As Sun (2009: 26) iterated, "*Guanxi* is established on the basis of the concept of 'reciprocity', it is reciprocal in nature. What one does in other's interest is considered as a kind of 'social investment', it is obvious he/she expects something in return." Simply put, one salient feature of Chinese interpersonal relationship is its instrumentalism.

To summarize, warming up in rural insurance sales is an indispensable part of the successful conclusion of business. It builds up rapport, facilitates the communication and paves the way for smooth communication between the insurance sales agents and their prospective clients. Moreover, it is based on the social concept of "reciprocity".

3.3.3 Introducing the Offer

Move 2, introducing the offer, is the most important move of all the moves in agent-client interactions, and it is an obligatory move which takes up the vast majority of the time of the interactions. The success or failure of the sales mostly depends on the effectiveness of the introduction.

Step 1 of Move 2, offering the product or service, is the formal initiation of the sales effort, and is the first time the topic of business brought up. In the sample in Table 3.2, "你那个怎么讲哦？" ("How about that (the insurance) we talked about last time?") is the indirect way of bringing up the topic, since they have already met for several times before and both parties are well aware of what they are talking about. It seems in the local settings, direct mentioning of insurance and money is dis-preferred, which may be due to the maintaining of face between the interactants. The concept of face, central to Brown and Levinson's (2011) theory, is derived from Goffman (1967) and the English folk terms "losing face" and "saving face". The theory assumes that all competent adult members of a society are concerned about their face, the self-image every member wants to claim for himself or herself and recognizes what others have. Brown and Levinson further distinguished negative face wants from positive ones. Negative face refers to basic claims of territory, freedom of action and freedom from imposition. While positive face refers to the desire of being appreciated and approved by others. It is in the reciprocal interest of the participants in conversation to maintain each other's face. There are in total five strategies offered:

(1) Bald on record, without redressive action;

(2) Positive politeness;

(3) Negative politeness;

(4) Off record;

(5) Don't do the face threatening act (FTA).

It is noted in the sample conversations that the fourth strategy "off record" and the fifth "don't do the FTA" are the most frequently employed among others, throughout the conversation. It is rarely direct asking of purchasing, but such an idea is implied and reinforced throughout, for example, "你看也花不了多少钱" ("It doesn't cost you much."), "分摊到每个月，就几百块。" ("If you divide it into each month, it will only cost you several hundred.").

Step 2 of Move 2, essential detailing of the offer. In this way, the prospective client would have a better understanding of the specific clauses, rights and obligations. Of course, as van Dijk (2006) argues, there are certain strategies adopted in the detailing, for example, emphasizing the benefits and downplaying the detriments, all in all, creating a favorable impression on the part of the prospective client.

Step 3 of Move 2, indicating the value of the offer, is the most important part of all the introduction. All the efforts, either directly or indirectly, serve the purpose of emphasizing the value of the offer. For example, in the sample dialogue in Table 3.2, the agent distinguishes the insurance under discussion with rural cooperative medical insurance by emphasizing the deposit function of the insurance: "我们这个有两个功能的，又存钱又保障" ("Ours has two major functions—both deposit and guarantee."); for another, "那点钱搞么东西噢" ("What can we do with so little money?") and "差这么两千块钱不得过日子啦。" ("It only costs you several thousand a year.") emphasizing the much lower cost and much greater benefit that it brings; more detailed, "假如健健康康的，20年后给你9万；万一有个什么事情，马上给你9万，合同终止；如果有重大疾病，医保那边照样报。这个保你100岁，就是你活多老保多老。" ("If keeping healthy, after 20 years, you'll have 90,000 yuan; in case anything bad happens, you will have 90,000 yuan right away, and the contract ends; if you have major diseases, you can get compensation from social security as well. This goes as long as your life."), "其实那钱放在那里也就放着了，买了之后如果自己有点压力反而还是好事……" ("Actually it's of no use if you just put your money there. After all, if you have this, a little pressure will do you good as well.."), "你像我们现在都是四十来岁了，慢慢年纪大了，也搞不动了" ("We are already in our forties, growing old and will be unable to buy insurance."), "我们虽然是妇女，也要给自己些保障哎，完全靠人家也都是靠不住，最起码自己有一点，好些哎" ("Though we are both women, we need to get ourselves insured as well; it's hard to rely on others. At least, we need to have something to get ourselves covered."), "小家伙负担也重得不得了……房价多贵" ("Our children have got much burden already. You know how expensive the housing is."), "最起码还是不给他

们增加负担啊，多少有个保障" ("The least we can do is to shoulder them with additional burden. At least it's an assurance.").

In this part, the agent employs mainly the strategy of "emphasizing the benefits and downplaying the detriments" by essential detailed introduction of the specific policy in question. All the interactions are centered on the purpose of persuading the client to make the purchase decision.

3.3.4 Offering Incentives

Move 3, offering incentives, is an optional move in the dialogues. It occurs when policies are rather larger in amount or there is some promotional efforts. The additional bonuses are normally some household apparatus, such as quilt, pot, electric blanket, etc. For example, "如果今天下单我们有礼品送。" ("If you sign the contract today, there will be presents."), "下单达到……（××数额）就有一套××纪念币" ("When the contract value reaches…, there will be… a set of commemorative coins."), "根据不同金额，现场下单有被子、微波炉、电炒锅等。" ("According to different contract values, we have different presents, such as blankets, micro-wave ovens, and electric frying pans."). This move is optional for most of the time. There is seldom such incentives, because they mostly happen when there is a promotion meeting on site, that is, some prospective clients will be invited to a certain location (such as a fancy hotel, a local school, the hall of a company, etc.) to carry out a promotion. The process goes as follows. First, the agent will seek support from the company. Then some renowned lecturer of insurance or beneficiary of some insurance policies is invited to introduce (educate) the participants about the importance of insurance for their lives, for example, the visible benefits they have received and enjoyed, clear contrast between having been insured and not having been insured offered. Of course sometimes, the clients are also attracted by the additional benefits of the gifts, which has already become a popular promotional method widely employed by institutions.

3.3.5　Establishing Credentials

Move 4, establishing credentials, is also an important move in realizing the persuasion process in insurance sales in transformational China's rural areas. The following offers evidence from the transcriptions of dialogues and also interviews with the agent.

1. Establishing credentials and trust

Move 4, establishing credentials, is an obligatory move and is found in all the conversations. It plays a vital role in the successful conclusion of the insurance sales. Since establishment of credentials is the foundation of trust, and meanwhile trust is the pillar stone in the conclusion of insurance sales. Trust can be classified into "interpersonal trust", "institutional trust", "particularistic trust" and "generalized trust" (Zhao, 2013; Liang, 2011; Li and Liang, 2002; Luo and Ye, 2007), in which interpersonal trust corresponds to particularistic trust and institutional trust corresponds to generalized trust. Since particularistic trust is also called personal trust, which refers to a particular dyads trust relationship and is the outcome of the interactions between the two parties. If there is no acceptance and reciprocity from both parties, there would be no trust. In many circumstances, people would prefer someone familiar or someone who can trust, as a manager of a private company said, "I'd rather do business with good friends for only 200,000 yuan profit, than for 500,000 yuan profit with someone without trust" (Yang and Peng, 1999). Such a statement expresses the earnest concern of the Chinese people when it comes to business, since if there is lack of trust, the party concerned would have to shoulder so enormous risk that he/she could even lost the investment once and for all. In the context of insurance sales in transformational China's rural areas, trust also plays a vital role. The trust is established, maintained and even enhanced not only in the actual dialogues, but more importantly in the casual interactions between the agent and the client. As one experienced insurance agent once put it in one interview sharing her experience in successfully concluding a major policy.

"这个客户其实之前非常反感保险,他对保险可以讲一点兴趣都没有。但是我这人是这样子的,我看准了的事情我一定会去做。那我就经常有事没事找他嘛,找他刮。开始其实他门都不让我进,那我就观察,我就发现他家有个小女儿,长得好得很。有一次一个偶然的机会我就晓得了他女儿生日,我就跑到超市买了一个学习机。那时候学习机蛮贵的唉,就是那种一捺就发声音的那一种啊,还能学英语,我就送给他女儿。这下子好了,因为他们工作忙啊,没时间想这些东西,那我就帮他们解决了这个问题。后来讲,他女儿喜欢得不得了,天天玩。这样子慢慢地,他就加了我微信了。那我经常在微信上面讲啊,宣传啊,也就是一个潜移默化的效果。半年多时间吧,后来有一次他就主动找我签了一个十万的单子。现在想想,其实也就是做人,先交人,再交心,最后才是交易。当然交易我们也不是讲一锤子买卖,后面他们有什么需要,我总是尽心尽力去做好服务。" (This client actually disliked insurance a lot in the past. He had no interest at all in insurance. But you know me, I am determined to have it done once I'm in. So I started to visit him from time to time, and chat casually to him. But at the beginning, they didn't even let me get in their house. So I noticed he has a beautiful little daughter, and occasionally I got to know her birthday, I bought a learning machine in the supermarket for her as birthday present. You know at that time, learning machines are rather expensive, the ones that once you touch, there will be sound, and you can even learn English with them. So I bought one for his daughter, and things just got much better from then. Since they are too busy to think about their daughter's study, I happened to solve the problem for them. I heard that their daughter loved the present a lot, and played on it everyday. Then gradually, we became friends on Wechat. I put some introductions and cases and other materials on Wechat to exert some imperceptible influence. Slowly in this way, about half a year later, he purchased a rather substantial policy about 100,000 yuan from me. Now when I look back, I firmly believe it's about making friends, being trustworthy, and deal at last. It's not a once-and-for-all deal; it takes a lot of patience and time. Even now, if there is anything I can do for them, I still do it.) (Interview,

February 14, 2013)

The above interview is a typical example of persuading successfully a prospective client, who was resistant to insurance at the beginning, and finally after the trust between the agent and the client established, concluding a major insurance policy (100,000 yuan is considered as a rather large sum with the local standard). "有事没事找他" ("visit him from time to time"), "找他刮" ("chat casually to him"), "帮他们解决了这个问题" ("solve the problem for them"), "这样子慢慢地"("slowly in this way"), "潜移默化" ("exert some imperceptible influence"), "做人" ("making friends"), "先交人，再交心，最后才是交易" ("making friends, being trustworthy, and deal at last") and "不是讲一锤子买卖" ("It's not a once-and-for-all deal.") are all clear manifestations of the central role of trust in insurance sales in transformational China's rural areas.

Establishing credentials in the actual dialogues is an obligatory move. It includes both the credibility of the agent and the insurance company that offers such policy. For example, "你晓得我"("you know me"), "我们在这边也不是一天两天，就是有什么问题，你到时候来找我"("We are here not for just one or two days; if there's any problem, you can come to me anytime."), "世界500强，中国最大的保险公司" ("world top 500, China's largest insurance company"), "参与了西部大开发" ("taking part in Western Development"), "在世界各地都有大投资" ("having major investment in all over the world"). All such expressions serve to establish the credentials of not only the agent himself/herself, but also the company, by presenting a credible, trustworthy and helpful image.

2. The role of trust and *Guanxi*

It has been generally accepted that the more modern the society is, the more institutional trust people have. Institutional trust is a kind of trust based on the guarantee of institutions, and therefore, people tend to have greater faith in people's general liability and responsibility. With the reliable and widely acknowledged institutional guarantee, even the behaviors of strangers are completely predictable (Zhao, 2013). Nevertheless, the conclusion of insurance sales in China's rural areas is mainly built on the basis of interpersonal trust. Moreover, with the impact of economic tides, there are some irregularities, abuse or even purposeful manipulation of interpersonal trust, which is also one of the concerns of the present study. For example, some people hold that the overuse of trust in local communities tends to compromise the social integrity and thus increases the cost of interpersonal communication. This is especially true when it comes to a society in which interpersonal trust overweighs institutional trust, which consequently gives rise to *Guanxi* manipulation or backdoor activities. Nonetheless, based on the data I collected and what I observe, we do not tend to impose value judgment upon such complex phenomenon, and what we can do is to present the facts and uncover the dynamics operating under the interactions. A more balanced view of not only trust, but also *Guanxi* seems to be more appropriate. As Wong (2007) argued that "*Guanxi*" is a very local, complex and delicate concept and its sophistication is far greater than the official formal bureaucratic institutions featured by their complexities.

3.3.6　Other Moves

There are other moves, Move 5 to More 8, enclosing documents, soliciting response, using pressure tactics and ending politely, among which, enclosing documents and using pressure tactics are optional, while the other two, soliciting response and ending politely are obligatory. It is quite evident that soliciting response should be obligatory, since the successful conclusion of the policies, as mentioned, for most of the time, requires several or even more visits of the agents to the prospective clients. Thus it's crucial for the agent to make sure further communication is possible. Some examples of each of the above mentioned moves are listed as follows.

Move 5, enclosing documents, is an optional move in this specific sample, "我这场子有个建议书" ("We have a suggestion form here").

Move 6, soliciting response, is an obligatory move, since the successful conclusion of the business usually takes rounds of visits and interactions. It is rather rare that the agent can secure a conclusion of business by just one visit, and thus further communication is vital in their sales performance. Just as one of the agents recalled, "想一次成功，那基本不太现实，一般都是要跑好几次，你不把关系搞好，他不相信你，还搞个鬼啊？" ("It's not likely that you succeed by visiting only once. Usually, we need to visit multiple times. Without making the relationship reliable, it's impossible.")

In the sample dialogue in Table 3.2, "我这场子有个建议书，我留到这场子，上面有我手机，你们到时候商量好了给我电话，我到时候过来就中了" ("We have a suggestion form here and I can leave it with you, and there is my contact. After you have made your decision, call me and I'll come over again.")

Move 7, using pressure tactics, is an optional move. This move should be employed with caution, because it is very likely that it might invoke antipathy from the part of the client. Nonetheless, sometimes it is also necessary to fasten the client's decision process, as one agent said, "有的时候要尽量叫他们快一点，比如讲我们有的保险有时间期限；有的有东西送，那当场签单就有，晚一点就没得了嘛" ("Sometimes we also urge them, for example, setting a time limit; some with presents, but only for those who sign on site; if later, there will be nothing."), "我们有的时候讲某些保险只针对特定客户，比如讲老客户啊，或者他们累计的保险买到多少啊，那种" ("Sometimes we would say certain insurance is only for quality clients, for example, existing clients, or if the total amount of the insurance they have bought reaches a certain amount, etc.").

In my observation, it is only used when the prospective client has almost made his/her mind in making the purchase. Specifically in the sample dialogue in Table 3.2, "现在这个保险是有个推广期，再有一个月就没有了" ("Nowadays for each type of insurance there is a promotional period which lasts for only a month."), "那个××我们就推广了几个月，你现在想买就没得了。" ("That ×× only lasted for several months, and it's impossible for people to buy it now.")

Move 8, ending politely, is an obligatory move. Generally they are small talks again, such as "那好，我们就这么讲，到时候再联系" ("Well then, that's it, and let's keep in touch."). The topics vary, they could be children, education, decoration, family, life, troubles... All in all, such ending would make the conversation more like what happens between friends, which will be analyzed in more detail in the next two chapters.

This move normally centers around such topics as family, children, education, in short, small talks, which serves important function as well. It echoes the beginning move of warming up, serving the purpose of strengthening rapport and laying a solid foundation for future further visits. To a certain extent, the establishment and maintenance of "ego-centric social network" (Zhao, 2013) facilitate the insurance sales in transformational China's rural areas on the one hand. It requires constant, frequent and careful attention as well, which on the other hand illustrates the nature of *Guanxi* being reciprocal. To be more specific, in this particular context, the conviction, determination and devotion of the insurance sales agent will largely determine the success of the sales efforts.

3.4 Summary

In terms of communicative purposes, insurance sales are promotional in nature, which reflects the highly motivated sales efforts on the part of insurance sales agents. Thus the most important function of the agent-(prospective) client interaction is to offer a clear, objective and attractive introduction to the products in terms of the perceived interests, needs or inhibitions of the (prospective) clients. In the meantime, agents serve as the first link between the insurance companies and prospective clients. In China, especially in contemporary transformational China's rural areas, the old value system has been, for a large part, demolished, and the new one has yet to be established; while generally trust still plays a vital role in concluding the business. In the process of agent-(prospective) client interactions, agents have a large room to play, or even sometimes, purposefully manipulate the arrangement of the content of their interactions. For example, as van Dijk (2006) argues, in order to fulfill the purpose of persuasion, various means can be employed. Such as the difficulty in understanding the terms and conditions involved and contract language, detailed elaboration of the benefits while ignoring or downplaying the problems, and overall strategy of positive self-representation. However, such nature may sometimes be taken advantage of, or even abused by the agents to achieve their economic goals. That is, on the one hand, such persuasive or even manipulative discourse is to discursively focus on those cognitive and social characteristics of the recipients that make the recipients vulnerable and less resistant to persuasion/manipulation by means of appealing to relevant ideologies, attitudes and emotions of the recipients. And on the other hand the insurance sales agents can be more advantageous by emphasizing the position, power, authority or moral superiority of them or their sources (where relevant, the inferior position, lack of knowledge of the recipients.) For instance, in one interview question regarding how she succeeding in doing insurance sales, one agent recalls as followed: "我感觉如果我的客户家庭各方面发展得比我好，或者好很多，那么这个客户相对较难搞定，如果与我发展得差不多，甚至不如我，这张保单相对较容易搞定。" ("I think it is relatively harder if the prospective client is better off than me in terms of family and other aspects, while if he/she is almost the same or even not as good as me, then it will be much easier.")Therefore, it can be concluded that the agents, as one member of the professional community, are well aware of the intent, positioning, form and functional value of the communicative purposes through their training and experience sharing meetings, i.e., their socialization process. They can either consciously or unconsciously exploit such constraints in their interactions with their prospective clients to achieve their intentions of concluding the sales.

The above summary can also reflect from a perspective that in China's rural areas, there seems to be a greater variety and larger difference in income, status, reputation among the local residents. Ever since reform and opening-up policy being implemented, the rural society has undergone tremendous and dramatic transformation. One of which is that the homogeneous group of people who are engaging in farming with relatively homogeneous income have diversified into different groups of people who engage in various occupations with growing gap in income (Yang, 2014). Such social stratum differentiation concerning former peasants are transferred into other areas of the national economy in large numbers, and the former peasants' social identities are changed to embody other identities.

In terms of the generic patterns in their sales efforts and communication between their clients, based on the model Bhatia (1993) offered, it is found that in each and every dialogue between the agent and the (prospective) client, the first move of warming up is obligatory. This is a significant finding due to the fact that in oral communication, warming up, often in the form of phatic expression, functions as social talks, as opposed to conveying information. As Malinowski (1923) and Anthony (1964) argued, people use language to establish and maintain social contact in free, purposeless social talks. This kind of communication establishes a contact without transmitting a precise content, where the container is more important than the content, as Casalegno and Mcwilliam (2004) put it. Meanwhile, we argue that such talks do perform important functions in the process of agent-(prospective) client interactions. In transformational China's rural areas, insurance sales are concluded mostly among friends, relatives and the familiar ones, or at least introduced through the third party whom both the agents and (prospective) client trust and are familiar with. Such small talks pave a solid foundation for further and more detailed business talks; moreover, they serve an important function for *Guanxi* maintenance. As we argue, *Guanxi* is one of the major dynamics of the Chinese society. It has been a pervasive part of the Chinese business world for the last few centuries, and millions of Chinese firms were bound into a social and business web. A company's performance is largely dependent on such intricate and delicate web of *Guanxi*. Meanwhile, such *Guanxi* web requires constant maintenance. As Zhai (2007a, 2009) and Luo (2007) put it, Chinese firms develop *Guanxi* as a strategic mechanism to overcome competitive and resource disadvantages by cooperating and exchanging favors with government authorities and other stakeholders. Simply put, corruption and other irregularities, against which have been heavily criticized. However, it is argued here that this may due a large part to different socio-cultural factors. The self in relation to other becomes the focus of individual experience in China, which is under the heavy influence of Confucianism. The interdependent self contrasts sharply to the Western view of an independent self, which sees each human being as an independent, self-contained, and autonomous entity who comprises a unique configuration of internal attributes and behaves primarily as a consequence of these internal attributes. According to many observers of Chinese social relations (Fei, 2007; Luo, 2007; Tsui and Farth, 1997; Yang, 1994), Chinese have a much stronger tendency to divide people to categories and treat them accordingly. This tendency of treating people in differentiation depending on one's relationship to them constitutes the basic reason why *Guanxi* is of such great importance to the Chinese society. Insurance sales in transformational China's rural areas is an explicit embodiment of *Guanxi* and offers strong endorsement to such tendency in *Guanxi* among the Chinese people.

To summarize, such discursive patterns as moves and steps in insurance sales in transformational China's rural areas reveal the intricate and delicate operating mechanism governing the insurance sales practices, represented by the interactions between the insurance sales agents and their (prospective) clients.

Chapter 4

Topic Management in Insurance Sales Dialogues

4.1　Introduction

This chapter analyzes the dialogues from the perspective of topic management, and the mediation of different frames. We find that both the agents and the clients consciously or unconsciously shift among topics to their respective interactive advantages. More specifically, three different types of talk, namely, friendship talk, institutional talk and task-oriented talk are employed to the analysis of the dialogue, representing the mediation of different frames and the two different discourse systems at large.

4.2　Topic Management

It has been known that in our daily life communication, we either consciously or unconsciously manage topic in order to fulfill different purposes; while in insurance sales dialogues, it is found that both the insurance sales agents and the prospective clients are attempting to assume topic control to fulfill their respective objectives.

　　As we argued all through the study, the objective of the study is to unveil the dynamic nature of insurance sales in transformational China's rural areas. On the part of the agent, he/she tries to keep the conversation in track and tries every means to make the sales; while on the part of the prospective client, he/she is also managing to assume the topic control to his/her own advantage. The shifting or maintaining of the different topics reflects the mediation of different frames, and thus the mediation of different discourse systems at large. In the following part, I will offer an objective account of the analysis of the insurance sales dialogues from the perspective of topic management.

It has also been argued that contemporary business activities have eroded human relationships and have made them subservient to instrumental goals (Fairclough, 1995). This decline of meaning at the expense of instrumental values is serious. According to Fairclough, since there will be confusion between personal interaction and promotional communication—people may imitate what they see and hear about promotion in their interactions with their friends or relatives. Business activities have been accused of causing and accelerating this decline of meaning, and customers are portrayed simply as the "victims". This position is somehow misplaced. Insurance sales can be the embodiment of business discourse in significant ways. Business discourse is a hybrid discourse site where voices from various domains, such as friendship and kinship, are appropriated by both the service providers and customers in order to achieve their goals. Instead of business discourse colonizing interpersonal discourse or vice versa, as Fairclough put it, they are interacting with each other to create new meaning of business and friendship. As we will see in our analysis, meaning is not the sole property of service providers, but a joint property negotiated interactively by participants for their respective interactional goals. This phenomenon of meaning manipulation for interactional goals is at least consistent and compatible with, if not conducive to, the practices of insurance sales.

4.3 Phatic Talk and Its Functions

About half a century after Malinowski (1923) and Laver (1975) provided detailed analyses of the sequential features and pro-social functions of phatic talk

(J. Coupland, N. Coupland and Robinson, 1992; Holmes, 2000; Coupland, 2010). Interaction, in Laver's view, can be generally divided into three phases sequentially: the opening, the medial, and the closing. And marginal phases of interaction, phatic talk, as Laver observed, is restricted only to the openings and closings of encounters. Holmes (2000), however, had shown that small talks may also appear in the middle of an interaction, especially when speakers intentionally get away from the ongoing business. The characteristics of the distribution of small talks are generalized as "elasticity", "flexibility", and "adaptability" (Homles, 2000: 7-48), with the medial phase reserved for "big talks" where business is done. Thus small talks serve a transformational or "time-filler" function among different activities. Phatic talk in both the opening and the closing phases serves as a transition, though in different directions. In the opening phase, phatic talk serves to establish relationship and achieves a transition from non-interaction to interaction. In the closing phase, however, phatic talk is adopted once again to make another transition from interaction to non-interaction. Though phatic talk may happen sequentially at the openings and endings of conversations, its importance for a successful interaction can be felt throughout the whole process. This function of lubricating and smoothening everyday conversation has been widely acknowledged. Thus, small talk fills a time gap with acceptable and valuable relationship-maintaining social interaction, and avoids problematic and embarrassing silent moments before the "main activity" can be started or resumed.

Laver also discusses three pragmatic functions of phatic talk in the opening phase. In the initial phase of a conversation, phatic talk is expected to fulfill a "propitiatory function of defusing the potential hostility of silence in situations where speech is conventionally anticipated" (Laver, 1975: 220). Here, phatic talk helps to establish a friendly atmosphere among participants, who may be acquaintances or strangers, and to make further interaction possible. Phatic talk also has an "explanatory function", "allowing the participants to feel their way towards the working consensus of their interaction" (ibid.: 221). This uncertainty-reducing function facilitates the revelation of each other's personal information, such as social status, personality, and mood. This function is also closely related to the choice of topics in the following interaction. Another function of phatic talk is the "initiatory function". Phatic talk allows the speakers to cooperate in getting the interaction under its way. By talking about conventional and uncontroversial topics, the speakers contribute to the initiation of an interaction, avoiding abruptness of speaking. In closing sequences, by picking up phatic communication once again, one can reduce possible sense of rejection and consolidate the relationship, thus ending the talk in a friendly way.

Similar to Malinlowski, Laver also recognizes the relational value of phatic talk. Apart from being a simple semantic phenomenon, it functions to create ties of union through subtle and complicated means rather than a mere exchange of words. As a relational phenomenon, phatic talk varies in its topics and ways of conducting interaction with people of different social relationships. Depending on their social status in relation to the other party, speakers may choose either self-oriented or other-oriented expressions to initiate talk. When an inferior opens an encounter, he/she is likely to open with self-oriented remarks. But if a superior initiates the encounter, he/she may choose other-oriented topics or questions about the inferior's personal matters. If the speakers are equals, a neutral topic is a probable choice. This speculative predictive mechanism specifies how speakers use phatic talk to demonstrate solidarity/intimacy and status relationships among them (J. Coupland, N. Coupland and Robinson, 1992: 212). This mechanism introduced by Laver is very similar to the politeness strategies proposed by Brown and Levinson (1987).

Having introduced phatic talk and business talk by previous scholars, it is imperative to examine their application in the analysis of the interactions between the insurance sales agents and their (prospective) clients. In the following part, the three dominant types of talk in the interactions will be identified for their content, organization, and pragmatic functions. There are three main sections: 1) Data of Analysis; 2) Three Types of Talk in Insurance

Sales Interactions; and 3) Summary.

In rural insurance sales settings, most of the prospective clients are either friends, relatives or at least familiar people introduced through a mutually acknowledged third party. The relationships between the agents and their clients are complicated and dynamic. On the one hand, prospective clients are insurance agents' friends, so it is expected that as friends, they should be supportive, honest, loyal, faithful and considerate. On the other hand, how much an insurance agent earns depends on how much the prospective client buys, according to a particular commission formula. Thus it is profit-driven and practical goal-oriented. Therefore, the insurance sales agent-client relationship is a dynamic, ambiguous and conflicting one. Nevertheless, a harmonious relationship between the agent and the client is important for both of them. The agents need the clients' cooperation and decision to make the purchase, and the clients need the agents' advice, both practical and spiritual, in order to facilitate their lives in the local community. As for most of the time, the agents possess much greater resources in the local settings. These dilemmas and the potential conflicts motivate insurance sales agents to invoke various identity categories in order to achieve their interactional goals.

4.4 Categories of Talk in Insurance Sales Interactions

The analysis is based on a detailed study of an approximately 20-minute conversation between an insurance sales agent and a prospective client, and three other interactions between the agents and the clients. Only female agents are represented to avoid gender differences (Actually, most of the local agents are female, probably due to the fact that females could be more suitable for insurance sales); their ages range from 30 to 50. All the agents are experienced insurance sales agents with at least five years' experience. The clients are mostly new to insurance; few of them have prior knowledge of insurance. This phenomenon has some important implications. On the one hand, since most of the prospective clients have little prior knowledge of insurance, it will take great efforts of the agents to introduce and explain the concept, rationale, function and necessity of insurance. While on the other hand, it leaves much room for the agents to tap into the unexplored huge potential market, which also makes the prospective clients potential victims of certain manipulation or misbehaviors if the agents build their sales solely on the blind trust that the clients have in them. It could be safe to say, whether or not there exists serious manipulation largely relies on two factors: One, the sense of conscience and responsibility the agents have; and the other, the willingness and the need of the clients to purchase the insurance in question. All the interactions occur in the working environment of insurance sales—in the clients' living room, the courtyard, store or corridors. All participants are aware that they are being recorded.

4.4.1 Three Types of Talk

In their interactions, three main types of talk—friendship talk, institutional talk, and task-oriented talk—have been identified, mainly by their content and their linguistic features. Among the three, the task-oriented talk is the most complex due to the fact that it contains the features of both friendship and institutional talk. The following explores the three categories of talk in insurance sales discourse and the detailed examination of how identities are interactionally managed within the three types of talk.

4.4.2 Friendship Talk

The friendship talk (the talk among friends), is identified by both its content and its organizational features. Talks play a significant role in the indexing, managing, and maintenance of friendship. As Simmel (1961) argued, talk is "an end in itself" in social gatherings where our human instinct for "sociability" is achieved. Because of the special nature of friendship talk, its content is quite varied. It could be anything about the agents or the clients, from their full-time jobs to trivial matters, such as buying things and seeing a doctor. Most friendship talk is conducted for its own sake, without any explicit purpose of the participants, nor are there any of the practical outcomes that characterize most institutional outcomes. Nonetheless, it is not suggested that friendship talk is not goal-oriented, indeed, friendship talk can be highly pragmatic in nature. This is especially true of the friendship talk in institutional settings, where the socio-emotional aspects of human behavior are brought to play for various purposes. While most institutional talk is goal-oriented in the sense that the participants' behavior is highly contingent upon their relevant identities in an institution. Moreover, friendship talk does not have the constraints of institutional talk.

In the interactions of insurance sales, friendship talk is fairly frequent and plays a significant role. Before turning to the functions of friendship talk in insurance sales, we need to focus on some excerpts of friendship talk in the data corpus. The following is an opening of a conversation between an experienced insurance sales agent and his prospective client who was identified to have the potential need for insurance coverage.

(A: Insurance sales agent, female, an experienced insurance sales agent with over five years' experience; B: Prospective client, male, a potential customer of insurance policies.)

They are familiar with each other but haven't seen each other for a while.

1. A: 哎呀,好久没见,发财了嘛? 这么大房子,真漂亮。(Well, long time no see, you've got rich? Beautiful big house.)

2. B: 好久没见。感觉好像好长时间喽,你现在在哪发财啊? (Long time no see. It seems it has been quite some time. Where do you work now?)

3. A: 唵,是的哦,我啊,我不就在家里混,呵呵。(Well, yes. Me? Stay at home, he he.)

4. B: 来啊, 家里坐下子。(Come on, and have a seat inside.)

5. A: 唵, 好啊, 刮下子。(Well, ok, That will be nice.)

 (到家里坐下, 倒水, 坐好) (Go inside the house, pour water, and have a seat.)

Chapter 4　Topic Management in Insurance Sales Dialogues

6. B: 现在在搞嘛子哦？(What are you doing now?)

7. A: 我不就在家里搞搞，一直在邮局上班嘛。(I stay at home, and have always been working with the post office.)

8. B: 邮局好哦，铁饭碗，旱涝保收。(It is good to work at the post office, very stable; you don't have to worry about any ups and downs.)

The above interaction contains the features of friendship talk identified by Tannen (2001) and Lakoff (1990)—such as preference for personal topics, turns of equal lengths, and mutual initiation of topics. Yet, some striking differences are found. First of all, as both Tannen and Lakoff pointed out, conversations among friends are reciprocal and cooperative. However, the greetings of the interactants are not a preferred sequence of question-answer. The agent initiated the conversation with "哎呀，好久没见，发财了嘛？这么大房子，真漂亮。" ("Well, long time no see, you've got rich? Beautiful big house.") The preferred sequence is not only the "answer" to this question "好久没见。感觉好像好长时间喽" ("Long time no see. It seems it has been quite some time."), but some modesty expected concerning the compliment to his house. Instead, the client asked the same question "你现在在哪发财啊？"（"Where do you work now?"）as a counter-question, and after that, initiated a new topic. In fact, this "counter-question" sequence is quite common in the data, not only at the opening of the conversations but also in the middles and closings of them. What is operating here is the two maxims of friendship engagement: the maxim of intimacy and control. Nevertheless, what they are doing is far from being "unfriendly" to each other. As argued in Chapter 2, the maxim of intimacy is the maxim of dependence, whereas the maxim of control is the maxim of independence. Being friends involves not only showing care about each other, but also respecting personal territories when necessary. As a result, when the agent first initiated the question in Turn 1, the client did not answer it, but asked the same question. In fact, when the client asked the question, he didn't expect an answer, because he had initiated a new topic by inviting the agent into his house. What they were doing here is negotiating the maxim of intimacy and maxim of control. In other words, they are negotiating the dependence and interdependence between friends.

Besides the negotiation of dependence and interdependence in the sample dialogue, the disagreement of the agent with the client's claim that he was rich, in Turn 7, is also an implicit indication of his current situation and very covert intention of hoping the client made the decision of making the purchase of the insurance policies under discussion. This ambivalence and contradictions, very common and frequently found in the data, will be further explored later in more detail.

Another striking difference between the friendship talk identified and the findings of Tannen and Lakoff is the rate of speech. As a prelude to the task-oriented talk later on, the friendship talk is slower in speech compared with the task-oriented talk that follows. The same is found in most of the other conversations. The contrast in the rate of speech distinguishes friendship talk from other types of talk. Rate of speech is not a static feature of talk, but one of the dynamic strategies which can be used to negotiate social identities during interactions.

Although friendship talk is one of the distinctive features of insurance sales interactions, it is also quite frequently seen in other institutional settings as well. For example, business deals are also intermingled with business and conversational talk (Scollon, 1998). Moreover, in doctor-patient interactions, socio-emotional talk is also widely employed at the beginning of the consultations as a lead-in to the professional talk in question, in order to address the increasingly holistic concern of patients in the health-care setting (J. Coupland and N. Coupland, 1994). It has also been found that in classroom settings, teachers may relax the institutional constraints from time to time in order to build rapport with their students. Nonetheless, within these institutional settings, the goal of friendship talk is only auxiliary to primary institutional goals in question. To be more specific, in doctor-patient interactions, there are restrictions constraining participants' topic contributions. For example, after a doctor greets the patient with a simple "Hey" ("How are you?"), although a patient can initiate any topic in his turn, his response is still largely constrained by the relevance to the institutional frame. That is why most patients' responses are about themselves related to the medical concerns, which can be used by the doctor as a lead-in to the medical consultation (J. Coupland and N. Coupland, 1994).

It is the friendship talk in insurance sales which makes use of the socio-emotional aspect of institutional talk to the fullest extent. The function of friendship talk is evident now. As insurance sales intermingles friendship and business, the insurance sales agents' main strategy is to exploit these seemingly contradictory ideologies. One of the important tasks of insurance sales is to exploit the intersectional space of friendship and business to the greatest possible extent and at the same time to reconcile the contradictions in this mediated interface. As talk is the most effective means of transferring ideas and concepts, friendship talk certainly plays its role in socializing between the agents and the prospective clients. Through friendship talk, prospective clients can experience the friendly atmosphere of the interactions, in contrast with the contractual business goals in the deal itself. As experienced agents, they are well socialized about how to intermingle the personal and business domains, and manage potential or imminent conflicts from this mediation. As an agent confessed in his interview, "其实我们做保险讲到底就是做人，人做好了，其他东西都好办。一般比如讲客户有这个需求，他要是能信任你，那他肯定找你做。所以最关键的东西我觉得就是做人，让人家能够信任你，这一点是最重要的。"("As a matter of fact, in my view, the essence of the business is to make friends. If they can trust you, things will be much easier. As long as they can trust you, it is almost for sure he will buy from you given there is a need. So the key is to make friends and gain trust."). Given this phenomenon, friendship talk or friendship identity can be strategically employed by the insurance sales agents to serve various purposes, as will be elaborated and analyzed later.

4.4.3 Institutional Talk

The criteria for determining the institutionality of a segment of speech are the three features of institutional talk identified by Drew and Heritage (1992b: 22), based on their work in conversation analysis. The three features can be categorized as follows: activities and goals, constraints, and inferences.

First of all, for activities and goals, institutional interaction involves an orientation by at least one of the participants to some core goal, task or identity (or set of them) conventionally associated with the institution in question. In short, institutional talk is normally informed by goal orientations of a relatively restricted conventional form.

Secondly, constraints may often involve special and particular constraints on what one or both of the participants will treat as allowable contributions to the business at hand.

Thirdly, for inference, institutional interaction may be associated with inferential frameworks and procedures that are particular to specific institutional contexts.

Being different from the ordinary conversations among friends, institutional talk in insurance sales is institutionally goal-oriented, that is, the participants' goal achievement is contingent upon their institutional affiliation, constrained by turn-taking rules, and made possible through institutional inferential procedures in question. The features can be unveiled by the following excerpt from a conversation between an experienced insurance sales agent and her prospective client. The agent was selling a kind of policy by showing the benefits. The policy being introduced was claimed to have both the functions of savings and investment. In the introduction, she showed how the policy works by presenting a table which showed the annual earning and other benefits possible.

> (A: Insurance sales agent, female, around 35 years old, experienced with over 5 years' experience; B: Prospective client, male, around 30 years old, relatively well-off, having a small privately owned business in

Chapter 4 Topic Management in Insurance Sales Dialogues

Guangzhou, now at home having his days off for the Spring Festival)

1. A: 现在我们推出的这种××会比较适合你的情况。我给你讲下子具体是怎么回事。这是我们公司特别针对一些家庭条件相对比较好，但是暂时没有足够保障的客户量身定制的。它的优势主要在这几个方面：首先，它是按年缴费，缴费额根据自己情况灵活掌握，可高可低，最高到 10 万，最低到 5800，所以它灵活、自由。第二，一般的保险我们讲它只是提供一个保障，比如讲，有什么意外情况，它能够提供比较好的保障，弥补一定损失；但这一种保险，它一方面在需要的时候提供一定保障，更重要它也是一种理财方式。只要你交够足够年限，到时全部所交金额都能得到返还，同时每年还能有分红……你可有搞理财啊？ (This policy will be suitable for you. Let me explain it to you. This product is specifically designed for those families who are well-off but with insufficient insurance coverage. It has the following advantages. Firstly, the premium is made annually. The amount is rather flexible, as high as 100,000 yuan and as low as 5,800 yuan. So it's very flexible. Secondly, the insurance we see can only offer you some assurance. For instance, if there is anything unfortunate, it can cover some losses for you. But our insurance is different. It offers not only some assurance to cover some losses on unfortunate occasions, but more importantly, it is a kind of wealth management. As long as you pay for certain years in time, all the money will be reimbursed to you, and every year you can have additional dividends… Do you have any wealth management?)

2. B: 理财啊？理财怎么讲啊？ (Wealth management? What about it?)

3. A: 理财——你现在也晓得，我们现在的环境，货币贬值厉害，每年钱是越来越不值钱。我们小时候到小店买糖，一分钱一个，你现在看看，一包糖就是十几块，算下来你看看贬值了多少倍啊。再你看看，我们去买菜，以前嘛拿个 100 的出来，能买一堆菜，肉啊鸡啊鱼啊蔬菜的，你现在再拿 100，随便买下子，看不到东西。再讲呢，我们现在还年轻，挣钱能力还比较强，在这个时候存一点钱，等我们老的了，干不动了，还能多少有点保障。最起码嘛，我们能自己保自己，现在小伢子们负担也重，等我们老的，要是能自己保自己，不要找他们要钱的，那其实也就是给他们做贡献了，再讲，找人要钱也不快活，可是的啊？ (Wealth management—as you know, nowadays, the money

depreciates quickly. Its value is getting lower and lower. When we were young, if we went to stores to buy some candy, one Cent for one, but what about now? One small bag is about 20 yuan. You can see how many times money has depreciated. For another, if we go to the market, one hundred yuan seemed a lot of money in the past. You can have a pile of stuff, pork, chicken, fish and vegetables, etc. what about now? You don't see much in your basket. What's more, now that we are still young, we can make money, so it is a good chance for us to make some deposits. When we get old and weak, it can offer us some basic subsistence. Now that our children are having enough burden already, in this way at least we can support ourselves and we don't have to ask them for money, which is already making contributions for them. What's more, it is not enjoyable to ask for money, isn't it?)

4. B: 那是的哦，呵呵。(Yeah, that's true, he he.)

5. A: 要碰到好的还好，要是碰个搭犟（"麻烦的，不好的"的意思，当地方言），那就真受罪了……(If we come across someone nice, we're lucky. What if we come across someone really troublesome? That'll be really unfortunate…)

6. B: 嗯，那也是一方面。(Yeah, true.)

7. A: 所以讲要是可能，我觉得你就可以考虑下子我们这个。(So if possible, I think it'll be a good idea if you consider this.)

8. B: 唵，你将讲分红是什么意思啊？(Err, you mentioned dividend just now, and what does it mean?)

9. A: 是这样的——你过来，到这边我给你看看这个表……（打开电脑，展示分红情况表）比如讲你现在买这一档，一年两万，交10年，那不就是总共交了20万嘛，你今年多大年纪了？(That is—Come over here. I'll show you this table [Turn on the computer, and demonstrate the dividend table] Suppose you buy this, 20,000 yuan for a year lasting for 10 years, and that makes 200,000 yuan in all. How old are you now?)

B: 我今年虚岁33，32周岁。(33 years old (in traditional way), but 32 for official record.)

A: 好，32周岁，交10年，到42周岁，总共交了20万，等你到60周岁的时候开始，每个月给你返还1666.67，也就差不多1700；连

Chapter 4　Topic Management in Insurance Sales Dialogues

续返 10 年，你看，10 年也就 120 个月，刚好 20 万。但是还不止，怎么讲呢？我们××公司你也晓得，世界 500 强，国家重点扶持。它拿了你的钱不是讲放在那里，它也拿去投资，比如讲你要看新闻也晓得，现在西部大开发、新能源、高铁、股票这些，它都有份参加。它投资赚了钱，就给我们这些客户分红，按照不同比例进行分红。根据前几年的情况，这个分红额差不多一年有 6%左右，也就是讲，你一年交两万，6%，那就是 1200，一年还能收 1200；这个 1200 呢，你可以自己拿回来，或者你觉得好，还能继续累加到你的保费中，就像利滚利那样子…… (OK, 32 years old, for 10 years— that's 42 years old with a sum of 200,000 yuan. When you are 60 years old, the reimbursement starts, 1666.67 yuan per month, roughly 1,700, for 10 consecutive years, which is 120 months, so 200,000 yuan in all exactly. But more than that, you will get more. Let's see, you know, our company is one of the world's top 500, and a national key enterprise. It takes your money in not for savings, but for investments. If you watch TV, the news is always about Western Development, new energies, express railways, stock market… It invests in these different projects and gives you dividends according to different ratios. For your case, based on the data of the last several years, the dividend could be about 6% a year, that is, if you pay 20,000 yuan a year, with 6%, that'll make a total of 1,200 yuan. For this 1,200 yuan, you can choose either withdrawing it or adding it to your premium as further investment, if you like the idea. Simply put, it works at compound interest…)

It can be clearly seen that this dialogue is marked with turns of unequal lengths, with most turns initiated and maintained by the insurance sales agent whose goal is obvious—to sell the policy in introduction and to promote the advantages, values and positive aspects of the policy. While in friendship talk, turns are normally equally distributed and maintained, not allowing participants to dominate a particular turn. Nevertheless, in promoting business and selling products, a salesperson should have longer turns to enable him/her to have more detailed introduction. In the above excerpt, the agent's upholding of much longer turns and her prospective client's cooperation in not interrupting indicate the agent's institutional affiliation to one of the major insurance companies as an expert, which can invoke the frames of superiors' authority and subordinates' obedience, to the agent's interactional advantage. Moreover, the change of footing is also achieved through the use of the inclusive "we" and "our insurance" in Turn 1, in which the institutional role of an insurance sales agent can be resumed. By invoking the institutional affiliation, the agent can resume the discourse identity of an expert (being an author and principal of an institution) and can more easily accomplish her objective of persuasion. In friendship talk, or in task-oriented talk, the discourse identities a salesperson can play are rather limited to the principal of his/her personal roles, that is, as a friend and the animator of the company he/she is representing. Being only an animator of the company, his/her selling is obviously less convincing and more subject to contention and challenge, especially in nowadays context of rampant overuse of such promotional efforts as commercials and advisements, in which people may resist or feel obnoxious.

Besides allowing the agent to adjust appropriate discourse identities, institutional talk also puts constraints on the participation of the prospective client, to the advantage of the agent. Resembling closely to the asymmetrical interactions of doctor-patient and teacher-student, institutional talk in insurance sales discourse allows the agents to question their prospective clients and to sustain a turn long enough to do their jobs. The question in the institutional talk in the above interaction serves a very important function. Firstly, by asking the prospective client questions, the agent was able to understand quickly how much technical knowledge the client knew, and thus she would be able to adjust the technical level of her talk. Secondly, by engaging in a question-and-answer sequence, as in other asymmetrical interactions, the agent was in a better position to control the introduction of topics and to convince her prospective client of what she was saying—establishing the impression that she was a person with technical knowledge, as in a doctor-patient or teacher-student interaction. To put it another way, the inferential procedures of those kinds of asymmetrical interactions are being invoked to the advantage of the agents, in place of the more familiar buying/selling inferential procedures in which the buyers and sellers are also in an asymmetrical relationship, but with advantage reversed. Apart from adjusting the discourse identity for selling, institutional talk can also be used to alienate the responsibility of the insurance agents when there is trouble, which will be addressed later. The following excerpt of a conversation between an agent and a client can illustrate this phenomenon.

The agent, female, in her forties, is an experienced insurance sales with more than four years' experience. About a month ago, the client purchased from her an insurance policy worth of 100,000 yuan with a term of ten years. Due to some reasons, the client wanted to withdraw from the contract. The conversation happened when the agent was called to the client's home. A refers to the insurance sales agent, and B is her client.

1. A: ××，你好啊. (Good morning, ××.)

2. B: ××，你那个怎么搞的哦？上次我跟你签了，回来我跟我家他一讲，他就觉得不好，现在我们不搞了。(××, what are the specific terms of the insurance? Last time after we signed the contract, I talked to my husband, and he didn't like it, so we'd like to quit.)

3. A: 啊？是怎么回事哦？你先别急，慢慢讲。但总的来讲你要不是特别特殊的原因，我建议你别退保。现在退保损失大哎。(Ah? What happened? Take it easy, let's see. But generally if it's not absolutely necessary, I don't think it will be a good idea to quit, since you might suffer huge losses.)

4. B: 不管了，反正我们就是不搞了，你这个东西划不来……(I don't care. We just want to quit. It's not a good deal…)

5. A: 瞎扯哦，哪场子划不来哦。其实你这个我还真是花了心思给你搞的。哎，你现在退保的话，根据合同，你不但本金拿不回来，还要损失违约费，那个数字也不小哎……(Nonsense. It is a good deal. Frankly, I've devoted a lot of efforts into your policy. Well, if you terminate the contract now, according to the contract, you will not only lose your deposit money, but also receive a penalty, and your losses would be substantial…)

6. B: 啊？违约费啊？(What? Penalty?)

7. A: 是的啊，呶，你看，我把合同都带来了。你看这个场子，第二页，现金价值表，你这个才刚刚买一个月，你就要退，那你损失太大了哎；它这场子写得很清楚。(Yes, of course. Look, I have got the contract with me. Look here, page 2, cash value statement. You bought it only one month ago. Now that you quit, you would suffer dearly. It's very clearly stated here.)

8. B: 啊？！那我这个现在要退，具体损失多少啊？(Ah? Now that I quit, how much exactly would I suffer?)

9. A: 你这个真要退那损失太大的，我给你算下子哦——其实真的，你这个退真划不来，人寿保险这个是中长期的投资，前期重的是保障，这是保险的真谛。你现在要提前解约，对你而言，你现在能拿到手的只是这几个：保单的现金价值，加累积生存金，再加累积红利，你这个才买一个来月，你这个就太划不来了。那你到底是什么原因要退保啊？(You would suffer dearly, let me see—To be frank with you, it's really not a good idea if you quit now. Life insurance is a mid- to long-term investment. For the first phase, we focus on guarantee, and it's the essence of insurance. If you want to quit now, for you, you can only have the following: cash value of the policy, plus cumulated survival insurance money, plus cumulated dividend. You have been buying it for only one month, so it is really not worthwhile. Why on earth do you want to quit?)

10. B: 反正我就是不想搞了……(I just don't want it anymore…)

11. A: 其实你假如要是急用钱，我们公司现在可以用保单现金价值贷款哎，最多能贷出现金价值的 80%。比如讲你现在这个保单，现金价值是…… 再乘以 80%，那就是…… 其实这个不也蛮好的嘛，你要是需要，我都能帮忙给你搞，这个肯定能搞到的。(In fact, if you need some money urgently, our company offers loan by your policy value. You can apply for the loan for a maximum of 80% of the policy value. Take your policy as an example, the value is… multiplies by 80%, that's … It will be a good deal. If you need it, I can do it for you. It's for sure.)

12. B: 哎呀，你这个真是搞死人了……(Oh, that's really troublesome…)

13. A: 另外一个，假如你是担心后面缴费压力，你还能选择减额缴清，也就是不再缴纳保费，但是合同还是有效力，只是保额会下降。

Chapter 4 Topic Management in Insurance Sales Dialogues

比如你这个的话，如果选择这一种，保额会下降到……(For another, if you worry about your payment later, you can choose lower the premium. That is to say, you stop paying the premium, and the contract is still valid, but the insured amount will drop. For your case, if you choose this, the insured amount will drop to…)

From the above dialogue, it can be clearly seen that the agent employed institutional talk to persuade the client to give up the idea of terminating the insurance contract, marked by unevenly distributed turn length (Turns 9, 11 and 13), and focused core goal (the agent tried to persuade the client to give up the idea of terminating insurance contract, but the client wanted to terminate it anyway). Most of the agent's talk is associated with the insurance company and insurance policy in question. In short, Turns 9, 11 and 13 are clear embodiment of being informed by goal orientations of a relatively restricted conventional form.

To be more specific, in Turn 5, the agent set the scene of "huge losses" if the client terminated the insurance contract, "瞎扯哦，哪场子划不来哦。其实你这个我还真是花了心思给你搞的。哎，你现在退保的话，根据合同，你不但本金拿不回来，还要损失违约费，那个数字也不小哎……" ("Nonsense. It is a good deal. Frankly, I've devoted a lot of efforts into your policy. Well, if you terminate the contract now, according to the contract, you will not only lose your deposit money, but also receive a penalty, and your losses would be substantial…") In the actual selling practice, when the agent is introducing the policy, most of them will emphasize the benefits, while downplay the constraints. It can be clearly captured in the client's surprised response in Turn 6 "啊？违约费啊？" ("What? Penalty?"), which indicates she had no or little prior knowledge about such "penalty" if she wanted to terminate the insurance contract. More importantly, the agent went on with long segments emphasizing the detriments or serious consequence if the client still insisted in the termination of the contract. Besides she offered options for the client to rule out some possible reasons and difficulties the client might have. For example, Turn 9, the essence of insurance, mid- and long-term investment, prior emphasis on guarantee ("中长期的投资，前期重的是保障，这是保险的真谛"), Turn 11, a possible loan ("保单现金价值贷款"), and Turn 13, a possible reduction in insurance money ("减额缴清"). After such tactics, the client softened her determination and anger, and became hesitant about the decision of terminating the contract, as in Turn 12 "哎呀，你这个真是搞死人了" ("Oh, that's really troublesome...").

It may be argued whether there are rampant uses of manipulation on the part of insurance sales agent. Nonetheless, our primary focus is to unveil the important functions institutional talk plays in the process of insurance sales, that is, not only for the necessary introduction of the insurance policy in promotion, but also in turning the client around if there is possible termination of the contract. Another focus is to present not only the dynamics between the agent and the client, but also the underlying mechanism under which such sales interactions take place.

There are significant implications for such interactions. On the one hand, besides the previous studies about asymmetrical distribution of turns in expert/layman interactions (Heath, 1992; Linell and Luckmann, 1991) and employer/employee interactions (Gavruseva, 1995). For example, Gavruseva (1995) pointed out that the asymmetrical pattern is discursively constructed and contested. Employees, despite their situational disadvantage, are able to resist and contest the existing asymmetrical structure by revoking changes in frames and footings. The interesting finding in the above analysis is that all institutional talk is asymmetrical, with the power going to the agent.

On the other hand, as we argue all through the study, *Guanxi* is the most important factor in insurance sales in transformational China's rural areas; the success or failure of the insurance agents' selling efforts largely depends on how well the agents are managing the relationship. In other words, sometimes it is not a matter of the insurance policy itself, rather it's the personal trust or credibility the agents enjoy from the prospective clients. Therefore, it sometimes enables the agents some room to exploit such trust and credibility; this is also why there are heated discussions on the malpractices of insurance sales nowadays in transformational China's rural areas. No matter what, there is a clear indication of inter-discursivity (Fairclough, 1989, 1992, 1995, 2001) in the process of insurance sales, and a greater tendency of confusion between friends and business, or as the post-modernist view of "commodification of self".

4.4.4 Task-oriented Talk

Task-oriented talk, the most predominant talk in my data, is different from institutional talk in several ways, although both have the same goal orientation. Task-oriented talk is embedded in the configuration of friendship talk, which in Fairclough's (1989, 1992, 1995, 2001) term as inter-discursivity, the constitution of a text from a configuration of other text types. As a result of this inter-discursive nature, task-oriented talk has the features of both friendship talk and institutional talk, but deviates itself from the others in the following several ways.

Task-oriented talk is marked with equal turn distribution, mutual topic initiation, and cooperative interruptions, as well as a lack of asymmetrical features, such as predominance of the question-answer sequence. Nonetheless, this type of talk had strong goal orientation as well, to get something done through the talk. The following is an example to illustrate task-oriented talk. Before this part, the agent had just finished presenting her prospective client some details of the policy in discussion regarding some of the details. She ended their conversation with a task-oriented talk in which the agent sounded more like a friend. But at the same time she was doing her job, advising the time that her prospective client should come to the promotional meeting at a fancy hotel.

1. A: 正月初八我们在××大酒店要搞一个招待会，你到时候能来看看哎。(We are going to have a reception dinner at ×× Hotel on the 8th day of the first lunar month. Are you coming over?)

2. B: 招待会啊？搞嘛子的哦？(Reception dinner? What about it?)

3. A: 就是招待一些我们客户，如果你现场签单有礼品，还有抽奖……(To entertain some of our clients. There are gifts and lucky draw if you sign on site…)

4. B: 那要交钱的吧？(Is it free?)

5. A: 不要的,对你们客户来讲都是免费参加的,买不买不要紧的,看看嘛,要不然你回去跟家里人商量下子嘛,我们都这么熟悉了,你放心……(Yes, it is free for you clients. It doesn't matter if you buy or not, and you can just have a look. Or you can come back talk to your family. We are friends, you can rest assured…)

6. B: 好啊，那到时候去我跟你讲。[停顿]你家xx（业务员丈夫）现在忙得不得了蛮，我那天在街上看到他……(OK then, I'll tell you if we can come over. [Pause] I saw your husband the other day in street. It seems he is pretty busy…)

7. A: 他哦，他不就瞎忙，现在在村里搞，杂七杂八的事情不晓得好多，一天到晚不归家……(Yeah, he is. He works at the village now with a lot of trivial things, barely coming back home…)

8. B: 那肯定的呀，村子里的事情哪讲得清楚，我回来都找了他好几回啦。我那个补贴还要找他搞，好像还有点什么问题吧，什么时候我还要找他去呢。(That's for sure, too many things with the village. I have come for him for several times already. I have to work out the subsidy. It seems there is some problem, so I need to go to him sometime.)

This short segment of talk is significantly characterized with the predominance of features of friendship talk, that is, almost equal turn length and topic contribution, lack of one-sided question-answer sequence, as compared with institutional talk analyzed above. Some interruptions are also common in both participants' turns. Nonetheless, the talk has a fairly strong institutional goal orientation—to get the prospective client to attend the gathering scheduled in a fancy hotel (where normally substantial purchase could be made). The embedding of goal-oriented talk in friendship talk serves the pivotal goal of creating a friendly environment for the interactions in insurance sales. Compared with the traditional sales encounters, such tendency blurs the boundary of friendship and business. To a certain extent, business is integrated into friendship now. Therefore, the insurance sales agents enjoy more egalitarian relationship. They are friends to each other even when they are talking about business. However, there is also a price to pay with the frequent occurrence of task-oriented talk. It is now becoming more difficult for the agent to control the talk, such as what to talk about, and where will the talk go. It becomes an intense struggle for both the agent and his/her prospective client in determining which one is more "powerful" in negotiating a friendly relationship. Task-oriented talk appears frequently at the juncture of other types of talks, where more changes in footing and frames are involved to negotiate to the participants' advantage. The next part presents a detailed analysis of this phenomenon in task-oriented talk.

The characteristics of each talk's mode are summarized in Table 4.1, and will be discussed in more detail later. Meanwhile, it should be noted that the talk categories are only proposed to enrich the analysis, and for the purpose of quantification of interactional devices, they are proposed for analytical purpose.

Table 4.1 Summary of the Characteristics of the Three Types of Talk

Characteristics	Types of talk		
	Friendship talk	Institutional talk	Task-oriented talk
Orientations	Interpersonal: rapport building	Institutional: giving instructions	Collaborative: negotiation of participants' advantage
Modes	Symmetrical	Asymmetrical	Symmetrical
Constraints on turn-taking, topic contribution	No	Yes	No
Interruptions (non-affiliative)	Yes	No	Yes
Aggravated oppositions	Yes	No	Yes
Prosodic and non-verbal signals	Slower/faster rate of speech to distinguish itself from former and subsequent talk, as well as change of tones and facial expressions		

4.5 Summary

The chapter analyzes in detail the conscious/unconscious control of topics in the conversations between agents and their (prospective) clients to reveal features of different discourse systems. It shows the negotiation, mediation and interplay of different frames, thus different discourse systems at large and further uncovers the intricacies of *Guanxi* involved in the sales interactions.

In terms of sequence of different types of talks, the interaction can be generally divided into three phases. The first phase is warming up. Both parties mainly socialize to establish a harmonious atmosphere in preparation for the next stages. The second phase is mainly the task-oriented talk and the institutional talk, with the agent managing to make the sales, which is also the most interesting phase with constant mediation and contestation of frames and identities. The third phase is the ending part, normally featured with friendship talk to end the interaction in a friendly and harmonious manner. As we mentioned, all the interactions are carried out between friends, relatives or at least the familiar people. Therefore, on the one hand, as friends, it is expected that they should be supportive, honest, loyal, faithful and considerate; on the other hand, the interactions are mainly driven by the agents' strong desire in pursuing economic benefit. It is profit-driven and practically goal-oriented. The insurance sales agent-client relationship is a dynamic, ambiguous and conflicting one. Nonetheless, a harmonious relationship between the agent and the client is important for both of them. Therefore, different frames are in constant mediation and contestation. The interactions are featured with strategic shifts among different types of talks, namely, friendship talk, institutional talk and task-oriented talk. More specifically, friendship talk reinforces the rapport between the agents and the clients and serves as significant lubricant in alleviating potential tension and conflict between them. Institutional talk is mainly employed by the agents to activate the institutional frame for controlling turns and initiating topics for persuasion. While task-oriented talk provides effective means for the agents in controlling and socializing the clients. The strategic shift between different frames represented by different types of talks reveals the constant mediation and contestation between the insurance sales agent and the client.

The above analysis of talk in agent-client interactions shows the dynamic process of insurance sales agent-client interactions through three different types of talk, namely, friendship talk, institutional talk and task-oriented talk. Friendship talk reinforces the rapport between the agents and the clients and reduces the potential tension between them. Institutional talk is mainly used by the agents to activate the institutional frame for controlling turns and initiating topics for persuasion. While task-oriented talk provides effective means for the agents in controlling and socializing the clients, and for the clients to assume more control in topics. Moreover, it is also an arena rampant with intense struggle owing to the contestation between the institutional frame and friendship frame. As will be shown in the next part, participants have to negotiate, activate and contest identities and their corresponding talks dynamically within and between talk categories. It also shows that the participants can utilize identities and corresponding talk features for their own interactional goals.

Chapter 5

Negotiation of Interactive Frames and Discourse Identities

5.1 Introduction

This chapter finds that both agents and clients are mobilizing the interactional devices available to them for their invoking the identities favorable to their own respective advantages. In other words, this part offers the fine analysis from the perspectives of interactive frames, footings and discourse identities. Through the analysis, the dynamics of agent-client interaction can be captured and described. Moreover, some discussions are made to shed light on the further understanding of *Guanxi*. It illustrates the complex nature of identities through the analysis of footing, interactive frames, contextualization cues and discourse identities.

5.2 Negotiation of Frames and Discourse Identites in Different Types of Talks

This part offers the analysis part. It first offers the context of the interaction, and then it analyzes the confrontation, mediation and co-construction of different identities, which is negotiated in different interactive frames, and it further discusses the implications.

5.2.1 The Context of the Interactions

The interaction to be analyzed is a talk between an experienced insurance sales agent and a prospective client in the client's house. The experienced agent is a female, just over 30 years, with over six years' experience in insurance sales in the local area. With her hard work and devotion, she has completed excellent sales volume and received financial incentives and other fringe benefits the company offers, for example, free tours to tourist spots. She is known as the star agent in the local branch and enjoys high acclaim and reputation in the company. She is well-aware that her income and well-being are largely dependent on her efforts and skills to make the sales. The prospective client is rather new about insurance but has some interest in understanding the necessity of insurance due to the fact he has been rather successful in business performance in Guangdong. (He does some trading business, purchasing some products from other remote areas and selling them afterwards to restaurants in large cities.) The agent owns a kindergarten where the prospective client's daughter goes to; the agent's husband is the director of the village who is well-recognized; and her father is a locally well-respected doctor. The two participants have met each other several times before the interaction takes place.

Some other agent-client interactions are also used for analysis. The context across all the interactions is similar: the agents are locally respected and well-known people who are trying to make the sales. All of them have more than five years' experience. While all the prospective clients have above-the-average income (compared with the local standard) and enjoy well-off life. Most of the interactions take place in the clients' house. All participants are aware of being recorded during their interactions.

The relationship between the agent and the prospective client is rather complicated and ambiguous. On the one hand, they are friends who are quite familiar with each other featured by spiritual support. On the other hand, the agent's income is based on the prospective client's decision in making the purchase and his possible recommendation of insurance to other friends or relatives. What is tricky here is that the agent needs to make efforts to make the sales and at the same time maintain the friendly relationship. The agent does not have the authority or power of regulation and control, as manifested in employer-employee relationships. This is exactly why insurance sales agents manage to exploit the mediated interface between business and friendship, in other words, by constantly intermingling friendship and business relationships.

As already summarized in Chapter 4, the interaction can be generally divided into three phases. The first phase is warming up, in which both parties mainly socialize to establish a harmonious atmosphere in preparation for the next stages. The second phase mainly focuses on task-oriented talk and institutional talk, with the agent making efforts to conclude the sales. The most outstanding characteristic is that this phase is rampant with constant mediation and contestation of frames and identities. The third phase is the ending part, which is generally featured with friendship talk to end the interaction in a friendly and harmonious manner. The following analysis mainly focuses on the second phase, in which their identities are at stake.

5.2.2 Co-construction of Different Identities in Task-oriented Talk

The dynamic management of identities is clearly captured in the mediation of different frames, which proves that our identities are not pre-determined identities, but discursively and cooperatively produced and managed, and that these dynamics are constituted in and activated by the conversational dynamics, such as changes in footings and interactive frames, and discourse identities as already mentioned above.

By analyzing conversations between the experienced insurance sales agents and their prospective clients, this study examines in detail how identities in insurance sales are interactively maintained, ratified and managed—through changes in footing, mediation of different frames and discourse identities—rather than being imposed by one of the participants concerned. Since power, trust and familiarity are inherent features of the interaction, the mediation of power between the agents and the prospective clients will also be examined and analyzed, as power in this kind of interaction is subject to negotiation, as we argued earlier.

1. The general pattern of agent-client interactions

The following reconstructed segment of agent-client interaction offers an analysis into the interactive management of identities to their respective advantages. First, we would generalize an overall pattern of agent-client interaction, and then we'll probe into different segments to have more detailed analysis.

(A: Insurance Sales Agent; B: Prospective Client)

1. A: 今天在家休息啊？（Taking a break at home today?）

2. B: 唵，在家里玩。(Yeah, staying at home.)

3. A: 哦，刘老师原来你们喊姐夫嗨？(Oh, do you call Teacher Liu brother-in-law?)

4. B: 是的哦。(Yes.)

5. A: 他原来就是我们中学老师哎。(He was our teacher when we were in middle school.) [停顿 1 秒(Pause for a second)]哦，两个毛毛，嗨？(Ah, you have two children, right?)

6. B: 嗯，在家里陪读。(Yeah, so I have to stay at home with them.)[停顿 0.5 秒(Pause for half a second)]你是保险公司的嗨？(Are you working in the insurance company?)

7. A: 嗯，我是××人寿公司的。刘店的×××你可认得？刘店那医生啊，我是她姐姐。你老婆在松树科，我们隔壁生产队嘛。(Yeah, I'm working in the ×× Life Insurance Company. Do you know ××× at Liudian? That doctor, I'm her elder sister. Your wife is at Songshuke, the neighboring production unit.)

8. B: 嗯。(Yes.)

9. A: 呵呵，我昨天听刘老师讲搞保险，(他)跟你们怎么讲的啊？(I heard that Teacher Liu talked about insurance to you yesterday. How

did he tell you about it?)

10. B: 嗯——也没怎么讲，就是讲就讲起头来了。就讲这保险那保险，讲保险种类上好多……(Well, nothing much, just some casual talk. About this insurance, that insurance, and many types of insurance…)

11. A: [停顿0.5秒 (Pause for half a second)] 嗯，那是的哦。(Yeah, that's true.)

12. B: 你们办的是什么保险呢？(What kind of insurance do you have?)

13. A: 我们办的有小家伙的教育保险、成长保险啊许多的。(We offer education insurance, growth insurance, etc.)

14. B: 小家伙在学校念书不是已经有保险了么？(Haven't the children already got covered by insurance at school?)

15. A: 不是的，那个保险钱是不退给你的，我们给你介绍的额保险，是积少成多，一次性给你还是三次给你，比你存银行利息高。(No, that kind of insurance won't reimburse you. What we are introducing here is more about deposits, with higher interest rates than what the banks offer, and you can choose once or three times.）

16. B: 什么险种啊？(What kind of insurance is that?)

17. A: 如果你给毛毛买的话，如果参加分红，分红有本金累计生息。具体情况我给你介绍下子，假如讲我们买十万的那种，分十年交，一年就是交一万，假如讲我们第一年交了一万，这就是你的本金，本金放那要生息，我们按照去年的情况，5.6%来算，一年就是560；第二年开始我们本金就是10 560了，这时候再加上你第二年交的保费一万，那就是20 560；然后第三年、第四年，以此类推，就是讲利生息、滚动的，到最后呢，等你交满十年了，你可以选择一次性拿回来，也可以分几次拿回来；假如讲你觉得利润还好，你也可以继续放那，就像是理财样的，也中；还有比如讲你每年想把那个分红拿出来，也中，那你就是本金放那，分红自己拿回来用，也一样……(If you buy for your child, and take part in dividend, it has cumulative interest. Let me give you some specific information. Suppose we buy 100,000 (yuan) for ten years, that's 10,000 (yuan) for each year. And further suppose we pay 10,000 (yuan) for the first year, that's your deposit, which generates interest rate, with the rate of last year, it's 5.6%, and that's 560 (yuan). That will make the deposit for the second year as 10,560 (yuan), and plus your deposit of

Chapter 5 Negotiation of Interactive Frames and Discourse Identities

the second year, that's 20,560 (yuan) in total. Then the third year, forth year, etc. Simply put, it's about cumulative interest. After you have been paying for ten years, you can take it all back altogether or in several different times; if you think the returns are satisfactory, you can also choose to put it there, just like wealth management. And if you want to withdraw the dividend each year, it's also OK. That is to say, you put the deposit there, and withdraw the dividend for your own use. It's just the same and it's totally up to you...)

18. B: 那假如讲我中间想要用钱，那怎么搞啊？(What if I need this amount of money during this period?)

19. A: 用钱的话呢，你最好是不动本金，本金一动，那就相当于违约，违约的话那你就划不来了。这个东西我们要实话实说，因为我们有合同，呶，这个场子，你看看（指出条款给客户看），那你就非常划不来了。(If you really need to use this money, you'd better not use the deposit money; once you use that, that's breach of contract, and you would suffer. I need to be frank with you. [Show the clauses to the client.] Here is the contract, here...)

20. B: 哦，那就是讲，我买了以后就不能动了……(Oh, that is to say, I can't use that money...)

21. A: 也不是那么讲，一般买保险我们不都是闲钱嘛；暂时没有其他比较好的地方投资啊或者怎样；再讲你家里这个情况，也不至于啊，这个也不多，呵呵，你讲可是的啊？(Not exactly, normally we buy insurance with our spare money or without any other better places to make investment or others; and also for you, you don't have to according to your condition. It's not too much. Don't you think so?)

22. B: 哎呀，那个东西难讲哦……(Well, it's hard to say...)

23. A: 我觉得呢，我们这么想，现在我们还比较年轻，挣钱能力比较强，年富力强的时候，这个时候买点保险，给我们小家伙有个保障，就像是存款样的，等他们长大了，最起码还有那么一笔钱在那儿。我们到时候万一讲的话，年纪大了，做不动了，他们能用这一笔钱还能做一点事情。再讲，现在钱存银行你也晓得，每年通货膨胀那么厉害，钱是越来越不值钱；我们这个就是讲一方面你是存那有利息，另外一方面公司还把这个钱拿去投资——××公司你也晓得，世界500强，中国最大的保险公司，它把这个钱收起来不是讲就放那或者放银行，它是要拿去投资的哎，比如讲现在什么西部大开发啊、风力发电啊、三峡工程哪，许多项目……(For me, I think right now we are still young, and we can make a lot of money. If we buy some insurance, and offer some guarantee for our children just like deposits, when they grow up, they would have this amount of money. In case we get old and weak, this money can be of some use. Moreover, if you deposit with the bank, with the current depreciation, the value would be lower and lower. What we have here is not only you can have interest rate, but also dividends; the company will make investment elsewhere—You know our company is one of the world top 500, China's largest insurance company. It doesn't leave your money just there or deposit it in the bank; it is to invest in, for example, the development of the West, wind power, project of the Three Gorges…)

24. B: ……你可买了啊？(…Did you buy it?)

25. A: 我给我家他和儿子还有我自己都买了啊，我家条件没你这么好，买不了太多，就这样子，我都买了不少呢……(I have bought it for my husband, my son and myself. Our financial situation is not as good as yours, and we can't afford too much. Even so, I still bought some…)

26. B: 你家××现在还在村里搞吧？(Your husband ×× is still working at the village?)

27. A: 唵，他不一直在那场子瞎忙嘛。(Yeah, he is.)

28. B: 那还瞎忙啊，主任多好，不过事情也确实多。(It is true that he has a lot of things at hand, as a village head.)

29. A: 是的啊，一天到晚不归家，不晓得在忙什么东西。(Yeah, barely at home. No idea what he is busy with.)

30. B: 哦，你儿子现在上大学了吧？在广州还是在哪可是的啊？(Your son is at university now, right? In Guangzhou?)

31. A: 唵，在广州，那个不成器的东西……[停顿2秒]其实你也可以考虑给你自己买一点哎。你看你现在挣钱多，但是我们国家现在养老啊、社会保险这一块还不怎么完善，将来年纪大了，我们不讲给小家伙们创造多大价值，最起码自己保自己，那就是给他们减轻负担了。呶，我们公司现在有一个险种我给你介绍下子啊……(Yeah, in Guangzhou, that naughty boy…[Pause for 2 seconds]… Actually you can think about buying some for yourself. Now that you make a lot of

Chapter 5 Negotiation of Interactive Frames and Discourse Identities

money, but our life insurance and social security are not sufficient. It's not that we make much contribution for our children when we are old, but for lessening their burdens by assuring ourselves' lives. Look at this one here...)

32. B: 哦？我们也有啊？(Oh, for us as well?)

33. A: 有啊，这一种是我们最近才推出来的，主要针对三四十岁、现在收入比较好的客户，它也是保本型的。就是讲，不管怎么搞，你到最后都能把本钱拿回来，就相当于一种储蓄。你想想看，钱存到银行，现在肯定不是一个好选择；买房子，现在不讲其他地方，就××县这个小场子，房价都已经高得不得了了；炒股吧，也是风险大得不得了——我家那个当时买了几万，到现在还没回本；我们这个险种呢，不光能保本，还能有分红，多少你可以根据你自己情况选，最低起步五万，十万、二十万、三十万，最高五十万，买得越多，相对应的收益也就越多，大概一般比如讲十年以后，十万的话一般一个月能拿到一两千块钱，一共拿十年，你想想看，这不就等于上班拿工资了嘛？最起码，生活有的了⋯⋯(Yes, of course, it's a newly launched one. It's mainly for those who are at the 30s or 40s with good income. It's safe. No matter what, you would have your deposits back, just like a kind of savings. Think about it, it's definitely not a good idea to deposit with banks. Real estate is not a good idea as well. Take our county as an example, such a small place with already sky-rocketing price. Security market, too high risks. For example, my husband once bought some and suffered great losses; even now he hasn't recovered yet. Our insurance not only saves for you, but with dividends. There are 50,000,100,000, 200,000, 300,000, tops at 500,000 (yuan); the more you buy, the more profits you would have. Generally speaking, about 10 years later, if you buy 100,000 (yuan) now, you would have one or two thousand yuan each month for consecutive 10 years. Think about it, it's like salary, you would at least be self-sufficient...)

34. B: 哦，那这个还不错呢，我也是在考虑，现在虽然讲挣点钱，不稳定啊。(Oh, that sounds good, I'm considering. Though we make some money now, it's not stable.)

35. A: 是的啊，拿我们来讲就是提前准备，那个成语啊怎么讲啊，哦——叫未雨绸缪，呵呵，反正这东西，有条件，搞下子还是好的，其他东西我不敢讲，最起码我搞的东西我有信心，其他可能也有业务员找了你吧？(Yes, exactly, we need to have some precautions. For this, if it does not pose too much burden, I think it's a good idea. I have faith in it. There might have already been some agent approached you?)

36. B: 唵，有……(Err, yeah…)

37. A: 是的啊，其实这东西我也不瞒你，你买得多我们有提成，但是我每次都跟我客户讲清楚，大家离得不远，又熟，你讲可是的啊？(That's right, I don't want to hide from you. The more you buy, the more bonus I would have. But I always make it clear with our clients. We live close to each other and are familiar with each other.)

38. B: 那是的哦，其他人是也找过我的，我当时就讲不了解，看看再讲，呵呵……(Yes, others did approach me before. I said I didn't know much about it and need to consider for a while, he he…)

39. A: 反正这一点你放心，我在这场子也这么多年了，大家都是抬头不见低头见的，那种事情我做不出来。(No matter what, please rest assured for one thing. I have been here for years, and we see each other quite often. I won't do bad things.)

40. B: 那我放心呶——要不是你来，我哪听你讲这么半天呢，你讲可是的。(Yes, of course—if it were not you, how could I listen to you for so long, right?)

41. A: 那是的哦——要不你这样子，我们公司下个星期六在××酒店搞个宣讲会，到时我们有省里请来的讲师介绍产品，现场签约的话还有礼品，还有抽奖活动，反正到时你不想买也不要紧，你要有时间的话就过去看看，我带你们一起……(That's right—how about you go to the promotion dinner next Saturday at ×× Hotel? We would have lecturers from the capital to introduce our products. If you sign on site, there will be gifts and lucky draw. You don't have to buy, but you can come over if you are free. I will take you there…)

42. B: 下个礼拜六啊？哦，我将好要到街上去，几点钟啊？(Next Saturday? I would be there, what time exactly?)

43. A: 上午九点半，这样子，我八点半到这来接你，我们一起过去，××酒店你也晓得，还是不错的啊，中午我们有招待会，公司请吃饭。(9:30 a.m., I can pick you up at 8:30, and we can go together. You know ×× Hotel, which is a luxury hotel. There will be a reception dinner.)

Chapter 5 Negotiation of Interactive Frames and Discourse Identities

44. B: 哦，那好啊。(OK, that sounds good.)

45. A: 好，那就这么讲，我先给你做个登记……(OK, that's it. Let me sign you up first…)

46. B: 唵。(OK.)

47. A: 哎也，你家里这装修搞得真好，真漂亮，上档次，花了不少钱吧？(AYA, the decoration in your house is really nice and classy. It must have cost you a lot.)

48. B: 这个啊，我们在外头，一年不回来趟把，我老婆讲自己住的场子要搞好一点，舒服些嘛。(For that, we work outside, and rarely come back. My wife says it's important to make our own living places comfortable.)

49. A: 那是的哦，自己住，搞好的，每天在里面，心情都不一样啊，呵呵……(That's true. It's important, it will make you feel good living inside, he he…)

50. B: 那也是的，所以那时候她讲要搞，我想想，搞就搞吧，反正都是自己住，我们在外面毕竟也不长久，总是要回来的，可是的啊？回来的话，毕竟怎么样也是自己一个窝啊……(Yeah. So when she said so, I agreed. It's for ourselves. We would come back eventually. It's our home after all…)

51. A: 唵，那你们想的是对的哦。(Yeah, that's right.)

This segment of an interaction between the agent and the prospective client presents a rather complete structure of the shifts between different types of talks. From this segment of a long conversation, the sequence of the three types of talk can be clearly seen, as we have summarized earlier: it initiates with friendship talk (Turn 1 to Turn 6); and then goes on with task-oriented talk (Turn 9 to Turn 10), and institutional talk (Turn 17 to Turn 24); if there is some kind of deadlock or hesitations, resumes friendship talk (Turn 26); and finally it ends with friendship talk.

In general, friendship identity is often invoked by friendship talk at the beginning of interactions, useful in maintaining the interpersonal tie and downplaying the business-oriented aspects of their activities. Agents may initiate an institutional talk by invoking the corresponding identities in order to control and justify their action. In the meantime, the client can invoke friendship talk to justify their action/inaction. Their interactions always end with a friendship talk to reinforce their friendship and rapport. Table 5.1 offers a summary of the sequence of the talk categories and their respective interactive functions in their interactions.

Table 5.1 Summary of the Sequence of Talk Categories and Their Respective Interactive Functions

Sequence	Topics	Initiators	Interactional functions
Friendship talk	Family, health, decoration, etc.	Agent or client	To create a friendly atmosphere
Task-oriented talk	Institutional topics	Agent or client	To introduce terms, conditions and other specifics
Friendship talk	Family, health, decoration, etc.	Client	To deal with business in a friendly manner
	Family, health, decoration, etc.	Client	To express disinterest or resistance
Institutional talk	Advice-giving, selling products	Agent	To resolve conflicts or resume control
Task-oriented talk	Institutional topics	Agent or client	To deal with business in a friendly manner
Friendship talk	Family, health, decoration, next meeting time	Agent or client	To end the interactions in a friendly manner

2. Interactive management of different identities in friendship talk

The following analyzes in detail the starting part of the conversation. It is mainly concerned with the interactive management of identities in friendship talk, followed with some discussions on its socio-cultural implications.

(A: agent; B: prospective client)
1. A: 今天在家休息啊？（Taking a break at home today?）
2. B: 唵，在家里玩。(Yeah, staying at home.)
3. A: 哦，刘老师原来你们喊姐夫嗨？(Oh, do you call Teacher Liu brother-in-law?)

Chapter 5 Negotiation of Interactive Frames and Discourse Identities

  4. B: 是的哦。(Yes.)

  5. A: 他原来就是我们中学老师哎。(He was our teacher when we were in middle school.)[停顿 1 秒 (Pause for a second)] 哦，两个毛毛，嗨？(Ah, you have two children, right?)

  6. B: 嗯，在家里陪读。(Yeah, so I have to stay at home with them.) [停顿 0.5 秒(Pause for half a second)] 你是保险公司的嗨？(Are you working in the insurance company?)

  One of the distinctive features of this conversation is the interactive management of different identities of both parties to their respective advantages. To be more specific, from Turn 1 to Turn 6 demonstrated above, the agent greeted the prospective client with "今天在家休息啊？"（"Taking a break at home today?"）, which clearly indicates the intimate relationship between the agent and the prospective client, since normally when Chinese people greet each other with "吃过了吗？"("Have you had your meal?"), "到哪儿去啊？"("Where are you going?"), which may be considered as personal or private topics. It serves as ice-breaking function. As is known, it is quite natural and normal for friends to greet each other. However, when it comes to insurance sales, there is financial interest at stake, and thus it must be treated with extreme caution. As one of the informants confesses, "开始的时候尚好重要，其实现在很多人都对保险有看法，他们觉得卖保险就是骗人。我们只能尽量让他们相信我们自己，然后再慢慢来。只要相信了我们，一般来讲就没什么太大问题了。怎么才能要他们相信我们呢？平时自己怎么做肯定很重要，另外一个就是开始尽量跟他们刮，慢慢刮，慢慢扯到理财啊、保险啊这些东西。"("It's very important to have a good start. Now that many people don't like insurance, they think it's about cheating. What we can do is to make them have faith in ourselves, and take it slowly. Once they have faith in us, it will be easy. How can we make them have faith in us? One thing is about how we do things in our life. The other is to talk to them, slowly, topics moving to wealth management, insurance, etc.") Due to the overuse and over-exploitation of the agents' personal credibility, many local people have negative opinion about insurance sales staff. such constraints even interfere with the agents' families or relatives. For example, one father of one of the insurance sales agents mentioned, "有时候真是觉得不好见人，这东西搞得好都好，搞得不好人家真骂哎！人家当面不一定讲，背后真是戳脊梁骨……" ("Sometimes it is really hard. If we do it right, it's OK. What if things go wrong, people won't curse you in your face, but they do afterwards…") (Personal communication, March 8, 2013) This segment of confession demonstrates the dilemma that most of the agents face—On the one hand, they need to shoulder enormous performance pressure from the insurance company. Moreover, the lure of the financial rewards stimulate them to further exploit their *Guanxi* network. On the other hand, they need to face the moral dilemma. After all, not only they themselves but also their close family members and relatives live in the local area, they are obliged to get along with other people. As one agent put it, "看我不做保险会不会饿死！" ("See if I would starve without doing insurance!")(Personal communication, July 9, 2013). Similar frustrations and desperation are quite prevalent among the agents. Therefore, they need to work very carefully in managing their identities in talking with their prospective clients. We may argue that it's actually a matter of degree, which depends on whether it is out of the free will of the clients to make the purchase, or whether the agent purposefully conceals the potential problems of the policy in discussion and purposefully manipulates their familiarity with the clients and the clients' trust into the agents. Nonetheless, we do not intend to impose any moral judgment on them. Our primary objective is to study the dynamic and interactive management of identities in the process of insurance sales.

Then in Turn 3 and Turn 5, the agent activated the friendship frame with "刘老师原来你们喊姐夫嗨"("do you call Teacher Liu brother-in-law"). Teacher Liu is a third party that both the agent and the client are familiar with, who acts as the bridge to a closer and more intimate interaction. As we have argued earlier, the Chinese society is a society of the familiar ones, a "differentiated mode of association" (Fei, 2007；Zhai, 2007b; Huang and Hu, 2004). Even though the agent and the client have been familiar already, nonetheless, if there is a

Chapter 5 Negotiation of Interactive Frames and Discourse Identities

trustworthy third party there, the interaction would be even more smooth and intimate partly due to the fact that school teachers are considered as a well-respected and prestigious group of people. In order to further strengthen the credibility of the agent, in Turn 7, the agent drew another one, a locally well-known doctor into the discussion, "刘店的×××……我是她姐姐。" ("Do you know ××× at Liudian?... I'm her elder sister"). By saying so, the agent was establishing a credible image, that is, "I'm not only your friend, but also many renowned people can vouch for me. You can rest assured about my credibility." The successful establishment of the image would be greatly conducive to the successful conclusion of business. The sales, for most of the time, are relying on such images to a certain extent. For most clients, the trust or confidence in the person is even more important than the product in sales, as one of my informants stated, "如果不是她在做，我也不会买，我觉得都是乡里乡亲的，大家又那么熟，那不会（骗我）的。"("If it were not for her, I definitely won't buy it. I think we are home fellows, so familiar with each other. She won't lie to me on this"). This statement expressly transmits the idea. The person who is selling the product is much more important than the product itself. It may be argued whether this virtually blind trust would do damage to the relationship among people in transformational China's rural areas. If some agents exploit such resources to the sole pursuit of profits only to their own advantage, there are such risks; but nevertheless, there are certain mechanisms which will work to avoid such things from happening. In China, especially rural China, a person is not considered as an individual, he/she is considered as a part of a group, for example, a family, a team or an integral part of something bigger. If the agent is doing something only for his/her own profit, then the reputation or fame of the whole group could be sabotaged, and finally the group may respond to such misbehaviors. Therefore, it seems there is a kind of underlying governing principles or hidden moral standards functioning to ensure the order of interactions among people in the local context.

1) Negotiation of identity in institutional talk

The following analysis probes into the negotiation of identity in institutional talk, where the agent presented a professional image, while the prospective client showed rather as a recipient.

17. A: 如果你给毛毛买的话，如果参加分红，分红有本金累计生息。具体情况我给你介绍下子，假如讲我们买十万的那种，分十年交，一年就是交一万，假如讲我们第一年交了一万，这就是你的本金，本金放那要生息，我们按照去年的情况，5.6%来算，一年就是560；第二年开始我们本金就是10 560了，这时候再加上你第二年交的保费一万，那就是20 560；然后第三年、第四年，以此类推，就是讲利生息、滚动的，到最后呢，等你交满十年了，你可以选择一次性拿回来，也可以分几次拿回来；假如讲你觉得利润还好，你也可以继续放那，就像是理财样的，也中；还有比如讲你每年想把那个分红拿出来，也中，那你就是本金放那，分红自己拿回来用，也一样……(If you buy for your child, and take part in dividend, it has cumulative interest. Let me give you some specific information. Suppose we buy 100,000 (yuan) for ten years, that's 10,000 (yuan) for each year. And further suppose we pay 10,000 (yuan) for the first year, that's your deposit, which generates interest rate, with the rate of last year, it's 5.6%, and that's 560 (yuan). That will make the deposit for the second year as 10,560 (yuan), and plus your deposit of the second year, that's 20,560(yuan) in total. Then the third year, forth year, etc. Simply put, it's about cumulative interest. After you have been paying for ten years, you can take it all back altogether or in several different times; if you think the returns are satisfactory, you can also choose to put it there, just like wealth management. And if you want to withdraw the dividend each year, it's also OK. That is to say, you put the deposit there, and withdraw the dividend for your own use. It's just the same and it's totally up to you…)

18. B: 那假如讲我中间想要用钱，那怎么搞啊？(What if I need this amount of money during this period?)

19. A: 用钱的话呢，你最好是不动本金，本金一动，那就相当于违约，违约的话那你就划不来了。这个东西我们要实话实说，因为我们有合同，哎，这个场子，你看看（指出条款给客户看），那你就非常划不来了。(If you really need to use this money, you'd better not use

Chapter 5 Negotiation of Interactive Frames and Discourse Identities

the deposit money; once you use that, that's breach of contract, and you would suffer. I need to be frank with you. [Show the clauses to the client.] Here is the contract, here…)

20. B: 哦，那就是讲，我买了以后就不能动了……(Oh, that is to say, I can't use that money…)

21. A: 也不是那么讲，一般买保险我们不都是闲钱嘛；暂时没有其他比较好的地方投资啊或者怎样；再讲你家里这个情况，也不至于啊，这个也不多，呵呵，你讲可是的啊？(Not exactly, normally we buy insurance with our spare money or without any other better places to make investment or others; and also for you, you don't have to according to your condition. It's not too much. Don't you think so?)

22. B: 哎呀，那个东西难讲哦……(Well, it's hard to say…)

23. A: 我觉得呢，我们这么想，现在我们还比较年轻，挣钱能力比较强，年富力强的时候，这个时候买点保险，给我们小家伙有个保障，就像是存款样的，等他们长大了，最起码还有那么一笔钱在那儿。我们到时候万一讲的话，年纪大了，做不动了，他们能用这一笔钱还能做一点事情。再讲，现在钱存银行你也晓得，每年通货膨胀那么厉害，钱是越来越不值钱；我们这个就是讲一方面你是存那有利息，另外一方面公司还把这个钱拿去投资——××公司你也晓得，世界500强，中国最大的保险公司，它把这个钱收起来不是讲就放那或者放银行，它是要拿去投资的哎，比如讲现在什么西部大开发啊、风力发电啊、三峡工程哪，许多项目……(For me, I think right now we are still young, and we can make a lot of money. If we buy some insurance, and offer some guarantee for our children just like deposits, when they grow up, they would have this amount of money. In case we get old and weak, this money can be of some use. Moreover, if you deposit with the bank, with the current depreciation, the value would be lower and lower. What we have here is not only you can have interest rate, but also dividends; the company will make investment elsewhere—You know our company is one of the world top 500, China's largest insurance company. It doesn't leave your money just there or deposit it in the bank; it is to invest in, for example, the development of the West, wind power, project of the Three Gorges…)

……

33. A: 有啊，这一种是我们最近才推出来的，主要针对三四十岁、现在收入比较好的客户，它也是保本型的。就是讲，不管怎么搞，你到最后都能把本钱拿回来，就相当于一种储蓄。你想想看，钱存到银行，现在肯定不是一个好选择；买房子，现在不讲其他地方，就××县这个小场子，房价都已经高得不得了了；炒股吧，也是风险大得不得了——我家那个当时买了几万，到现在还没回本；我们这个险种呢，不光能保本，还能有分红，多少你可以根据你自己情况选，最低起步五万、十万、二十万、三十万，最高五十万，买得越多，相对应的收益也就越多，大概一般比如讲十年以后，十万的话一般一个月能拿到一两千块钱，一共拿十年，你想想看，这不就等于上班拿工资了嘛？最起码，生活有的了……(Yes, of course, it's a newly launched one. It's mainly for those who are at the 30s or 40s with good income. It's safe. No matter what, you would have your deposits back, just like a kind of savings. Think about it, it's definitely not a good idea to deposit with banks. Real estate is not a good idea as well. Take our county as an example, such a small place with already sky-rocketing price. Security market, too high risks. For example, my husband once bought some and suffered great losses; even now he hasn't recovered yet. Our insurance not only saves for you, but with dividends. There are 50,000, 100,000, 200,000, 300,000, tops at 500,000 (yuan); the more you buy, the more profits you would have. Generally speaking, about 10 years later, if you buy 100,000 (yuan) now, you would have one or two thousand yuan each month for consecutive 10 years. Think about it, it's like salary, you would at least be self-sufficient...)

As analyzed and argued in the last part, one of the salient features of institutional talk in insurance sales interactions in transformational China's rural areas is marked with the unequal contribution/length to the conversation. For example, from Turn 17 to Turn 23 and Turn 33 (listed above) are typical examples of such a feature. The agent explained the characteristics of the insurance in discussion, highlighted the advantages of such insurance of itself and compared with other means of investment. Such turns have important implication to the sales. On the one hand, it enables the agent to have control over the conversation as what to talk about and where this conversation went. On the other hand, through the introduction in detail, the agent established an image of being professional, knowledgeable and more importantly, as a friend, caring for the interests of the prospective client, which also has some implication to the prospective client. The message implied here is: The agent is my good friend; she is professional, she is caring for my interest, and more importantly, she is trustworthy. This kind of institutional talk bears great significance in the successful conclusion of business. Nonetheless, institutional talk needs to be carefully managed. Otherwise, it may evoke resistance from the part of the client. As one of my informant agents introduced her first successful conclusion of a substantial policy worth 4.5 million yuan, "在朋友家的一次聚会上，邻座的夫妻俩戴的手表引起了我的注意，感觉价值不菲，我便与他妻子聊了几句，还蛮投缘，就彼此留了电话，成了朋友。再后来就是关注她关注的，比如企业资讯、企业网站；通过微信啊、手机短信啊这些慢慢进行理念的渗透。比如讲了解她的需求之后，通过服务增进友谊，告诉她保险是一种财富传承，是身份的象征，像他们这样的，资产也需要合理的配置，是一种理财；同时，尽可能提供高品质的服务。"("At a friend's party, the watches that the neighboring couples wear aroused my attention. They are luxury brands, then I talked to the wife and we had a nice talk, so we exchanged our phone numbers and became friends gradually. After that I followed what she followed, like enterprise news, and corporate websites. I also tried to introduce such ideas as insurance through Wechat or text messages. After increasing friendship through services, I told her insurance is a kind of wealth inheritance. It's a kind of personal identity. They need to manage their wealth. Meanwhile, I offer high-quality services.") This short segment of confession reveals that agents do make careful analysis and preparation for institutional talk—identify prospective clients' needs and relate the needs to the products they are selling. In actual conversation, such topics can be arranged in the form of institutional talk and thus the agents assume the identity of professional service providers. Since it's obvious in normal conversations between counterparts, both parties are supposed to contribute roughly equally to the topic in discussion, instead of one party dominating, which gives rise to another important type of talk—task-oriented talk.

2) Negotiation of identity in task-oriented talk

For task-oriented talk, Turn 25 "我给我家他和儿子还有我自己都买了啊，我家条件没你这么好，买不了太多，就这样子，我都买了不少呢……" ("I have bought it for my husband, my son and myself. Our financial situation is not as good as yours, and we can't afford too much. Even so, I still bought some…") and Turn 41 "那是的哦——要不你这样子，我们公司下个星期六在××酒店搞个宣讲会，到时我们有省里请来的讲师介绍产品，现场签约的话还有礼品，还有抽奖活动，反正到时你不想买也不要紧，你要有时间的话就过去看看，我带你们一起……" ("That's right — how about you go to the promotion dinner next Saturday at ×× Hotel? We would have lecturers from the capital to introduce our products. If you sign on site, there will be gifts and lucky draw. You don't have to buy, but you can come over if you are free. I will take you there…") offer good examples. In Turn 25, after several segments of long introduction in Turns 17, 19, 21 and 23, and after the prospective client had already got some idea about the insurance in discussion, the prospective client attempted to strengthen his confidence in the policy by asking a question in Turn 24, "你可买了啊？" ("Did you buy it？"), given the simplicity of the question, the implication here could be significant—even though the agent and client are friends and they are familiar with each other; however, when it comes to money, both need to be more careful: The prospective client needs to make sure the insurance is safe and to his advantage. If the agent herself has also bought the insurance, then it should be no problem at all; otherwise, the prospective client may reconsider more carefully. The agent needs to be careful about not pushing too hard, since it might scare away the prospective client. As I argue earlier in Chapter 2, the Chinese society is, to a certain extent, a *Guanxi* society, or more broadly, a society typified with Confucianism discourse system, in which particularistic trust plays a more important role in interpersonal relationship (Zhao, 2013; Huang, 2004; Zhai,

2011). Confucianism influences are deeply rooted in the Chinese people, which also has been argued to be one of the reasons that there is high level of particularistic trust and a lower level of generalized trust. Specifically in the above example, whether the agent herself had bought the insurance is important, which has become one of the focal factors that determined the prospective client's decision in making the purchase.

In Turn 41, after the prospective client had made clear his confidence in the agent, the agent made a further attempt to invite the prospective client to attend a seminar in a fancy local hotel. It is also presented in the best interest of the prospective client, "现场签约的话还有礼品，还有抽奖活动"("If you sign on site, there will be gifts and lucky draw."), and the agent also left room for the prospective client, "反正到时你不想买也不要紧"("You don't have to buy"), which saves the prospective client's negative face, not to impose. Such flexibility also contributes to the successful conclusion of business.

From the above analysis, it can be seen that the conversation is constitutive of different types of talks, which indicates the shifts and mediation of different frames. The conversations mostly start with friendship talk, followed by institutional talk or task-oriented talk, and end with friendship talk. To be more specific, if there is some deadlock or difficulties in institutional talk or task-oriented talk, the agents would shift back to friendship talk consciously or unconsciously to maintain the harmony and rapport between the agents and the clients. Meanwhile the clients also manage to shift between different types of talk to their own advantage due to lack of interest while maintaining the harmonious atmosphere in the interaction. Therefore shifts and mediation of different frames unveil the dynamics of the interactions between the agents and the clients, and they also offer an illustration to friendship (Kong, 2003; Zhai, 2011; Huang and Hu, 2004), business and insurance sales discourses. Insurance sales discourse is a platform for the mediation and contestation of business and friendship discourses.

By analyzing this segment of conversation between the agents and the prospective clients, this part examines in detail how identities in insurance sales are interactionally maintained, contested, and managed through changing interactive frames and discourse identities. As I argued all through that identities are not something preordained, rather than being imposed by one of the parties concerned, and they are maintained, ratified, contested, and interactionally managed. Moreover, since power is an inherent feature of all interactions, it can be revealed that in insurance sales, power is never a stable element, but rather is subject to negotiation, especially in the increasingly common situations in which power structure is not well-defined—such as insurance sales interactions. The identities can be complex and overlapping.

3. Footing in different types of talk

From Turn 1 to Turn 9, both participants exhibit a different footing, that is, the friendship footing, as shown by a topic change. The topic they turned to is an informal one about the agent's job, "我是××人寿公司的"("I'm working in the ×× Life Insurance Company."). The change of footing is also accompanied by a change in prosodic features. Both of them were rather casual and tended to speak more slowly and use more emotional markers. The average rate of characters per second for the agent in this casual talk is about 5 characters, while in the institutional talk that follows in Turn 17, the rate is about 7 or 8 characters per second. This feature of friendship talk is the opposite of what Tannen (2001) found in her study of interactions among middle-class American acquaintances. Is it due to cultural differences in friendship? Or is it just not representative of the real interactions between friends in the Chinese context? It could be that the rate of speech alone is not a defining feature of friendship talk, but the contrast with the previous talk. Due to the fact that if both of them already spoke very fast in the friendship talk, it would be virtually impossible to speak even faster in the following institutional talk and task-oriented talk. Thus what they can do is to speak more slowly to distinguish between their friendship talk and other types of talk.

Chapter 5 Negotiation of Interactive Frames and Discourse Identities

In the above interaction, the agent tends to be rather indirect in her efforts to make the sales, mostly in institutional talk and task-oriented talk, in contrast to the regulating and controlling that an employer and employees in ordinary work settings do (Gabrenya and Hwang, 1996; Kong, 1998b). Even though the agent's husband is the director of the village, and her father and brother are both locally well respected doctors, she does not possess the legitimacy in regulating and controlling the prospective client. Rather she initiated the actual sales efforts by starting very indirectly with the introduction of a third party that both participants were familiar with. In Turn 9, "我昨天听刘老师讲搞保险,(他)跟你们怎么讲的啊？" ("I heard that Teacher Liu had talked about insurance to you yesterday. How did he tell you about it?") She also asked and answered several questions pertaining to the issue of insurance in discussion. "你们办的是什么保险呢？" ("What kind of insurance do you have?"), "……我们给你介绍的额保险，是积少成多……" ("…What we are introducing here is more about deposits…") This more resembles advice given by a friend than a command given by a superior to a subordinate. In order to make her sales more convincing, she made a more detailed introduction to the features of the insurance in discussion in Turn 17, the bonus type insurance. In order to reduce the imposition, she carefully formulated the introduction into examples and figures, which would be much more tangible and easily understandable to the prospective client.

Despite the careful formulation of the sales by the agent, the prospective client still saw it as a face-threatening move. Naturally resistance and hesitation are possible, and after long segments of institutional talk and task-oriented talk, Turn 26, "你家××现在还在村里搞吧？" ("Your husband ×× is still working at the village?") marks a clear signal of the prospective client's resistance and reluctance. By a rather abrupt change of topic, a change in footing from "business" to "friends" is made. The prospective client's discourse identity has also been shifted to the related discourse identities a friend can assume in an interpersonal interaction. By changing to the friendship identity, the prospective client's construct of self—the principal—cannot be challenged, in the sense that her own personal experience and relations should be respected by his friend. This strategic shift of footing was cooperatively echoed by the agent, who co-constructed cooperatively the friendship talk with the prospective client in the next two turns (Turn 27 and Turn 29). Until Turn 31, after responding to the second casual question of the agent's son, "唵，在广州，那个不成器的东西……"("Yeah, in Guangzhou, that naughty boy...") there is a short pause for 2 seconds. This pause is a contextualization cue (Gumperz, 2001) to indicate the agent's effort to resume to the previous topic of insurance, and continue to convince the prospective client in purchasing another type of insurance designed for himself instead of his children.

As already shown in the above segment, friendship talk is as "goal-oriented" as other types of talk. Both participants see the identity in question as a strategy to achieve their respective goals. Nevertheless, the nature of the goals in this talk category is different. While the goals of task-oriented and institutional talks are to get something done, the goal of friendship talk resembles to that of ordinary conversations among friends in terms of reciprocity and topic contribution. Friendship talk here can serve as an important lubricant to get things done as well, just as the claim that no interaction is power-free.

In task-oriented talk, there is a mismatch of different discourse systems and frames, as illustrated in Figure 5.1.

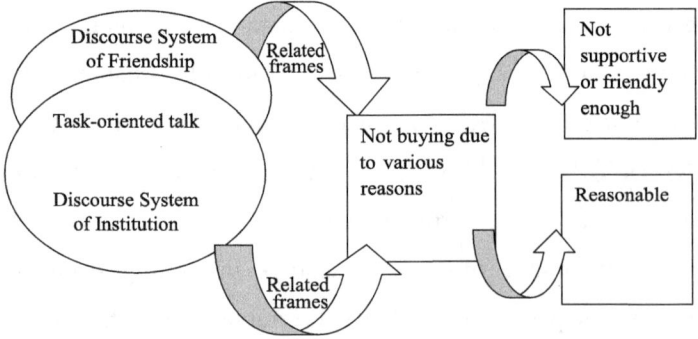

Figure 5.1 Mismatch of Discourse System and Frames in Task-oriented Talk

The indecision of the prospective client is not expressly stated, rather it is

Chapter 5 Negotiation of Interactive Frames and Discourse Identities

indicated and inferred in the hesitation, unwillingness to continue the current topic or, long pauses, or sometimes even abrupt interruptions to change the topic. As in the discourse system of friendship, it is expected that the client should be supportive and cooperative, as what friends will do at most times. Nevertheless, if it is interpreted in the discourse system of institution, then business is business, and friends are friends; they are two completely different things. In the meantime, the confrontation and conflict between different discourse systems have become a site of struggle for the mediation of different frames and identity negotiation, in which the participants manipulate the frame to the advantage of the identities they are constructing. Therefore, it can be argued that the inter-discursivity of discourse systems can be strategically employed not only by business enterprise and their representatives (agents), but also by their (prospective) clients, who can play an active role in resisting agents' profit-making interests. According to the interviews with one of the agents, among about 100 of her clients, around 90 are working away from their hometown and earn their living in different large cities. About 10 are employed with the local factories or other service sectors, only several of them are working as peasants who earn their living by farming. This occupational distribution is similar to clients of other agents (personal communication with the agents). Another feature of the relationship between the agents and their (prospective) clients is that they know each other, sometimes very well. They are either relatives, friends or home fellows, or at least they are referred to by a third party with whom both of them are familiar. As one of my respondents said in the interview on June 6, 2010, "从2002年开始做保险，当时是表妹（大姑的女儿）她在做保险，然后刚好戴汇这里准备做网点，她就介绍我做。后来她就走了，然后我就接下来在这里开始做了。刚开始做的时候基本就在这一条街，都是隔壁啊、邻居啊的。当时我还带着小孩，只做这一条街道，熟悉嘛。" ("I started doing insurance in 2002. At that time, my cousin (my aunt's daughter) was doing it. It happened that they were planning to set up a network here at Daihui. She then introduced me. After some time, she left, and then I continued to do it. In the beginning, it's just about this street. They (the clients) are all my neighbors. I was raising a child, but I only focused on this street, because we were familiar.")

Such a view is echoed by the second respondent (an existing client) in the interview on August 20, 2010:

Respondent: "我签第一笔单子的时候是 2002 年了。那时候小杨（保险销售员）家里困难得很，又有老又有小的，负担重；那时候他还才刚刚做，开始做得不好，后来就找到我，我也就签了一个小单子。哎嘿，签了那个单子后他做得就好了，我旁边一群人都签了。" ("My first sales was in 2002. At that time, Yang, the agent, had a difficult time, and heavy burden with the old and the young to care for. He just started selling and was not doing well. He then came to me, but I just bought a policy of limited value. Well, just after that, he began to do well, and a large group of people around me all bought insurance.")

Interviewer: "那也就是人情单了？" ("Then it's a compliment policy?")

Respondent: "是的啊，是人情单啊。后来也觉得那个东西还不错，就又给毛毛买了。只要家庭条件允许，搞搞还是不错的。" ("Yes, it is. But later, it turned out that it was good, so I bought some for my child. As long as it's affordable, it's good to buy.")

To expand the findings in this study further, it can be argued that modern China is undergoing profound changes in its relationship orientations, from more collectivistic to more individualistic, as seen in the mixing and crossing of in-group and out-group domains. Nonetheless, more cross-cultural studies seem necessary—between China's and foreign countries' rural cultures, and even between China's rural and urban cultures—in order to confirm the findings.

To sum up, this part has illustrated the complex nature of identities. Both interactional sociolinguistics and conversation analysis have been employed to examine how participants construct identities for accomplishing interactional goals. The notions of footing, interactive frames, contextualization cues and discourse identities in interactional sociolinguistics are useful in examining how participants mobilize the interactional devices available to them for invoking the identities favorable to them. Meanwhile, the conversational analysis of turn-taking and interruption patterns show how identities can be co-constructed and contested. Both interactional sociolinguistics and conversation analysis bear the assumption that language can shape and be shaped by the context. Conversation analysis is more focusing on studying participants' sense-making practices through sequential devices, without paying more attention to the interactional devices within utterances, while interactional sociolinguistics focuses more on the interactional properties of verbal and non-verbal signals. The above analysis attempts to integrate the two in an effort to make the analysis more thorough and complete.

5.3 Summary

In general, the present chapter probes into the dynamics of agent-client interactions through interactive devices such as changes in footing, frames, and discourse identities. Friendship identity is often invoked by friendship talk at the beginning of interactions, useful in maintaining the interpersonal tie and downplaying the business-oriented aspects of their activities. Agents may initiate an institutional talk by invoking the corresponding identities in order to control and justify their action. In the meantime, the client can invoke friendship talk to justify their action/inaction. Their interactions always end with a friendship talk to reinforce their friendship and rapport.

Moreover, both parties are striving to employ different identities in fulfilling their different interactional objectives. Such strategic shifts between different frames, and the struggle in the co-construction of different identities reveal the intricacies of Chinese *Guanxi*, and show that identities are dynamic entities subject to negotiation. They are discursively and cooperatively produced and managed. These dynamics are captured in the activation of conversational dynamics, such as changes in footings and interactive frames, signaled by conversational cues. At the micro-level, friendship identity reinforces the rapport between the agents and the clients, and serves as significant lubricant in alleviating potential tension and conflict between them. Corporate identity is mainly employed by the agent to activate the institutional frame for controlling turns and initiating topics for persuasion, and initiates the personification of a corporate. While in task-oriented talk different identities are at constant mediation, they provide effective means for the agent in controlling and socializing the client. The strategic shift between different frames represented by different types of talks and different discourse identities reveals the constant mediation and contestation between the insurance sales agents and the prospective clients.

The negotiation and shifts in identities between the agents and clients reveal the dramatic changes in rural areas. Ever since the initiation of reform and opening-up policy, the rural community has undergone tremendous changes. Different social strata differentiate and new classes emerge. Such tremendous changes consequently lead to tremendous changes in the communication patterns among participants. It has been generally acknowledged that such differentiations in rural strata are not the result of social enclosure mechanisms which restrict social mobility, but due to increased social mobility induced by market and institutional reform, and thus consequently the transformation from relative equalization in the planned economy to strata differentiation (Yang, 2014). The social background of our informants and the researcher's immersion and observation in the local area can prove such differentiation is present. And the interactional patterns of insurance sales agent-client interactions can reflect such tremendous transformations in contemporary China's rural areas.

More specifically, this chapter illuminates the dynamics of insurance sales in transformational China's rural areas. Insurance sales agents in China's rural areas exploit the intersection between friendship and business. Nevertheless, as agents can employ friendship talk to create meanings, clients can evade and justify their action/inaction. In short, both the agents and the clients can use friendship talk for their respective interactional advantages. Moreover, identities can be the products of mobilization by human agents, rather than preordained entities, and can be invoked linguistically for interactional purposes.

Through linguistic resources, insurance sales agents are able to strike a balance between the pragmatic business purpose and the personal emotion style, and they try to convince not only their prospective clients but themselves that insurance sales through *Guanxi* is a socially acceptable and legitimate activity. Beliefs and emotions are commercialized and even manipulated to serve the purpose of successful conclusion of policy sales, supporting the sociological argument of insurance sales as "the business of belief" (Biggart, 1989). After all, from the above analysis, it can be seen that insurance sales agents are eager and deliberate in trying to employ linguistic resources to give meanings and construct appropriate identities for themselves, which indicates that insurance sales as a social activity is still built upon a weak foundation and yet to be widely accepted, let alone applauded.

Due to the fact that an important task of post-modern enterprise is to reconcile the business goals of the company and the personal needs of their individual employees, there are corresponding changes in discourse as well. It has been recognized that traditional bureaucratic control measures are no longer appropriate and effective in satisfying the nowadays employees' needs of searching for meaning. Such changes have been characterized by the shift from the rational bureaucratic control discourse to "entrepreneur of self" discourse (Du Gay, 1996), in which employees are encouraged to be autonomous and self-regulating individuals. Such an identity is argued to be constructive to both entrepreneurs and employees themselves. Nonetheless, changes in discourse do not necessarily mean a total disappearance of power but only changes in power structure (Foucault, 1977). As argued by Wodak (1995) that there is basically no power-free discourse. In the context of China's rural insurance, the insurance companies still enjoy the power advantage since they are in a more advantageous position to ascribe meanings to, and define identities for, their institutional benefits. Given the fact that insurance sales agents are encouraged to be the "entrepreneur of self", they do so more for the benefit of the institution than for themselves, as they are not equipped with enough means to do so. They at most accept and identify themselves to the meanings, and practice them and transmit such meanings in their interactions with others. In the Chinese rural insurance context, agents work for their companies, but with a different label. By exploiting and commercializing peoples' beliefs and trust through linguistic resources, insurance companies are attempting to construct an identity for themselves as organizations that are doing "social good" for the society and the agents are offering a new form of self for themselves as well. However, with the inherent problems in the insurance sales system, such as lack of an effective selection system and sufficient training, insurance sales may produce even more disappointment, helplessness, frustration and fragmentation of individual identities.

Chapter 6

Epilogue and Discussions

6.1 Summary of Discursive Features, Frame Mediation and Discourse Identity

The study is implemented for the intention of exploring the dynamics of interactions between the insurance sales agents and the prospective clients in transformational China's rural areas. It reveals some interesting findings in the following aspects: First, it demonstrates how such insurance sales communications are structured. More specifically it shows how such discursive features as communicative purpose, moves and steps, topic management, and discourse identities are applied to demonstrate the interactants' relational negotiations, interactional motives, perceptions of the world, negotiation goals and interpersonal values in transformational China's rural areas. These findings have provided significant insights into the understanding of relational discourse, manifested by insurance sales negotiations from the linguistic perspective. In other words, by applying a society-based and a language-based discourse approach to insurance sales agent-client interactions in transformational China's rural areas, the study has explored how *Guanxi* and socialization influence the communication structure with a focus on the interaction patterns from the perspectives of genre analysis, topic management and discourse identity.

From the above analysis and study, at the micro-level, we can conclude that the present study offers empirical evidence, that is, linguistic representation that the agents deliberately utilize or even sometimes manipulate by mobilizing their social identities to achieve their economic goals in sales. Meanwhile, the clients are also employing their identities to their own advantages as well. From the analysis, identity is not a static entity, but rather subject to negotiation and to the interactants' respective interactional purposes. Moreover, during the interactions, two distinct discourse systems are at constant mediation and interplay. Through footing change (alignment) or persuasion, sales can be successfully concluded in the insurance sales interactions.

At the macro-level, the rapid commercialization of the economy that marked the period had profound and far-reaching social implications, perhaps the most significant of which were the increased opportunities for social mobility and the consequent emergence of a new and prosperous merchant class.

6.2 Discussions

After the analysis and relative findings, this part offers some discussions on the theoretical framework, analytical framework, analytical concepts and methodology, and then it goes on discussing the socio-cultural implications.

6.2.1 Theoretical Framework, Analytical Framework, Analytical Concepts and Methodology

R. Scollon and S. W. Scollon's overarching framework discourse system has been widely and handily applied beyond intercultural contexts to various sites where communication is the core of social actions and practices and is adopted as the general framework for this study, since the study is an attempt to integrate the macro and the micro.

As argued earlier, insurance sales discourse offers exciting arena for analysis since it is a place where different identities are at constant interplay and even conflict. It is even safe to say that it is the agent's social identities (no matter what specific social identities they have or display, in all they are locally trusted and respected) that greatly contribute to the successful conclusion of the sales. Meanwhile, the Chinese people attach great importance to face (*Mianzi*), which is an individual's public or social image gained by performing one or more specific social roles that are well organized by others. Though highly abstract, the concept of face is treated by the Chinese people as something that can be defined quantitatively. Generally how much face an individual has depends partly on his or her *Guanxi* network. The larger one's *Guanxi* network is, and the more powerful the people connected within it are, the more dignity one has. One needs to have a certain amount of dignity in order to cultivate new *Guanxi*. *Mianzi* also provides the leverage one needs to successfully expand and manipulate a *Guanxi* network. Enjoying the prestige of not losing face and saving other people's face are key components in the dynamics of *Guanxi*. *Mianzi* is therefore an intangible form of social currency and personal status, often determined by social position and material wealth.

While Chinese people weave networks of *Guanxi*, they also weave webs of *Renqing* obligations that must be repaid in the near future (Hwang, 1987). In essence, *Renqing* provides the moral foundation for the reciprocity and equity that are implicit in all *Guanxi*. *Guanxi* is embedded in *Renqing* formulation as an endless flow of interpersonal exchanges and reciprocal commitments. The discourse of *Renqing* articulates the moral and decorous character of social conduct. It implies the necessity for reciprocity, obligation, and indebtedness in human relations. What activates reciprocal relations and imbues these relationships with a sense of obligation and indebtedness is relational sentiments and ethics.

One of my informants (client of an insurance sales agent) once commented, "如果当时不是她在做保险的话，我肯定不会买的" ("If it is not she who was selling insurance, I definitely will not buy it"). The above statement has rich connotation. "If it is not she" clearly articulates that the client carefully observed certain unspoken underlying logic in their interaction, that is, due to the agent's personal relationship with him, the agent's social status, credibility and other social capital that he/she possessed. For this client, it seems there are certain necessity for him/her to observe and perform reciprocity, obligation and indebtedness.

After a further question of the reasons why he bought the insurance policy, he said, "我觉得我相信她——她可信得很，我们是亲戚，又住在一个村子里，她肯定不会害我的呀。我一点不懂保险，就是现在过了这么久，我还搞不清楚我买的是什么保险。就是相信她呗。" ("I think I just trust her. She is rather believable. We are relatives and live in the same village. I don't think she will do anything bad to me or against my interest. I don't know anything about insurance, and even now after several years I am still not clear about what policy I have purchased, let alone the terms and conditions. I just trust her.")

From the above short segments of interview, it is clearly seen the vital role of trust and familiarity play between the agent and the client. In the local area, without trust, virtually no business can be done. What also worth our attention is that in the local area, the relationship between the local residents is quite close and resembles the features of a traditional rural community (Family members live close to each other for generations, maintain close and frequent contacts, and relatives and friends support each other.). Thus it gives rise to another concept, credibility (可信, *Kexin* in Chinese pinyin).

Kexin refers to the degree of a party's trustworthiness. A high level of *Kexin* boosts *Guanxi* and its sustainability over the long run. A *Guanxi* with someone who has little *Kexin* is unreliable, unpredictable, and unstable. In order to develop long-standing, solid *Guanxi*, one has to assess the party's *Kexin*. This can be identified from his or her social reputation, educational background, previous examples of trustworthiness or opportunism, and solidity of *Guanxi* with other people. *Kexin* does not depend on how many *Guanxi* he or she has established (quantity), but rather how good the relationships are (quality). A party's *Kexin* can be gauged from whether he or she always keeps promises and whether he or she does his or her best to help *Guanxi* partners when they badly need help. People normally give high credit to those who are more concerned about their *Guanxi* partners than themselves when their partners need help. A person willing to make sacrifice on the behalf of others, repay debts no matter what difficulties he or she faces, or return favors no matter what the personal cost, possesses utmost *Kexin*. In the above cases, the agent possesses a very high degree of *Kexin*, which gives rise to the client's almost blind trust of decision making in purchasing the insurance.

Another important aspect of the trust is based on household registration system established in 1958, under which geographical migration is restricted. The system stipulates that every single urban or rural household had to register all its members with a local public security station. Registration at birth gives citizens the right to live in a particular village or district of a city. No household member can move to another city or province without filing for a change in household registration, which is a long, arduous and usually unsuccessful bureaucratic procedure. Although China is now experimenting with less strict registration rules, the local residents are still bound by the close connections linked by blood, clan, friendship and other ties. For example, Beijing, Shanghai, Guangzhou and some other major cities have already opened the gate for DIY tourists to visit Hong Kong, Macau, Taiwan and other regions of China. However, Nanling county of Wuhu city has not approved such arrangement yet. If they want to visit the above mentioned areas, they have to go on packaged tours.

The Chinese society is a society of the familiar ones, a "differentiated mode of association" (Fei, 2007; Zhai, 2007b; Huang and Hu, 2004). It has been generally agreed that Chinese people tend to categorize different people into different groups characterized by so called "insider" versus "outsider". It is argued that the Chinese culture built its foundation on the basis of agriculture as its economic foundation. While this kind of self-sufficient lifestyle restricts mobility and constrains that people are "attached to earth" and "dependent on land", which consequently also accounts for some moral qualities of the Chinese people, particularly, the virtue of patience and great importance attached to reputation.

Nevertheless, industrial world attempts to shorten the period of time needed for production, it requires everything to speed up. In China's rapid process of transforming itself from an agricultural society into an industrial society, diverse and various concepts and ideologies interact and collide with each other. As we have argued, with the old system demolished and the new one yet to be established, there is a growing confusion and not knowing what course to take. It is represented in the malpractices of some insurance agents' ways of promotion of policies. For example, they solely emphasize the advantages, purposefully ignore the problems or even some hidden clauses not in favor of the clients, or consume on their credibility and integrity established over time. These, in my view, are necessary pains and a process we need to undergo and can echo, to a certain extent, the post-modernist view of "commodification of self". The process of growing mature in the agents' socialization process indicates that the ultimate harmony not only between the agents and the clients but also how the agents can live with themselves in peace would largely depend on a naturalistic view of "nature does nothing, but everything is done". As the philosophy of Taoism upholds, simplicity and a naturalistic view of life is the way of nature, and should also be the way of human being, given the complications of modern life. Associated with the principle of simplicity is the attitude of contentment towards material living. Only one is contented with what he/she has and lives with it, can he/she live in peace deep in his/her heart. However, this contradicts sharply with the modern view of industrialization, exploitation as much as possible. One may criticize this view of life as a form of asceticism which may not fit the life of a highly developed civilization. However, contentment is not the same as the denial of any enjoyment at all. A life of contentment is a life free from frustration, anxiety, and sense of misery. Once a less extreme and more moderate view is established, most of the conflicts and disputes can and will be resolved.

6.2.2 A Socio-cultural Perspective

This study analyzes the discursive patterns through move analysis, topic management and discourse identities in conversations between the insurance sales agents and their (prospective) clients in transformational China's rural areas. What's more, it interprets the analytical results with the salient cultural values and communicating norms in China's rural areas. Generally speaking, the study has at least the following theoretical contributions.

Firstly, the study develops a systematic and comprehensive theoretical framework to study the discursive patterns and functions of the communicative purposes, the moves and steps, topic management, strategic activation and shifts of different discourse identities in the interactions between the insurance sales agents and their (prospective) clients in transformational China's rural areas, represented by a county in Central China. Following this theoretical framework, the study generalizes the moves, steps in the interactions, the strategic management of different topics through different types of talks and different discourse identities with references to their linguistic features. Then the functions of the strategic management are sorted out based on the linguistic devices that realize the goal of persuasion. Consequently, the underlying cultural sources that account for the features are interpreted according to the functions in the collected data (both recordings of dialogue and interviewing) of the study.

Secondly, the study has enriched the socio-cultural study of transformational China's rural areas in examining insurance sales agent-client interactions in terms of exploring the discursive features in such interactions. In other words, money has become more important in rural *Guanxi*, as manifested in language, more specifically, discursive features. As most of the current studies of transformational China's rural areas, either focus on ethnographic study or logical reasoning. In contrast, this study manages to incorporate macro-analysis of socio-cultural environment with micro-analysis of more detailed discursive features in insurance sales interactions in transformational China's rural areas. Moreover, it manages to combine the macro- and the micro-analysis, and thus it offers a useful approach in studying other contexts.

Thirdly, the study explains the cultural implications with various dimensions of cultural sources. Mainly two sets of cultural sources are taken as reference for the explanation of cultural diversities. At the over-arching level, it is rooted in the two salient ideologies of the two cultures: collectivism in the Chinese traditional culture and individualism, more or less, manifested in the Chinese society after the initiation of reform and opening-up policy. Nonetheless, the explanations for communicating style or behaviors at the cultural level with reference to the two ideological constructs are believed to be too general and not adequate enough (Wilson, 2010). Therefore, socio-ideological construction and communication style are employed at the micro-level to further our interpretation of cultural features in the study, which resort to a variety of cultural sources. We believe this way helps to increase the validity of and add triangulation to our cultural interpretation in the study.

Last but not the least, by integrating modern social theories and concepts (Fei, 2007; Zhai, 2007b, 2009; Cao and Chen, 1997; Sun, 2001; Lu, 2002), it describes and generalizes the communication patterns for insurance sales in transformational China's rural areas, and in the meantime, comes to uncover the hidden agenda of agent-client interactions with some interpretations from the perspective of socio-cultural interpretation with empirical data.

In conclusion, the study aims to investigate the dynamics of insurance sales agent-client interactions in transformational China's rural areas, and it is found that in rural areas, the decision of making the purchase of insurance policy can be summarized as follows.

Firstly, there is an emergence of understanding of the necessity of such a service, given that fact of the insufficiency of social securities that the government offers in such areas as education, medical expenses and pension plans. While at the same time, due to the rising standard of living of local residents, simply put, there is financial feasibility to purchase more services with wider coverage to improve their well-being.

Secondly, in transformational China's rural communities, *Guanxi* and *Renqing* connections are still quite rampant and pervasive in everyday life, from daily life to dealing with others. While currently, insurance sales in rural areas are still mostly conducted through the agents' extensive connections with the local residents. For most of the time, the sales are achieved, for a major part, through the trust of the clients in the agents, which requires almost impeccable credibility and reputation of the agents. That is also why almost all agents who are doing well (indicated by having good sales performance) are locally well-respected individuals.

Thirdly, the changing social conditions, or the decentralization of central authority, presupposes a downward responsiblization, individuals are becoming more and more independent and assume more responsibility, not only greater freedom in earning, making a living, but also more risks taken by themselves, compared with the state allocation of resources. It's unwise and dangerous to impose a simple moral judgment of which is better. However, it's a general fact and tendency in current transformational China's rural areas.

Fourthly, agents' efforts in selling insurance are almost irresistible. In the investigation, there are certain extreme cases that the agents' constant, inexhaustible and repeated visits and talks make the prospective client annoyed and thus the whole situation turn into a mess, which could also be one of the reasons that in current transformational China's rural areas, many people have certain bias or prejudice against insurance sales agents.

Last but not the least, given the fact that people's living standard is getting higher and higher, and wealth is being accumulated more and more through various means, many people just don't have much knowledge or expertise on how to manage their wealth. Thus they have to resort to someone who seems to have the relative knowledge and expertise, which then offers some room for the insurance agents to take advantage of and make the sales. Moreover, the rapid improvement in life makes the local residents to be eager to show off, just as an old Chinese saying goes, "If not return home after getting rich, it's just like parade with beautiful dress at night." The idea of face in Chinese people's minds is deeply ingrained. Therefore, the work of agents can, to some extent, satisfy the need and fill this vanity.

References

曹红欣(Cao Hongxin). 2009. 我国保险营销制度改革探讨. 公共管理, (13X): 43-45.

车瑜, 杨宇科(Che Yu, Yang Yuke). 2017. 社会连带、资源优势与销售绩效的实证研究——基于保险销售中强连带与桥连带的影响. 财经科学, (3): 110-122.

陈平(Chen Ping). 1999. 外贸英语写作教学新思路: 语篇体裁分析理论及其应用. 外语教学, (3): 28-30.

丁孜山(Ding Zishan). 2008. 我国保险经济市场发展研究. 保险研究, (4):76-78.

董笑(Dong Xiao). 2017. 银行代理保险销售风险的法律规制研究. 时代金融, (11): 130-131.

杜金榜(Du Jinbang). 2008. 司法语篇隐性说服研究. 现代外语, (3):253-262.

费孝通(Fei Xiaotong). 2007. 乡土中国. 南京: 江苏文艺出版社.

郭影(Guo Ying). 2009. 浅析中国保险经济行业. 当代经济, (4): 38-40.

胡涛(Hu Tao). 2004. 论信函的体裁分析. 外语教学, (1): 87-91.

胡皖, 王海霞(Hu Wan, Wang Haixia). 2009. 社会学视野下保险业的科学发展. 保险研究, (3): 33-42.

黄光国, 胡先缙(Huang Guangguo, Hu Xianjin). 2004. 面子: 中国人的权力游戏. 北京: 中国人民大学出版社.

黄晓琴(Huang Xiaoqin). 2001. "体裁"分析及其在 ESP 教学中的应用. 绍兴文理学院学报(哲学社会科学版), (2): 75-78.

霍永寿(Huo Yongshou). 2004. 弱化与语用调节论: 以中医诊谈为个案. 昆明: 云南大学出版社.

李桂香(Li Guixiang). 2008. 浅议中国保险的营销体制. 经济论坛, (14):129-130.

李俊, 赵毅(Li Jun, Zhao Yi). 2013. 农村阶层分化与农村统一战线. 河南科技学院学报, (1): 30-33.

李伟民, 梁玉成(Li Weimin, Liang Yucheng). 2002. 特殊信任与普遍信任: 中国人信任的结构与特征. 社会学研究, (3): 11-12.

梁莹(Liang Ying). 2011. 特殊信任视野中的公民法治观念——基于两次延续性调查的研究视角. 学海, (3): 97-105.

林礼汉, 陈鸣凤 (Lin Lihan, Chen Mingfeng). 1998. 实用金融业务英文写作. 广州: 广东经济出版社.

刘怡, 谢洋(Liu Yi, Xie Yang). 2009. 中国保险中介制度的历史变迁及其完善发展的对策. 经济研究导刊, (1): 95-96.

卢倩云(Lu Qianyun). 2000. 当代中国农民阶层分化与现代化关系的社会学探视. 广西师

范大学学报, (S2): 19-22.

陆学艺(Lu Xueyi). 2002. 当代中国社会阶层研究报告. 北京: 社会科学文献出版社.

罗家德, 叶勇助(Luo Jiade, Ye Yongzhu). 2007. 中国人的信任游戏. 北京: 社会科学文献出版社.

马振涛(Ma Zhentao). 2018. 保险科技浪潮下寿险公司核心能力建设研究. 海南金融, (1): 69-74.

裴小林(Pei Xiaolin). 2014. 中国经济转轨的真实起源. 中国乡村研究, (1): 1-48.

沈烈(Shen Lie). 2009. 保险公司资产负债管理. 北京: 经济科学出版社.

舒俊辉, 李健(Shu Junhui, Li Jian). 2006. 保险中的道德风险与委托——代理模型. 重庆工学院学报, (8): 130-131.

孙立平(Sun Liping). 2009. 重建社会——转型社会的秩序再造. 北京: 社会科学文献出版社.

王国军, 李康乐(Wang Guojun, Li Kangle). 2009. 中国保险营销模式的反思与建构. 甘肃行政学院学报, (2): 49-58.

王露璐(Wang Lulu). 2016. 新乡土伦理——社会转型期的中国乡村伦理问题研究. 北京: 人民出版社.

王淑芹(Wang Shuqin). 2017. 中国乡土伦理的转型——评王露璐著《新乡土伦理——社会转型期的中国乡村伦理问题研究》. 伦理学研究, (1): 137.

王艳萍(Wang Yanping). 2013. 转型经济的国际最新研究//中华外国经济研究会. 外国经济学说与中国研究报告: 5. 北京: 社会科学文献出版社.

徐伊俐, 朱静(Xu Yili, Zhu Jing). 2017. 保险销售人员情绪智力对员工绩效的影响. 经营与管理, (11): 48-51.

许菊(Xu Ju). 2004. 商务英语公函的体裁分析. 西安外国语学院学报, 12(1): 26-29.

许闲(Xu Xian). 2009. 中国保险问题国外学术研究探析. 上海保险, (3): 60-62.

杨舸(Yang Ge). 2017. 社会转型视角下的家庭结构和代际居住模式——以上海、浙江、福建的调查为例. 人口学刊, (2): 5-17.

杨中芳, 彭泗清(Yang Zhongfang, Peng Siqing). 1999. 中国人人际信任的概念化: 一个人际关系的观点. 社会学研究, (2): 3-23.

俞国良(Yu Guoliang). 2017. 社会转型: 社会心理服务于社会心理建设. 心理与行为研究, (4): 433-439.

原琳(Yuan Lin). 2008. 浅谈我国保险经纪人制度的现状及问题. 当代经济, (9): 128-129.

曾祥娟(Zeng Xiangjuan). 2001. 体裁分析与科技英语写作教学. 外语教学, (5): 51-55.

翟学伟(Zhai Xuewei). 2007a. 报的运作方位. 社会学研究, (1): 83-98.

翟学伟(Zhai Xuewei). 2007b. 关系研究的多重立场和理论重构. 江苏社会科学, (3): 118-130.

翟学伟(Zhai Xuewei). 2009. 是"关系", 还是社会资本. 社会, (1): 109-121.

翟学伟(Zhai Xuewei). 2011. 中国人的关系原理——时空秩序、生活欲念及其流变. 北京: 北京大学出版社.

张知新, 王辰(Zhang Zhixin, Wang Chen). 2016. 商业健康保险本土化发展的探索与思考. 保险理论与实践, (1): 30-39.

赵福利(Zhao Fuli). 2001. 英语电视新闻导语的语步结构分析. 外语教学与研究, (2):

99-104.

赵建国(Zhao Jianguo). 2013. 中国式关系批判. 北京: 新华出版社.

朱俊生(Zhu Junsheng). 2009. 2009 中国保险市场前瞻. 中国保险, (1): 24-27.

朱俊生(Zhu Junsheng). 2010. 2009 年中国保险市场发展回顾. 中国保险, (1): 21-26.

Allen, W. 2007. Australian political discourse: Pronominal choice in campaign speeches. In I. Mushin & M. Laughren (Eds.), *Selected Papers from the 2006 Annual Meeting of the Australian Linguistic Society* (pp. 1-13). Brisbane: University of Queensland.

Androutsopoulos, J. K. & Georgakopoulou, A. 2003. Discourse constructions of youth identities. In A. de Fina, D. Schiffrin & M. Bamberg (Eds.), *Discourse and Identity* (pp. 1-25). Cambridge: Cambridge University Press.

Anthony, B. 1964. *Language Made Plain*. Madison: International Universities Press.

Askehave, I. & Swales, J. M. 2001. Genre identification and communicative purpose: A problem and a possible solution. *Applied Linguistics*, 22(2): 195-212.

Atkinson, P. & Delamont, S. 2006. Rescuing narrative from qualitative research. *Narrative Inquiry*, 16(1): 164-172.

Baker, T. & Simon, J. 2002. *Embracing Risk: The Changing Culture of Insurance and Responsibility*. Chicago: University of Chicago Press.

Bamberg, M. 2010. Blank check for biography? Openness and ingenuity in the management of the "who-am-I-question". In D. Schiffrin, A. de Fina & A. Nylund (Eds.), *Telling Stories: Language, Narrative, and Social Life* (pp. 109-121). Washington, D.C.: Georgetown University Press.

Bargiela-Chiappini, F. 2009. *The Handbook of Business Discourse*. Edinburgh: Edinburgh University Press.

Barnouw, V. 1979. *Anthropology: A General Introduction*. New York: Dorsey Press.

Bateson, G. 1972. A theory of play and fantasy. *Psychiatric Research Reports*, 2: 39-51.

Beck, U. 1992. *Risk Society: Towards a New Modernity*. London: Sage.

Beebe, L. & Cummings, M. 1985. Speech act performance: A function of the data collection procedure? (Paper presented at the TESOL Convention). New York.

Bellack, A. A. 1966. *The Language of the Classroom*. New York: Mimeo.

Bettinghaus, E. P. & Cody, M. J. 1987. *Persuasive Communication* (4th edn.). New York: Holt, Rinehart and Winston.

Bhatia, V. K. 1993. *Analyzing Genre—Language Use in Professional Settings*. New York: Longman.

Bhatia, V. K. 1995. Genre-mixing in professional communication: The case of "private intentions" v. "socially recognized purposes". In P. Bruthiaux, T. Boswood & B. Bertha (Eds.), *Explorations in English for Professional Communication* (pp. 1-19). Hong Kong: City University of Hong Kong Press.

Bhatia, V. K. 1997a. Applied genre analysis and ESP. In T. Miller (Ed.), *Functional Approaches to Written Text: Classroom Applications* (pp. 134-149). Washington, D. C.: United States Information Agency.

Bhatia, V. K. 1997b. Genre-mixing in academic introductions. *English for Specific Purposes*, 16 (3): 181-196.

Bhatia, V. K. 2004. *Worlds of Written Discourse—A Genre Based View*. London: Continuum Publishing.

Bhatia, V. K. 2005. Generic patterns in promotional discourse. In H. Helena & V. Tuija (Eds.), *Persuasion Across Genres: A Linguistic Approach* (pp. 213-225). Amsterdam and Philadelphia: John Benjamins.

Bhatia, V. K. 2008. *Worlds of Written Discourse*. London: Continuum Publishing.

Biggart, N. W. 1989. *Charismatic Capitalism: Direct Selling Organizations in America*. Chicago: University of Chicago Press.

Bilbow, G. T. 1997. Cross-cultural impression management in the multicultural workplace: The special case of Hong Kong. *Journal of Pragmatics*, 28(4): 461-487.

Blum-Kulka, S. 1982. Learning how to say what you mean in a second language: A study of speech act performance of learners of Hebrew as a second language. *Applied Linguistics*, 3(1): 29-59.

Blum-Kulka, S., House, J. & Kasper, G. 1989. *Cross-cultural Pragmatics: Requests and Apologies*. Norwood: Ablex.

Boden, D. 1983. Talk international: An examination of turn-taking in seven Indo-European languages (Paper presented at the American Sociological Association meetings). Detroit. August 31-September 4, 1983.

Bond, M. H. 1986. *The Social Psychology of the Chinese People*. Oxford: Oxford University Press.

Bond, M. H. 1992. *The Psychology of the Chinese People*. Oxford: Oxford University Press.

Bond, M. H. 1994. *Beyond the Chinese Face: Insights from Psychology*. Oxford: Oxford University Press.

Borchers, T. A. 2002. *Persuasion in the Media Age*. Boston: McGraw-Hill.

Braet, A. C. 1992. Ethos, pathos and logos in aristotle's rhetoric: A re-examination. *Argumentation*, 6(3), 307-320.

Bremer, K. 1996. *Achieving Understanding: Discourse in Intercultural Communication*. London: Longman.

Brown, P. & Levinson, S. C. 1987. *Politeness: Some Universals in Language Usage*. Cambridge: Cambridge University Press.

Brown, P. & Levinson, S. C. 2011. Politeness: Some universals in language usage. In A. Dawn & G. Peter (Eds.), *The Pragmatics Reader* (pp. 321-335). London: Routledge.

Brunner, J. A. & Wang, Y. 1988. Chinese negotiating and the concept of face. *Journal of International Consumer Marketing*, 1(1): 27-44.

Bublitz, W. 1988. *Supportive Fellow-Speakers and Cooperative Conversations: Discourse Topics and Topical Actions, Participant Roles and Recipient Action in a Particular Type of Everyday Conversation*. Amsterdam and Philadelphia: John Benjamins.

Butterfield, J. 1990. State response to informal groups. *Journal of Nationalism & Ethnicity*,

18(2): 56-64.

Cameron, D. & Taylor, T. J. 1988. Analysing conversation: Rules and units in the structure of talk. *Language & Speech*, (1): 87-94.

Cao, J. Q. & Chen, Z. Y. 1997. *Walking out of the Ideal Castle: Study on the Chinese "Danwei" Phenomenon*. Shenzhen: Haitian Press.

Caroline, L. 2008. Constructing affiliation and solidarity in job interviews. *Discourse and Communication*, 2 (4): 411-432.

Casalegno, F. & Mcwilliam, I. M. 2004. Communication dynamics in technological mediated learning environments. *International Journal of Instructional Technology and Distance Learning*, 1(11): 15-34.

Chang, H. C. 1999. The "well-defined" is "ambiguous": Indeterminacy in Chinese conversation. *Journal of Pragmatics*, 31(4): 535-556.

Chen, R. 1993. Responding to compliments: A contrastive study of politeness strategies between American English and Chinese speakers. *Journal of Pragmatics*, 20 (1): 49-75.

Cheng, W. 2003. *Intercultural Conversation*. Amsterdam and Philadelphia: John Benjamins.

Chouliaraki, L. & Fairclough, N. 1999. *Discourse in Late Modernity: Rethinking Critical Discourse Analysis*. Edinburgh: Edinburgh University Press.

Christie, F. 1986. Writing in schools: Generic structures as ways of meaning. In B. Couture (Ed.), *Functional Approaches to Writing Research Perspective*(pp. 221-240). London: Pinter.

Church, A. 2009. Preference organization and peer disputes: How young children resolve conflict. *Journal of Language & Social Psychology*, 29(4): 502-504.

Coupland, J. 2010. Past the "perfect kind of age" ? Styling selves and relationships in over-50s dating advertisements. *Journal of Communication*, 50(3): 9-30.

Coupland, J. & Coupland, N. 1994. "Old age doesn't come alone": Discursive representations of health-in-aging in geriatric medicine. *International Journal of Aging & Human Development*, 39(1): 81-95.

Coupland, J., Coupland, N. & Robinson, J. 1992. "How are you?": Negotiating phatic communion. *Language in Society*, 21(2): 207-230.

Creese, A. 1991. Speech act variation in British and American English. *PENN Working Papers*, 7 (2): 37-58.

Crosby, L. A., Evans, K. R. & Cowles, D. 1990. Relationship quality in services selling: An interpersonal influence perspective. *Journal of Marketing*, 5(4): 68-81.

de Fina, A., Schiffrin, D. & Bamberg, M. 2006. *Discourse and Identity*. Cambridge: Cambridge University Press.

Dechert, W. D. 1983. Increasing returns to scale and the reverse flexible accelerator. *Economics Letters*, 13(1): 69-75.

Diana, B. 2002. *Applying Sociolinguistics*. Amsterdam and Philadelphia: John Benjamins.

Dion, P. A. & Notarantonio, E. 1992. Salesperson communicator style: The neglected dimension in sales performance. *The Journal of Business Communication*, 29: 63-77.

dos Santos, V. B. M. P. 2002. Genre Analysis of Business Letters of Negotiation. *English for Specific Purposes*, 21(2): 167-199.

Drew, P. & Heritage, J. 1992a. *Talk at Work: Interaction in Institutional Settings*. Cambridge: Cambridge University Press.

Drew, P. & Heritage, J. 1992b. Analyzing talk at work. In P. Drew & J. Heritage (Eds.), *Talk at Work: Interaction in Institutional Settings* (pp. 1-65). Cambridge: Cambridge University Press.

du Gay, P. 1996. Organizing identity: Entrepreneurial governance and public management. In S. Hall & P. du Gay (Eds.), *Questions of Cultural Identity* (pp. 151-169). London: Sage.

Du, P. D. 1996. *Consumption and Identity at Work*. London: Sage.

Duranti, A. 1988. Ethnography of speaking: Towards linguistics of the praxis. In F. J. Newmyer (Ed.), *Linguistics: The Cambridge Survey, Vol. VI. Language: The Socio-cultural Context* (pp. 210-228). Cambridge: Cambridge University Press.

Duranti, A. & Goodwin, C. (Eds.) 1992. *Rethinking Context: Language as an Interactive Phenomenon*. Cambridge: Cambridge University Press.

Durkheim, E. 1915. *The Elementary Forms of the Religious Life*. London: Allen and Unwin.

Duszak, A. 1997. *Culture and Styles of Academic Discourse*. Berlin: Mouton de Gruyter.

Egbert, M. 1993. *Schisming: The Transformation from a Single Conversation to Multiple Conversations* (Unpublished doctoral dissertation). University of California, Los Angeles.

Egbert, M. 1996. Context-sensitivity in conversation: Eye gaze and the German repair initiator bitte. *Language in Society*, 25: 587-612.

Egbert, M. 1997a. Schisming: The collaborative transformation from a single conversation to multiple conversations. *Research on Language and Social Interaction*, 30(1): 1-51.

Egbert, M. 1997b. Some interactional achievements of other-initiated repair in multi-person conversation. *Journal of Pragmatics*, 27: 611-634.

Eggins, S. & Slade, D. 1997. *Analyzing Casual Conversation*. London: Cassell.

Ensink, T. 1997. The footing of a royal address: An analysis of representativeness in political speech, exemplified in Queen Beatrix's address to the knesset on March 28, 1995. In C. Schaaffner (Ed.), *Analyzing Political Speech*(pp. 5-32). Clevedon: Multilingual Matters Ltd.

Ericson, R. & Doyle, A. 2003. *Risk and Morality*. Toronto: University of Toronto Press.

Ericson, R. & Doyle, A. 2004a. *Uncertain Business: Risk, Insurance and the Limits of Knowledge*. Toronto: University of Toronto Press.

Ericson, R. & Doyle, A. 2004b. Catastrophe Risk, Insurance and Terrorism. *Economy and Society*, 33: 135-173.

Ericson, R. & Doyle, A. 2004c. Criminalization in private: The case of insurance fraud. In Law Commission of Canada (Ed.), *What is a Crime? Defining Criminal Conduct in Contemporary Society* (pp. 99-124). Vancouver: University of British Columbia Press.

Evans, F. B. 1963. Selling as a dyadic relationship—A new approach. *American Behavioral Scientist*, 6: 76-79.

Fairclough, N. 1989. *Language and Power*. London: Longman.
Fairclough, N. 1992. *Discourse and Social Change*. Cambridge: Polity Press.
Fairclough, N. 1995. *Critical Discourse Analysis: The Critical Study of Language*. London: Longman.
Fairclough, N. 2001. The dialectics of discourse. *Textus*, 14 (2): 3-10.
Fairclough, N. 2003. *Analyzing Discourse: Textual Analysis for Social Research*. London: Routledge.
Fairclough, N. & Clive, H. 1995. *Critical Discourse Analysis: The Critical Study of Language*. Longman.
Fairclough, N. & Wodak, R. 1997. Critical discourse analysis. In T. A. van Dijk (Ed.), *Discourse Studies: A Multidisciplinary Introduction* (pp. 258-284). London: Sage.
Fang, T. 1999. *Chinese Business Negotiating Style*. London: Sage.
Ferraro, G. P. 1990. *The Cultural Dimension of International Business*. Upper Saddle River, NJ: Prentice Hall.
Fetzer, A. & Bull, P. 2008. "Well, I answer it by simply inviting you to look at the evidence": The strategic use of pronouns in political interviews. *Journal of Language and Politics*, 7(2): 271-289.
Fiske, S. T. & Taylor, S. E. 1991. *Social Cognition* (2nd edn.). New York: McGraw-Hill.
Flick, U. 2009. *An Introduction to Qualitative Research* (4th edn.). London: Sage.
Flowerdew, J. 1997. Competing public discourses in transitional Hong Kong. *Journal of Pragmatics*, 28: 533-553.
Flowerdew, J. 2003. Signaling nouns in discourse. *English for Specific Purposes*, 22: 29-346.
Foucault, M. 1977. *Discipline and Punish*. London: Allen Lane.
Fox, B. 1990. *China: Alive in the Bitter Sea*. Manhattan: Crown.
Gabrenya, W. K. & Hwang, K. K. 1996. Chinese social interaction: Harmony and hierarchy on the good earth. In M. Bond (Ed.), *Handbook of Chinese Psychology* (pp. 309-321). Oxford: Oxford University Press.
Gao, S. 1993. Taking a market-oriented direction and pushing forward in a gradual way: The basic experience of China's economic reform. *China Economic Review*, 4(2): 129-136.
Gass, R. H. & Seiter, J. S. 2007. *Persuasion, Social Influence, and Compliance Gaining*. London: Pearson Education, Inc.
Gavruseva, L. 1995. Positioning and framing: Constructing interactional asymmetry in employer-employee discourse. *Discourse Processes*, (20): 325-345.
Geertz, C. 1973. Thick description: Toward an interpretive theory of culture. In C. Geertz (Ed.), *The Interpretation of Cultures: Selected Essays* (pp. 3-30). New York: Basic Books.
Geluykens, R. 1993. Topic introduction in English conversation. *Transactions of Philosophical Society*, 91(2): 181-214.
Ghauri, P. & Fang, T. 2001. Negotiating with the Chinese: A socio-cultural analysis. *Journal of World Business*, 36(3): 303-325.
Goffman, E. 1967. *Interactional Ritual: Essays on Face-to-Face Behavior*. New York: Doubleday

Anchor.

Goffman, E. 1975. *Frame Analysis: An Essay on the Organization of Experience*. London: Penguin.

Goffman, E. 1981. *Forms of Talk*. Philadelphia: University of Pennsylvania Press.

Gong, W. B. 2001. *Social Development and Choice of Systems: Study on the Social Changes in China since 1978*. Hohhot: The People's Press of Inner Mongolia.

Goodwin, C. 1984. Notes on story structure and the organization of participation. In J. M. Atkinson & J. Heritage (Eds.), *Structures of Social Action: Studies in Conversation Analysis* (pp. 225-246). Cambridge: Cambridge University Press.

Goodwin, C. 1986. Audience diversity, participation and interpretation. *Text*, 6 (3): 283-316.

Goodwin, C. & Duranti, A. 1992. *Rethinking Context: Language as an Interactive Phenomenon*. Cambridge: Cambridge University Press.

Goodwin, C. & Goodwin, M. H. 1987. Concurrent operations on talk: Notes on the interactive organization of assessments. *IPRA Papers in Pragmatics*, 1(1): 1-54.

Grice, P. 1967/1975. Logic in conversation. In P. Cole & J. Morgan (Eds.), *Syntax and Semantics: Speech Acts 3* (pp. 41-58). New York: Academic Press.

Gu, Y. G. 1990. Politeness phenomena in modern Chinese. *Journal of Pragmatics*, 14(2): 237-257.

Gu, Y. G. 2001. The changing orders of discourse in a changing China. In H. H. Pan (Ed.), *Studies in Chinese Linguistics* (pp. 31-58). Hong Kong: Linguistic Society of Hong Kong.

Gudykunst, W. B. 1998. *Bridging Differences: Effective Intergroup Communication*. London: Sage.

Gumperz, J. 1982. *Languages and Social Identity*. Cambridge: Cambridge University Press.

Gumperz, J. 1992a. Editor's introduction to "contextualization and understanding". In A. Duranti & G. Charles (Eds.), *Rethinking Context: Language as an Interactive Phenomenon* (pp. 229-230). Cambridge: Cambridge University Press.

Gumperz, J. 1992b. *Discourse Strategies*. Cambridge: Cambridge University Press.

Gumperz, J. 2001. Interactional sociolinguistics: A personal perspective. In S. Deborah, T. Deborah & H. Heidi (Eds.), *The Handbook of Discourse Analysis* (pp. 215-228). Oxford: Blackwell.

Gumperz, J. & Hymes, D. 1972. *Directions in Sociolinguistics: The Ethnography of Communication*. Oxford and New York: Basil Blackwell.

Habermas, J. 1973. Dogmatism, reason, and decision: On theory and praxis in our scientific civilization. In J. Viertel (Ed.), *Theory and Practice* (pp. 253-282). Boston: Beacon Press.

Hage, J. & Powers, C. H. 1992. *Post-industrial Lives: Roles and Relationships in the 21st Century*. London: Sage.

Hall, E. T. 1989. *Beyond Culture*. New York: Anchor Press.

Halmari, H. 2008. On the language of the Clinton-Dole presidential campaign debates: General tendencies and successful strategies. *Journal of Language and Politics*, 7(2): 247-270.

Hamilton, H. 1996. Intra-textuality, inter-textuality, and the construction of identity as patient in Alzheimer's disease. *Text*, 16(1): 61-90.

Hara, K. & Kim, M. 2004. The Effect of self-construals on conversational indirectness. *International Journal of Intercultural Relations*, 28: 1-18.

Harris, P. & Moran, R. 1996. *Managing Cultural Differences: Leadership Strategies for a New World of Business* (4th edn.). Houston: Gulf.

Hasan, R. 1995. The conception of context in text. In P. H. Fries & M. Gregory (Eds.), *Discourse in Society: Systemic Functional Perspective* (pp. 183-283). Norwood: Ablex.

Hayashi, M. 1999. Where grammar and interaction meet: A study of co-participant completion in Japanese conversation. *Human Studies*, 22: 475-499.

Hayashi, M. 2001. Postposition-initiated utterances in Japanese conversation: An interactional account of a grammatical practices. In M. Selting & E. Couper-Kuhlen (Eds.), *Studies in Interactional Linguistics* (pp. 317-343). Amsterdam and Philadelphia: John Benjamins.

Hayashi, M. 2003. *Joint Utterance Construction in Japanese Conversation*. Amsterdam and Philadelphia: John Benjamins.

Hayashi, M., Mori, J. & Takagi, T. 2002. Contingent achievement of co-tellership in a Japanese conversation: An analysis of talk, gaze and gesture. In C. E. Ford, B. A. Fox & A. Thompson (Eds.), *The Language of Turn and Sequence* (pp. 81-122). Oxford: Oxford University Press.

Heath, C. 1992. The delivery and reception of diagnosis in the general practice consultation. In P. Drew & J. Heritage (Eds.), *Talk at Work: Interaction in Institutional Settings* (pp. 235-267). Cambridge: Cambridge University Press.

Herbert, R. K. 1986. Say "Thank you"—or something. *American Speech*, 61 (1): 76-88.

Herbert, R. K. 1989. The ethnography of English compliments and compliment responses: A contrastive sketch. In W. Oleksy (Ed.), *Contrastive Pragmatics* (pp. 3-35). Amsterdam and Philadelphia: John Benjamins.

Herbert, R. K. 1991. The sociology of compliment work: An ethno-contrastive study of Polish and English compliments. *Multilingua*, 10(4): 381-402.

Heritage, J. 1984. A change-of-state token and aspects of its sequential placement. In J. M. Atkinson & J. Heritage (Eds.), *Structure of Social Action: Studies in Conversation Analysis* (pp. 299-345). Cambridge: Cambridge University Press.

Hofstede, G. 1991. *Cultures and Organizations: Software of the Mind*. London: McGraw-Hill.

Holmes, J. 1986. Compliments and compliment responses in New Zealand English. *Anthropological Linguistics*, 28(4): 485-508.

Holmes, J. 1988. Paying compliments: A sex-preference politeness strategy. *Journal of Pragmatics*, 12: 445-465.

Holmes, J. 2000. Doing collegiality and keeping control at work: Small talk in government departments. In J. Coupland (Ed.), *Small Talk* (pp.1-45). Harlow, UK: Pearson.

Holmes, J. & Stubbe, M. 2003. *Power and Politeness in the Workplace: A Sociolinguistic Analysis of Talk at Work*. London: Longman.

Hopkins, A. & Dudley-Evans, T. 1988. A genre-based investigation of the discussion sections in articles and dissertations. *English for Specific Purposes*, 7: 113-121.

Hu, H. 1944. The Chinese concepts of "face". *American Anthropologist*, 46(1): 45-64.

Hutchby, I. & Wooffitt, R. 1998. *Conversation Analysis*. Cambridge: Polity Press.

Hwang, E. R. 1987. Face and favor: The Chinese power game. *American Journal of Sociology*, 92 (4) : 35-41.

Hymes, D. 1972. Models of the interaction of language and social life. In J. Gumperz & D. Hymes (Eds.), *Directions in Sociolinguistics: The Ethnography of Communication* (pp. 35-71). New York: Holt, Rinehart and Winston.

Ip, M., Gilligan, T., Koenig, B., et al. 1998. Ethical decision-making in critical care in Hong Kong. *Critical Care Medicine*, 26(3): 447-451.

Jamie, C. & Gary, H. 1997. Appropriate relational messages in direct selling interaction: Should salespeople adapt to buyers' communication style. *Journal of Business Communication*, 34: 401-418.

Jefferson, G. 1984. On stepwise transition from talk about a trouble to inappropriately next-positioned matters. In J. Atkinson & J. Heritage (Eds.), *Structure of Social Action: Studies in Conversation Analysis* (pp. 191-222). Cambridge: Cambridge University Press.

Jefferson, G. 1987. On exposed and embedded correction in conversation. In G. Button & J. R. E. Lee (Eds.), *Talk and Social Organization* (pp. 86-100). Clevedon: Multilingual Matters.

Jefferson, G. 2004. Glossary of transcript symbols with an introduction. In G. Lerner (Ed.), *Conversation Analysis: Studies from the First Generation* (pp. 13-31). Amsterdam and Philadelphia: John Benjamins.

Jones, J. & Moore, T. 2007. Language and politics. In L. Horn & G. Ward (Eds.), *The Handbook of Pragmatics* (pp. 35-55). Malden: Blackwell.

Kahneman, D. & Tversky, A. 1979. Prospect theory: An analysis of decision under risk. *Econometrica*, 47(2): 263-291.

Kindel T. 1990. Chinese consumer behavior: Historical perspective plus an update on communication hypotheses. In J. N. Sheth & C. T. Tan (Eds.), *SV-Historical Perspective in Consumer Research: National and International Perspectives* (pp.186-190). Singapore: Association for Consumer Research.

King, R. 1992. A man that could be trusted: Sexual difference and analytic technique in the work of Sigmund Freud. *Analysis*, 3: 13-22.

Knapp, M. L., Hooper, R. & Bell, R. A. 1984. Compliments: A descriptive taxonomy. *Journal of Communication*, 34 (4): 12-31.

Kong, C. K. 1998a. Are simple business request letters really simple: A comparison of Chinese and English business request letters. *Text*, 19: 103-141.

Kong, C. K. 1998b. Politeness of service encounters in Hong Kong. *Journal of Pragmatics*, 8: 555-575.

Kong, C. K. 2001. Marketing of belief: Intertextual construction of network marketers' identity. *Discourse and Society*, 11(4): 473-503.

Kong, C. K. 2002. Managing the ambiguous and conflicting identities of "up-line" and "down-line" in a network marketing firm. *Discourse Studies*, 3(4): 49-74.

Kong, C. K. 2003. "Are you my friend?": Negotiating friendship in conversations between network marketers and their prospects. *Language in Society*, 32: 487-522.

Labov, W. 1966. *The Social Stratification of English in New York*. New York: City Center for Applied Linguistics.

Labov, W. 1969. The logic of non-standard English. In F. William (Ed.), *Language and Poverty* (pp.153-187). Chicago: University of Chicago Press.

Labov, W. 1972. *Language in the Inner City*. Philadelphia: University of Pennsylvania Press.

Lakoff, G. & Johnson, M. 1980. *Metaphors We Live by*. Chicago: University of Chicago Press.

Lakoff, R. T. 1973. The logic of politeness; or minding your P's and Q's. (Papers from the 9th Regional Meeting of the Chicago Linguistic Society: 292-305.)

Lakoff, R. T. 1990. *Talking Power: The Politics of Language*. New York: Basic Books.

Larson, C. U. 2001. *Persuasion: Reception and Responsibility* (10th edn.). Cambridge: Wadsworth Publishing.

Laver, J. 1975. Communicative functions of phatic communion. In A. Kendon, R. Harris & M. Key (Eds.), *Organization of Behavior in Face-to-Face Interaction* (pp. 215-238). The Hague: Mouton.

Lee-Wong, S. M. 2000. *Politeness and Face in Chinese Culture*. Frankfurt: Peter Lang.

Lei, Y. 1995. Complimenting in Mandarin Chinese. In G. Kasper (Ed.), *Pragmatics of Chinese as Native and Target Language* (pp. 207-302). Honolulu: Second Language Teaching and Curriculum Center, University of Hawaii at Manoa.

Levine, M. 2007. Challenging the culture of affluence. *Independent School*, 67(1): 28-36.

Li, Q. 2010. *Thirty Years of Reform and Social Changes in China*. Beijing: Social Science Academic Press and Koninklijke Brill NV.

Lim, T. S. 1994. Facework and interpersonal relationships. In S. Ting-Toomey (Ed.), *The Challenge of Facework: Cross-cultural and Interpersonal Issues* (pp. 209-229). Albany, New York: State University of New York Press.

Lin, H. D. 2004. Initiating, sustaining, and concluding social transactions: An analysis of roleplay performance in the oral proficiency interview. *Journal of Language and Linguistics*, 3(1): 109-137.

Linell, P. & Luckmann, T. 1991. Asymmetries in dialogue: Some conceptual preliminaries. In I. Markova & K. Foppa (Eds.), *Asymmetries in Dialogue*(pp.6-13). Hemel Hempstead: Harvester Wheatsheaf.

Liu, Z. X. 1999. *Marching Towards Democracy and Nomocracy in China*. Jinan: The Shandong People's Press.

Livari, N., Kinnula, M., Kuure, L., et al. 2014. Video diary as a means for data gathering with children—Encountering identities in the making. *International Journal of Human-Computer Studies*, 72(5): 507-521.

Lobov, W. 1969. The logic of non-standard English. In F. William (Ed.), *Language and Poverty* (pp.153-189). Chicago: University of Chicago Press.

Luke, K. K. 1990. *Utterance Particles in Cantonese Conversation*. Amsterdam and Philadelphia: John Benjamins.

Luo, Y. D. 2007. *Guanxi and Business*. Singapore: World Scientific.

Makaya, P. & Bloor, T. 1987. Playing safe with predictions: Hedging, attribution and conditions in economic forecasting. *Applied Linguistics*, 16: 3-18.

Malinowski, B. 1923. The problem of meaning in primitive languages. In K. O. Charles & A. R. Ian (Eds.), *The Meaning of Meaning* (pp. 146-152). London: Routledge.

Manes, J. & Wolfson, N. 1981. The compliment formula. In F. Coulmas (Ed.), *Conversational Routine: Explorations in Standardized Communication Situations and Prepatterned Speech* (pp.115-132). New York: Mouton.

Mao, L. M. R. 1994. Beyond Politeness Theory: "Face" revisited and renewed. *Journal of Pragmatics*, 21(5): 451-486.

Martin, J. R. 1984. *Language, Register and Genre: A Reading in the Deakin University B. ED Children's Writing Course, Course Reader*. Geelong: Deakin University Press.

Martin, J. R. 1987. Process and text: Two aspects of human semiosis. In J. D. Benson & W. S. Greaves (Eds.), *Systemic Perspective on Discourse*. Vol. 1. (pp. 248-274). Norwood: Ablex.

Martin, J. R. 1992. *English Text: System and Structure*. Amsterdam and Philadelphia: John Benjamins.

Martin, J. R. 1999. Grace: The logogenesis of freedom. *Discourse Studies*, 1(1): 29-56.

Mary, I., Gilligan, T., Koenig, B., et al. 1998. Ethical decision-making in critical care in Hong Kong. *Critical Care Medicine*, 26(3): 447-451.

Mccall, G. J. & Simmons, J. L. 1966. *Identities and Interaction*. Columbus: Free Press.

Mentis, M. 1994. Topic management in discourse: Assessment and intervention. *Topics in Language Disorders*, 14 (3): 29-54.

Micali, P. J. 1971. *The Lacy Techniques of Salesmanship*. New York: Hawthorne.

Miles, M., Arnold, D. & Nash, H. 1990. Adaptive communication: The adaption of the seller's interpersonal style to the stage of the dyad's relationship and the buyer's communication style. *Journal of Personal Selling and Sales Management*, 10: 21-27.

Miller, D. 1984. Group fantasies and organizational functioning. *Human Relations*, 37(2): 111-134.

Mills, C. W. 1970. *The Sociological Imagination*. Harmondsworth: Penguin.

Minsky, M. 1975. *The Psychology of Computer Vision*. New York: McGraw-Hill.

Mokros, H. 1996. *Interaction and Identity*. Piscataway, NJ: Transaction Publishers.

Montgomery, B. M. 1988. Quality communication in personal relationships. In S. Duck, D. F. Hay, S. E. Hobfoll, W. Ickes & B. M. Montgomery (Eds.), *Handbook of Personal Relationships: Theory, Research and Interventions* (pp. 343-359). Oxford: John Wiley & Sons.

Mullany, L. 2004. Gender, politeness and institutional power roles: Humour as a tactic to gain compliance in workplace business meetings. *Multilingua*, 23: 13-37.

Mullany, L. 2006. Girls on tour: Politeness, small talk, and gender in managerial business meetings. *Journal of Politeness Research,* 2: 55-77.

Neale, M. A. & Bazerman, M. H. 1985. The effects of framing and negotiator overconfidence on bargaining behaviors and outcomes. *Academy of Management Journal,* 28(1): 34-49.

Neustupny, J. V. 1968. Two faces of Kokusaika. *Japanese Studies,* 8(2): 19-22.

Nunan, D. 1993. Task-based syllabus design: Selecting, grading and sequencing tasks. In G. Crookes & S. M. Gass (Eds.), *Tasks in a Pedagogical Context* (pp.55-68). Clevedon: Multilingual Matters.

Ochs, E. 1992. Indexing gender. In A. Duranti & C. Goodwin (Eds.), *Rethinking Context: Language as an Interactive Phenomenon* (pp. 335-358). Cambridge: Cambridge University Press.

Oetzel, J., Garcia, A. J., & Ting-Toomey, S. 2008. An analysis of the relationships among face concerns and facework behaviors in perceived conflict situations: A four-culture investigation. International *Journal of Conflict Management,* 19(4), 382-403.

Ouyang, H. H. 2004. *Remaking of Face and Community of Practice: An Ethnography of Local and Expatriate English Teachers' Reform Stories in Today's China.* Beijing: Beijing University Press.

Pan, Y. 2000. Facework in Chinese service encounters. *Journal of Asian Pacific Communication,* 10(1): 25-61.

Pan, Y., Scollon, S. W. & Scollon, R. 2009. *Professional Communication in International Settings.* New York: Wiley.

Pan, Y. L. 2010. *Intercultural Communication and Ron Scollon: A Reflection.* Washington, D.C.: Georgetown University.

Philips, N. & Hardy, C. 2002. *Discourse Analysis: Investigating Processes of Social Construction.* New York: Palgrave.

Pilegaard, M. 1997. Politeness in written business discourse: A textlinguistic perspective on requests. *Journal of Pragmatics,* 28(2): 223-244.

Planken, B. 2005. Managing rapport in lingua franca sales negotiations: A comparison of professional and aspiring negotiators. *English for Specific Purposes,* 24: 381-400.

Pomerantz, A. 1978. Compliment responses: Notes on the cooperation of multiple constraints. In J. Schenkein (Ed.), *Studies in the Organization of Conversational Interaction* (pp. 79-112). New York: Academic Press.

Pomerantz, A. 1984. Agreeing and disagreeing with assessments: Some features of preferred/dispreferred turn shapes. In J. M. Atkinson & J. Heritage (Eds.), *Structures of Social Action: Studies in Conversation Analysis* (pp. 57-101). Cambridge: Cambridge University Press.

Potter, S. J. & McKinlay, J. B. 2005. From a relationship to encounter: An examination of longitudinal and lateral dimensions in the doctor-patient relationship. *Social Science and Medicine,* 61: 465-479.

Prevignano, C. L. & di Luzio. 2003. A discussion with John J. Gumperz. In L. E. Susan, L. P.

Carlo & J. T. Paul (Eds.), *Language and Interaction: Discussions with John J.Gumperz* (pp. 7-29). Amsterdam and Philadelphia: John Benjamins.

Psathas, G. 1979. *Everyday Language: Studies in Ethnomethodology.* New York: Irvington.

Psathas, G. 1995. *Conversation Analysis: The Study of Talk-in-Interaction.* London: Sage.

Punch, K. F. 1998. *Introduction to Social Research.* London: Sage.

Putnam, H. 1981. *Reason, Truth and History.* Gambridge: Cambridge University Press.

Reid, I. 1987. *The Place of Genre in Learning: Current Debates.* Geelong: Deakin University.

Roger, D. 1989. Experimental studies of dyadic turn-taking behavior. In D. Roger & P. Bull (Eds.), *Conversation* (pp. 75-95). Philadelphia: Multilingual Matters.

Rogers, L. E. & Millar, F. E. 1988. Relational communication. In S. Duck, D. F. Hay, S. E. Hobfoll, W. Ickes & B. M. Montgomery (Eds.), *Handbook of Personal Relationships: Theory, Research and Interventions* (pp. 289-305). Oxford: John Wiley & Sons.

Rose, K. 1992. Speech acts and questionnaires: The effect of hearer response. *Journal of Pragmatics*, 17(1): 49-62.

Ru, X., Lu, X.Y. & Li, P. L. 2008. *2008: Analysis and Prediction of Chinese Society.* Beijing: Social Sciences Literature Press.

Russell, D. A. 2001. *Quintilian: The Orator's Education, Books I through XII.* Cambridge: Harvard University Press.

Sacks, H. 1972. An initial investigation of the usability of conversational data for doing sociology. In D. Sudnow (Ed.), *Studies in Social Interaction* (pp. 31-74). New York: Free Press.

Sacks, H. 1974. An analysis of the course of a joke's telling in conversation. In R. Bauman & J. Sherzer (Eds.), *Explorations in the Ethnography of Speaking* (pp. 337-353). Cambridge: Cambridge University Press.

Sarangi, S. & Slembrouck, S. 1996. *Language, Bureaucracy and Social Control.* London: Longman.

Saville-Troike, M. 1982. *The Ethnography of Communication: An Introduction.* Oxford: Basil Blackwell.

Schegloff, E. A. 1972. Sequencing in conversational openings. *American Anthropologist*, 70: 1075-1095.

Schegloff, E. A. 1979. The relevance of repair to syntax-for-conversation. In T. Givon (Ed.), *Syntax and Semantics 12: Discourse and Syntax* (pp. 261-286). New York: Academic Press.

Schegloff, E. A. 1987. Recycled turn beginnings: A precise repair mechanism in conversation's turn-taking organization. In G. Button & J. R. E. Lee (Eds.), *Talk and Social Organization* (pp. 70-85). Clevedon: Multilingual Matters.

Schegloff, E. A. 1990. On the organization of sequences as a source of "coherence" in talk-in-interaction. In B. Dorval (Ed.), *Conversational Organization and Its Development* (pp. 51-77). Norwood: Ablex.

Schegloff, E. A. 1992a. On talk and its institutional occasions. In P. Drew & J. Heritage (Eds.), *Talk at work: Interaction in Institutional Settings* (pp. 101-134). Cambridge: Cambridge

University Press.
Schegloff, E. A. 1992b. Repair after next turn: The last structurally provided defense of intersubjectivity in conversation. *American Journal of Sociology,* 97(5): 1295-1345.
Schegloff, E. A. 1995. *Sequence Organization* (Unpublished manuscript). University of California, Los Angeles.
Schegloff, E. A. 1996. Turn-organization: One intersection of grammar and interaction. In E. Ochs, E. A. Schegloff & S. A. Thompson (Eds.), *Interaction and Grammar* (pp. 52-133). Cambridge: Cambridge University Press.
Schegloff, E. A. 1997a. Practice and actions: Boundary cases of other-initiated repair. *Discourse Processes,* 23(3): 499-545.
Schegloff, E. A. 1997b. Third turn repair: Towards a social science of language. In G. R. Guy, C. Feagin & D. Schiffrin, et al. (Eds.), *In Honor of William Labov, Volume 2: Social Interaction and Discourse Structures* (pp. 31-40). Amsterdam and Philadelphia: John Benjamins.
Schegloff, E. A. 2000a. Overlapping talk and the organization of turn-taking for conversation. *Language and Society,* 29(1): 1-63.
Schegloff, E. A. 2000b. When "others" initiate repair. *Applied Linguistics,* 21(2): 205-243.
Schegloff, E. A. 2001. Accounts of conduct in interaction: Interruption, overlap and turn-taking. In J. H. Turner (Ed.), *Handbook of Sociological Theory* (pp. 287-321). New York: Plenum.
Schegloff, E. A., Jefferson, G. & Sacks, H. 1977. The preference for self-correction in the organization of repair in conversation. *Language,* 53: 361-382.
Schiffrin, D. 1981. Tense variation in narrative. *Language,* 57 (1): 45-62.
Schiffrin, D. 1990. The management of a cooperative self during argument: The role of opinions and stories in arguments. In A. D. Grimshaw (Ed.), *Conflict Talk* (pp. 241-250). Cambridge: Cambridge University Press.
Schiffrin, D. 1994. *Approaches to Discourse.* Oxford: Blackwell.
Schiffrin, D., Tannen, D. & Hamilton, H. 2001. *Handbook of Discourse Analysis.* Malden: Blackwell.
Scollon, R. 1995a. Matching discourse identity to social identity: One source of confusion in intercultural communication. (A paper presented at the 5th International Conference on Cross-Cultural Communication: East and West, August 15-19, 1995, Harbin, China.)
Scollon, R. 1995b. Plagiarism and ideology: Identity in intercultural discourse. *Language in Society,* 24(1): 1-28.
Scollon, R. 1997. Handbills, tissues, and condoms: A site of engagement for the construction of identity in public discourse. *Journal of Sociolinguistics,* 1(1): 39-61.
Scollon, R. 1998. *Mediated Discourse as Social Interaction: A Study of News Discourse.* London: Longman.
Scollon, R. & Scollon, S. W. 1991. Topic confusion in English-Asian discourse. *World Englishes,* 10 (2): 113-125.

Scollon, R. & Scollon, S. W. 2001. *Intercultural Communication: A Discourse Approach*. Malden: Blackwell.

Scollon, S. W. 1997. Metaphors of self and communication: English and Cantonese. *Multilingua*, 16(1):1-38.

Seligman, B. B. 1990. *Main Currents in Modern Economics*. Piscataway, NJ: Transaction Publishers.

Sheer, V. C. & Chen, L. 2003. Successful Sino-western business negotiation: Participants' account of national and professional cultures. *Journal of Business Communication*, 40(1): 50-85.

Shi, X. 2005. *A Cultural Approach to Discourse*. New York: Palgrave Macmillan.

Simmel, G. 1961. The sociology of sociability. In T. Parsons, D. Barrett, E. Shils, K. Naegele & J. Pitts (Eds.), *Theories of Society: Foundations of Modern Sociological Theory* (pp. 254-261). New York: Free Press.

Simons, H. W. 1986. *Persuasion: Understanding, Practice, and Analysis*. New York: Random House.

Sinclair, M. H. & Coulthard, R. M. 1977. Towards an analysis of discourse: The English used by teachers and pupils. *TESOL Quarterly*, 11(2): 203-206.

Skinner, G. 1977. *The City in Late Imperial China*. Stanford: Stanford University Press.

Sorkhabi, N. 2012. Care reasoning in interpersonal relationships: Cognition about moral obligation and personal choice. *North American Journal of Psychology*, 14(2): 221-244.

Spencer-Oatey, H. 2002. Managing rapport in talk: Using rapport sensitive incidents to explore the motivational concerns underlying the management of relations. *Journal of Pragmatics*, 34(5): 529-545.

Spencer-Oatey, H. 2008. *Culturally Speaking: Culture, Communication and Politeness Theory*. London: Continuum.

Spencer-Oatey, H. & Xing, J. 2003. Managing rapport in intercultural business interactions: A comparison of two Chinese-British welcome meetings. *Journal of Intercultural Studies*, 24: 33-46.

Spitzberg, B. H. & Cupach, W. R. 1984. *Interpersonal Communication Competence*. London: Sage.

Stenstrom, A. 1994. *An Introduction to Spoken Interaction*. London: Longman.

Strange, S. 1996. *The Retreat of the State: The Diffusion of Power in the World Economy*. Cambridge: Cambridge University Press.

Sun, X. L. 2001. *Nation and Society in China's Process of Modernization*. Beijing: Chinese Social Science Press.

Swales, J. 1990. *Genre Analysis—English in Academic and Research Settings*. Cambridge: Cambridge University Press.

Tanaka, H. 1999. *Turn-taking in Japanese Conversation: A Study in Grammar and Interaction*. Amsterdam and Philadelphia: John Benjamins.

Tannen, D. 1986. Frames revisited. *Quaderni de Semantica*, 7: 106-109.

Tannen, D. 1993. *Framing in Discourse*. New York: Oxford University Press.

Tannen, D. 2001. *I Only Say This Because I Love You: How the Way We Talk Can Make or Break Family Relationships throughout Our Lives*. New York: Random House.

Tannen, D. 2005. *Conversational Style: Analyzing Talk Among Friends*. Oxford: Oxford University Press.

Tannen, D. & Wallat, C. 1986. Medical professionals and parents: A linguistic analysis of communication across contexts. *Language in Society*, 15(3): 295-311.

Taylor, R. L. 2000. *Assessment of Exceptional Students: Educational and Psychological Procedures*. Upper Saddle River: Prentice Hall.

Terpstra, D. E. & Baker, D. D. 1991. Sexual harassment at work: The psychosocial issues. In M. J. Davidson & J. Earnshaw (Eds.), Wiley Series on Studies in Occupational Stress. *Vulnerable Workers: Psychosocial and Legal Issues* (pp. 179-201). Oxford, England: John Wiley & Sons.

Thomas, J. 1986. *The Dynamics of Discourse: A Pragmatic Analysis of Confrontational Interaction* (Unpublished doctoral dissertation). University of Lancaster, Lancashire.

Thompson, G. & Yiyun, Y. 1991. Evaluation of the reporting verbs used in academic papers. *Applied Linguistics*, 12: 365-382.

Tomlin, R., Forest, L. & Pu, M. M. 1997. Discourse semantics. In T. van Dijk (Ed.), *Discourse as Structure and Process* (pp. 63-111). London: Sage.

Touraine, A. 1971. *Post-Industrial Society*. New York: Random House.

Tsui, A. & Farh, J. L. 1997. Where *Guanxi* matters: Relational demography and *Guanxi* in the Chinese context. *Work and Occupation*, 24: 56-79.

Tsui, A. B. M. 1994. *English Conversation*. Oxford: Oxford University Press.

Turner, R. 1974. Words, utterances and activities. In R. Turner (Ed.), *Ethnomethodology: Selected Readings* (pp. 197-215). Harmondsworth: Penguin.

Urry, J. 1987. Some social and spatial aspects of services. *Society and Space*, 5(1): 5-26.

van der Valk, I. 2003. Right-wing parliamentary discourse on immigration in France. *Discourse & Society*, 14(3): 309-348.

van Dijk, T. 1997. Political discourse and racism: Describing others in western parliaments. In S. Riggins (Ed.), *The Language and Politics of Exclusion: Others in Discourse* (pp. 31-64). London: Sage.

van Dijk, T. 2006. Discourse and manipulation. *Discourse and Society*, 17(3): 359-383.

Verschueren, J. 2008. Context and structure in a theory of pragmatics (special issue with papers from the 10th international conference). *Studies in Pragmatics*, 10: 14-24.

Wang, J. 2010. *English for New Scientists*. Harbin: Harbin Institute of Technology Press.

Wang, N. 2000. The popularization of English in the age of globalization and the construction of Chinese critical discourse. *Foreign Languages & Their Teaching*, (8): 48-51.

Watson, T. J. 2008. *Sociology, Work and Industry* (5th edn.). London: Routledge.

Watzlawick, P. & Fisch, R. 1974. Change: Principles of problem formation and problem resolution. *Family Process*, 13(3): 399-400.

Weitz, B. A. 1978. The relationship between salesperson performance and understanding customer decision making. *Journal of Marketing Research*, 15: 501-506.

Wetherell, M. & Maybin, J. 1996. The distributed self: A social constructionist perspective. In R. Stevens (Ed.), *Understanding the Self* (pp. 219-279). London: Sage.

Wieland, M. 1995. Complimenting behavior in French/American cross-cultural dinner conversations. *French Review*, 68(5): 796-812.

William, S. 1977. Regional urbanization in 19th century China. In N. Ginsburg (Ed.), *The City in Late Imperial China* (pp. 143-148). Palo Alto: Stanford University Press.

Williams, K., Spiro, R. & Fine, L. 1990. The customer-salesperson dyad: An interaction/communication model and review. *Journal of Personal Selling and Sales Management*, 10: 29-43.

Wilson, D. C. 2010. *Institutionalization, technology, and power: The ideological context of style organizations* (Order No. 1480648). (755050753). https://search.proquest.com/docview/755050753?accountid=11232[2018-1-20]

Wilson, J. 2009. On the topic of conversation as a speech event. *Research on Language & Social Interaction*, 21(1-4): 93-114.

Wilson, T. P. 1991. Social structure and the sequential organization of interaction. In D. Boden & D. H. Zimmerman (Eds.), *Talk and Social Structure* (pp. 22-43). Cambridge: Polity Press.

Wodak, R. 1995. *Disorders of Discourse*. London: Longman.

Wodak, R. 2001. What CDA is about—A summary of its history, important concepts and its developments. In R. Wodak & M. Meyer (Eds.), *Methods of Critical Discourse Analysis* (pp. 1-13). London: Sage.

Wolfson, N. 1981. Compliments in cross-cultural perspective. *TESOL Quarterly*, 15(2): 117-124.

Wolfson, N. 1983. An empirically based analysis of complimenting in American English. In N. Wolfson & E. Judd (Eds.), *Sociolinguistics and Language Acquisition* (pp. 82-95). Cambridge: Newbury House.

Wolfson, N. 1984. Pretty is as pretty does: A speech act view of sex roles. *Applied Linguistics*, 5: 236-244.

Wolfson, N. 1989. The social dynamics of native and non-native variation in complimenting behavior. In M. Eisenstein (Ed.), *The Dynamic Interlanguage: Empirical Studies in Second Language Variation* (pp. 219-236). New York: Plenum Press.

Wong, M. 2007. Guanxi and Its Role in Business. *Chinese Management Studies*, 1(4): 257-276.

Wu, D. 2008. *Discourses of Cultural China in the Globalizing Age*. Hong Kong: Hong Kong University Press.

Yang, M. 1994. *Gifts, Favors, and Banquets: The Art of Social Relationships in China*. Ithaca: Cornell University Press.

Yates, L. 2000. *Ciao Guys: Mitigation Addressing Positive and Negative Face Concerns in the Directives of Native-speaker and Chinese Background Speakers of Australian English*

(Unpublished doctoral dissertation). La Trobe University, Melbourne.

Yule, G. 1980. Speakers' topics and major paratones. *Lingua*, 52(1): 33-47.

Zhang, Q. 1998. Fuzziness - vagueness - generality - ambiguity. *Journal of Pragmatics*, 29(1): 13-31.

Zhang, W. 1995. Context-dependent interpretations of linguistic terms in fuzzy relational databases. The 11th International Conference Collection on Data Engineering (pp. 139-146). IEEE. April 16-19 1995, Paris.

Zhou, K. X. 1996. *How the Farmers Changed China: Power of the People*. Boulder: Westview.

Zimmerman, D. H. 1988. On conversation: The conversation analytic perspective. In J. Anderson (Ed.), *Communication Yearbook II* (pp. 406-432). Newbury Park: Sage.

Zimmerman, D. H. & Boden, D. 1991. *Talk and Social Structure: Studies in Ethnomethodology and Conversation Analysis*. Cambridge: Polity Press.

Appendixes

Appendix I A Reconstructed Dialogue between an Insurance Sales Agent and a Prospective Client

(A: Insurance Sales Agent   B: Prospective Client)

1. A: 今天在家休息啊?
2. B: 唵，在家里玩。
3. A: 哦，刘老师原来你们喊姐夫嗨?
4. B: 是的哦。
5. A: 他原来就是我们中学老师哎。[停顿 1 秒]哦，两个毛毛，嗨?
6. B: 嗯，在家里陪读。[停顿 0.5 秒]你是保险公司的嗨?
7. A: 嗯，我是××人寿公司的。刘店的×××你可认得? 刘店那医生啊，我是她姐姐。你老婆在松树科，我们隔壁生产队嘛。
8. B: 嗯。
9. A: 呵呵，我昨天听刘老师讲搞保险，（他）跟你们怎么讲的啊?
10. B: 嗯——也没怎么讲，就是讲就讲起头来了。就讲这保险那保险，讲保险种类上好多……
11. A: [停顿 0.5 秒]嗯，那是的哦。
12. B: 你们办的是什么保险呢?
13. A: 我们办的有小家伙的教育保险、成长保险啊许多的。
14. B: 小家伙在学校念书不是已经有保险了么?
15. A: 不是的，那个保险钱是不退给你的，我们给你介绍的额保险，是积少成多，一次性给你还是三次给你，比你存银行利息高。
16. B: 什么险种啊?

17. A: 如果你给毛毛买的话，如果参加分红，分红有本金累计生息。具体情况我给你介绍下子，假如讲我们买十万的那种，分十年交，一年就是交一万，假如讲我们第一年交了一万，这就是你的本金，本金放那要生息，我们按照去年的情况，5.6%来算，一年就是560；第二年开始我们本金就是 10 560 了，这时候再加上你第二年交的保费一万，那就是 20 560；然后第三年、第四年，以此类推，就是讲利生息、滚动的，到最后呢，等你交满十年了，你可以选择一次性拿回来，也可以分几次拿回来；假如讲你觉得利润还好，你也可以继续放那，就像是理财样的，也中；还有比如讲你每年想把那个分红拿出来，也中，那你就是本金放那，分红自己拿回来用，也一样……

18. B: 那假如讲我中间想要用钱，那怎么搞啊？

19. A: 用钱的话呢，你最好是不动本金，本金一动，那就相当于违约，违约的话那你就划不来了。这个东西我们要实话实说，因为我们有合同，呶，这个场子，你看看（指出条款给客户看），那你就非常划不来了。

20. B: 哦，那就是讲，我买了以后就不能动了……

21. A: 也不是那么讲，一般买保险我们不都是闲钱嘛；暂时没有其他比较好的地方投资啊或者怎样；再讲你家里这个情况，也不至于啊，这个也不多，呵呵，你讲可是的啊？

22. B: 哎呀，那个东西难讲哦……

23. A: 我觉得呢，我们这么想，现在我们还比较年轻，挣钱能力比较强，年富力强的时候，这个时候买点保险，给我们小家伙有个保障，就像是存款样的，等他们长大了，最起码还有那么一笔钱在那儿。我们到时候万一讲的话，年纪大了，做不动了，他们能用这一笔钱还能做一点事情。再讲，现在钱存银行你也晓得，每年通货膨胀那么厉害，钱是越来越不值钱；我们这个就是讲一方面你是存那有利息，另外一方面公司还把这个钱拿去投资——××公司你也晓得，世界 500 强，中国最大的保险公司，它把这个钱收起来不是讲就放那或者放银行，它是要拿去投资的哎，比如讲现在什么西部大开发啊、风力发电啊、三峡工程哪，许多项目……

24. B: ……你可买了啊？

25. A: 我给我家他和儿子还有我自己都买了啊，我家条件没你这么好，买不了太多，就这样子，我都买了不少呢……

26. B: 你家××现在还在村里搞吧？

27. A: 唵，他不一直在那场子瞎忙嘛。

28. B: 那还瞎忙啊，主任多好，不过事情也确实多。

29. A: 是的啊，一天到晚不归家，不晓得在忙什么东西。

30. B: 哦，你儿子现在上大学了吧？在广州还是在哪可是的啊？

31. A: 唵，在广州，那个不成器的东西……[停顿2秒]其实你也可以考虑给你自己买一点哎。你看你现在挣钱多，但是我们国家现在养老啊、社会保险这一块还不怎么完善，将来年纪大了，我们不讲给小家伙们创造多大价值，最起码自己保自己，那就是给他们减轻负担了。哎，我们公司现在有一个险种我给你介绍下子啊……

32. B: 哦？我们也有啊？

33. A: 有啊，这一种是我们最近才推出来的，主要针对三四十岁、现在收入比较好的客户，它也是保本型的。就是讲，不管怎么搞，你到最后都能把本钱拿回来，就相当于一种储蓄。你想想看，钱存到银行，现在肯定不是一个好选择；买房子，现在不讲其他地方，就××县这个小场子，房价都已经高得不得了了；炒股吧，也是风险大得不得了——我家那个当时买了几万，到现在还没回本；我们这个险种呢，不光能保本，还能有分红，多少你可以根据你自己情况选，最低起步五万，十万、二十万、三十万，最高五十万，买得越多，相对应的收益也就越多，大概一般比如讲十年以后，十万的话一般一个月能拿到一两千块钱，一共拿十年，你想想看，这不就等于上班拿工资了嘛？最起码，生活有的了……

34. B: 哦，那这个还不错呢，我也是在考虑，现在虽然讲挣点钱，不稳定啊。

35. A: 是的啊，拿我们来讲就是提前准备，那个成语啊怎么讲啊，哦——叫未雨绸缪，呵呵，反正这东西，有条件，搞下子还是好的，其他东西我不敢讲，最起码我搞的东西我有信心，其他可能也有业务员找了你吧？

36. B: 唵，有……

37. A: 是的啊，其实这东西我也不瞒你，你买得多我们有提成，但是我每次都跟我客户讲清楚，大家离得不远，又熟，你讲可是的啊？

38. B: 那是的哦，其他人是也找过我的，我当时就讲不了解，看看再讲，呵呵……

39. A: 反正这一点你放心，我在这场子也这么多年了，大家都是抬头不见低头见的，那种事情我做不出来。

40. B: 那我放心哎——要不是你来，我哪听你讲这么半天呢，你讲可是的。

41. A: 那是的哦——要不你这样子，我们公司下个星期六在××酒店搞个宣讲会，到时我们有省里请来的讲师介绍产品，现场签约的话还有礼品，还有抽奖活动，反正到时你不想买也不要紧，你要有时间的话就过去看看，我带你们一起……

42. B: 下个礼拜六啊？哦，我将好要到街上去，几点钟啊？

43. A: 上午九点半，这样子，我八点半到这来接你，我们一起过去，××酒店你也晓得，还是不错的啊，中午我们有招待会，公司请吃饭。

44. B: 哦，那好啊。

45. A: 好，那就这么讲，我先给你做个登记……

46. B: 唵。

47. A: 哎也，你家里这装修搞得真好，真漂亮，上档次，花了不少钱吧？

48. B: 这个啊，我们在外头，一年不回来趟把，我老婆讲自己住的场子要搞好一点，舒服些嘛。

49. A: 那是的哦，自己住，搞好的，每天在里面，心情都不一样啊，呵呵……

50. B: 那也是的，所以那时候她讲要搞，我想想，搞就搞吧，反正都是自己住，我们在外面毕竟也不长久，总是要回来的，可是的啊？回来的话，毕竟怎么样也是自己一个窝啊……

51. A: 唵，那你们想的是对的哦……[停顿1秒]其实像你们这个情况，还是可以考虑考虑买点保险哎，反正也不要紧嘛，你有空就了解了解情况，要是有什么问题随时给我打电话。

52. B: 其实讲真的，你我肯定相信，保险我还真不是很感冒……

53. A: ……那你真错了。保险其实现在尚好重要呢，哎，一方面是一个保障——反正我们有话照讲，你别怪哦——不怕一万就怕万一，真万一有什么事情的话，最起码它还能保障一点，这个东西现在是越来越重要了。你想，现在你小伢子还小，他将来的教育、医疗、结婚、成家你都是要——不讲多嘛，最起码我们作为父母是要尽力，你讲可是的呀。

54. B: 那是的哦。

55. A: 这些东西算下来，不得了哎——呶，其他的不讲，你就看看我家儿子，现在在上大学了。我现在想想，他这么多年，花的钱真的是堆起来一大堆。

56. B: 呵呵，那是的哦。

57. A: 其他东西不讲，学费、生活费，那时候在××陪读，他一陪读不要紧哪，我们一天到晚在那儿服侍他，烧饭、洗衣裳，一个人一点事不能做，完全是消耗。我想想，我们那时候是经济太困难，我家情况你也晓得，他家爸爸死得早，什么东西都没留，留了一屁股债；我们搞了这么多年，才算差不多搞下来了。好不容易搞下来的，小伢子又大了，念书，负担真是重得不得了……

58. B: 你们是不容易哦，不过他家爸爸人好啊。

59. A: 人好有鬼用啊，他一天到晚在村里忙，晚上有时候都不归家，我就搞死人哪！

60. B: 你是能干，你那幼儿园搞得不错嘛——讲什么时候还到××表演获得奖啊？

61. A: 唵，是的哦。那是那时候县教育局搞个节目，要求我们底下的幼儿园报节目上去。我们当时就排练的一个舞蹈，小伢子们还真不错，呵呵，得了二等奖。那时候排练真的是没日没夜，天天要想啊，搞什么节目啊，怎么搞啊，那些小伢子怎么才练得好啊，我那一天到晚嗓子搞哑了……

62. B: 那是的哦，我家一个小伢子都搞死人了，不讲你那四五十个一把搞，呵呵。

63. A: 那你有什么办法呢？还是你们好哦，家里搞得又好，收入又可以，房子搞得这么漂亮，装修又这么上档次。开玩笑讲的话，我家兄弟经常讲"这才是生活啊"，哈哈。

64. B: 我们不就混日子，搞来搞去都是为了小家伙。

65. A: 那肯定的啊，老古话讲得好嘛——人往高处走，水往低处流。

66. B: 是的哦，可怜天下父母心哪。

67. A: 唵，你讲，不养儿不知父母恩哪。

68. B: 是的哦，我们现在也是养了小家伙才晓得他家爹爹奶奶那时候真是不容易，把我们几个拉扯大……

69. A: 是的啊——哦，你家大大妈妈现在多大年纪啦？

70. B: 我大大65，我家妈妈63嘛。

71. A: 也，那他们可买得什么医疗保险哎？

72. B: 哎哟，你就别讲了，那时候才搞合作医疗，我讲给他们买，他们不舍得嘛。他们讲他们身体好得很，一年白白交几百块钱，划不来，就没买。哪晓得今年3月份先是我大大生病，一下子搞掉两万多，住院都住了15天。15天搞下来，我妈妈那时候天天在医院陪得哦，哪晓得大大好了，妈妈又累倒了，又一下子干掉七八千——现在医院真是不能去，一去那就是搞死人——不死也是塌层皮……

73. A: 是的哦，现在看病看不起，念书念不起，买房子买不起，所以我讲你们现在呢趁着经济条件还好，赶紧提前做好准备。不讲其他的嘛，最起码一个你有个保障——你家大大妈妈他们年纪大了，现在保险买不了了，你们现在买正是好时候——咹，这是一个；再一个，你也是当存钱，先我跟你介绍那个，真的是特别适合你们，负担也不重，你再加一个大病保险，这种包括38种大病，基本上常见不常见的病都包括了，这是一个；再呢，也是当作一种强制储蓄，我们现在挣钱还可以，花钱也厉害——可是的啊？

74. B: 哎哟，你就别讲了，现在钱真不经花。

75. A: 是的啊，买了这种，你别想那么多，就当是强制储蓄，这么一搞嘛，我们在花钱的时候就会稍微注下意——咹，你看我家他那个小舅子，挣钱也厉害啊，一年二三十万，花得更厉害，第一年挣了头10万，就买的一个十几二十万的车子；还讲天天在外头鬼搞——

76. B: 哪个哎？小××啊？

77. A: 不是他是哪个——一下子花光了，现在一天到晚在我家蹲，找我家他借钱。我真是搞不懂，好好的一个人，怎么就搞成这样子。

78. B: 他噢，赌嘛，那个东西嘛，好赌如命，一赌起钱，那真是嘛眼睛都是红的，真是不要命。

79. A: 哪不是讲，他家日子要不然多好过哦。

80. B: 那也是的。

81. A: 所以讲，来得快，去得更快，呵呵。

82. B: 呵呵，钱确实不经花。

83. A: 所以讲，你现在有能力的时候多存一点，以后嘛，各方面都要好不少，不讲以后再为小家伙做什么事情——那个反正有多大力，发多大光——最起码我们自己保自己没问题也就基本上差不多了……

84. B: 唵，我们能做多少呢，还不就是给他们念书，到他们结婚的时候要是能买套房子那就最好了。

85. A: 是的哦，呶，要像这种情况，你就可以考虑买高一点。现在不是好多人都讲嘛"你不理财，财不理你"。你现在买，其实就是挣钱，像你们在外面可炒股哎？

86. B: 炒股那个东西我们不搞，前两年买了六万，最后剩两万，那个东西都是骗人的……

87. A: 那也不是那么讲哎，这个东西呢，要比较专业的知识——我们公司有专业的人去处理这方面的事情。呶，比如讲，我们客户买了保险以后，积少成多哦，一个人一年几千几万；几千几万个人，那加起来就是一个很大的数字哪，那这个钱肯定不能放那哦。你也晓得，现在钱存银行那肯定是越来越少，越存越少，这个东西你也晓得撒。

88. B: 那钱确实不能存银行，你们公司那些人把这个钱拿去炒股啊？

89. A: 不是讲全部拿去炒股，一部分吧。你想啊，股市里面有人亏钱，那肯定也有人赚钱啊，要不然那钱到哪儿去了呢，可是的啊？

90. B: 呵呵。

91. A: 高头我也讲了，一部分是拿去投资，比如讲什么三峡工程啊、西部大开发啊、高速公路啊这些东西，还有其他的呢。比如讲投资基金哪，还有一部分呢，那他们就拿去做股票。所有的这些投资盈利都是有分红，这个分红就不一定讲多少，一年一年不一样——去年的情况大概是有七个点，不讲多高嘛，最起码我那么多钱还是那么多钱，保值了。

这个其实也就不错了你讲可是的哎——要不然那钱存银行你存定期最多一年，也就三四个点左右，那多划不来哦。

92. B: 银行是不想存，其实我们现金也不多，呵呵。

93. A: 这个不要紧的嘛，多有多买，少有少买。买一个你觉得还好，下次还可以再追加或者讲再买个其他的，这个不影响的。

94. B: 主要我们这方面还是不怎么懂，虽然讲我相信你，但这么大一个数字，我还是要等我家那个回来，我们商量下子再讲——不要紧的嘛，我还要在家里蹲一向子的。

95. A: 哦，那好啊，那你大概什么时候走啊？

96. B: 我们大概过了十五吧。

97. A: 那好，那我到过年边再来找你啊。

98. B: 好嘛——哦，我家呢，有个哥哥、一个姐姐，一个在贵池，一个在马鞍山，他们过年也要回来。他们那个条件也都蛮好，要不你到时候也过来看看。

99. A: 哦，那好啊，他们什么情况？多大年纪了？

100. B: 我家哥哥42，姐姐38，都是做生意的。

101. A: 哦，那好，那到时候他们回来我再过来哦。

102. B: 好嘛。

103. A: 好，那就这么讲的呢，今朝真是要感谢你呢，还给我介绍，呵呵。

104. B: 那没事的，都是乡里乡亲的，客气嘛子哦。

105. A: 那到时候有空到我家去玩哎。

106. B: 好嘛。

107. A: 那我走了哦。

108. B: 唵，好啊，那我送你出去。

109. A: 哎哟，你真是礼节多，呵呵。

……

Appendix II   Questionnaire for Insurance Sales Agents

问卷（对保险业务员）

1. 您已从事保险业务员多久？
2. 您如何形容（描述）当代中国保险业务员和客户之间的关系？
3. 您觉得业务员与客户之间关系与之前相比（两年前、五年前、十年前）是变好了，变坏了，还是差不多？
4. 您觉得您的工作报酬是很好、合理，还是很差？
5. 您的工作给您很大压力吗？压力来自何处？
6. 您觉得与（潜在）客户沟通时有压力吗？压力来自何处？
7. 您觉得您和客户之间是平等的吗？或您觉得应当是平等的吗？
8. 您觉得哪一种客户最难打交道？您喜欢和哪种客户打交道？
9. 在您和客户的交往中，是否有极端冲突的例子？请详细描述。
10. 您希望客户参与到决策过程中吗？如买哪种保险，如何组合，购买什么价格的等。
11. 您如何应对客户的挑战？如不相信保险，怕没保障，等等。
12. 您如何说服您的客户相信保险，相信您所介绍的险种？
13. 您觉得哪种客户最难沟通，甚至觉得很烦？
14. 您是否有和客户之间不愉快的经历？请详细描述。

Appendix III   Questionnaire for Clients

问卷（对客户）

1. 您选择保险公司的标准是什么？
2. 您选择保险业务员的标准是什么？
3. 您如何描述当代中国保险业务员与客户之间的关系？
4. 您觉得如今保险业务员与客户之间关系与之前（两年前、五年前、十年前，甚至二十年前）相比是变好了，变坏了，还是基本没变？
5. 您信任保险业务员的程度是：A. 完全信任；B. 信任，但有所保留；C. 完全不信任。您觉得客户应该相信保险业务员吗？
6. 您觉得您与保险业务员是一种平等关系吗？您觉得应该是一种平等的关系吗？
7. 在购买保险过程中，您是否与业务员共同决策？（即业务员参加到做决定过程中，如买还是不买，买哪一种，哪种档次，如何组合。）
8. 当您有疑虑或需要更多信息时，您会直接询问保险业务员吗？您是如何问的？最好举例说明。
9. 您觉得哪一种保险业务员友善、可信度高？
10. 您觉得哪一种保险业务员难打交道，甚至有些烦人？
11. 您与您的保险业务员之间是否有不愉快的经历？可否详述？（越详细越好）

Appendix IV A Sample Answer to the Questionnaire from an Agent

业务员问卷示例

1. 您已从事保险业务员多久？
   2006 年至 2013 年，7 年多了。
2. 您如何形容（描述）当代中国保险业务员和客户之间的关系？
   有的会是好朋友，业务员真心为客户服务，客户也确实能体会到业务员的诚意。有的业务员给客户提供的帮助最终很可能让客户实在不好意思，作为回报往往会带来一系列保单。当然很多客户也知道业务员的薪酬很高。归结起来终究还是有利益关系的。有的却会成为敌人，当客户退保一下损失惨重内心一时无法接受时。假如一旦退保，必定损失惨重，即使有的客户嘴上不怪，内心还是有抱怨的。而有良知的业务员内心也会很愧疚，甚至就此罢手，再也不做保险了。
3. 您觉得业务员与客户之间关系与之前相比（两年前、五年前、十年前）是变好了，变坏了，还是差不多？
   因人而异，有的业务员做完保险就把客户丢到脑后，有的却保持联络。其实经营好老客户是个不错的选择，我们可以索取转介绍，并且老客户认同保险，有条件时更容易加保。
4. 您觉得您的工作报酬是很好、合理，还是很差？
   很好。
5. 您的工作给您很大压力吗？压力来自何处？
   压力很大。主要来自公司上级领导，一级压一级。当然自己想挣钱也是一方面。没办法，要业绩嘛。还要增员，不断为公司注入新鲜血液。
6. 您觉得与（潜在）客户沟通时有压力吗？压力来自何处？
   看什么样客户。面对条件特别好，又没有保险意识的，言谈中知道的比我还多的大客户时有压力，感觉自己很难搞定他。
7. 您觉得您和客户之间是平等的吗？或您觉得应当是平等的吗？

感觉有些财大气粗的客户不跟我们平等，有点高高在上的压抑。我认为当然应当平等。我们做的是一份工作，是帮客户制订理财计划，是帮客户规避人生和财产的风险，我们绝不低三下四，绝不！

8. 您觉得哪一种客户最难打交道？您喜欢和哪种客户打交道？

   财大气粗的人，自以为是，其实什么都不懂还装懂。我喜欢和容易沟通、和颜悦色、没有架子、愿意聆听、不固执己见、能够接受不同观点的人打交道。

9. 在您和客户的交往中，是否有极端冲突的例子？请详细描述。

   极端冲突应该只能是退保时或退保前后才会有。曾经一客户办了份 5 年期交，保费每年 10 000 元，第二年交续保前回乡路上遭遇小偷，全年收入洗劫一空，无条件缴费，然后要求退保，损失一小半。客户自己倒没说什么，可他妈妈心疼钱，在路上遇见我差不多是把我骂了一顿，至今伤疤犹在。骂我不要脸，不买保险我就赖在她家不走，要不是我非要劝他儿子买什么保险，她儿子也不会莫名其妙损失许多钱！农村老奶奶，我又不能跟她一样不讲道理地骂街，我强忍怒火与委屈，好口气地对她说："奶奶，你真没必要这么生气，我也不知道你儿子今年要破财，也不知道他今年交不起保险啊。大家都是乡里乡亲的，抬头不见低头见，你这么跟我撕破脸皮，以后我们哪就不打交道啦？再说宣传保险是我的工作，是我的义务。"不过后来我们见面又客客气气的了。

10. 您希望客户参与到决策过程中吗？如买哪种保险，如何组合，购买什么价格的等。

    那是必须的，但是客户往往会举棋不定，通常需要我们在关键时刻做出最后决定。

11. 您如何应对客户的挑战？如不相信保险，怕没保障，等等。

    不相信保险的话，现场我可以告诉她××人寿保险公司连续 11 年荣登世界 500 强企业，募集资金超过工商银行。参与国家大型稳健投资项目三峡工程、西部开发、华东电网、西气东输……年收益率 8%~12%。社保是保险，合作医疗是保险，新农保是保险，汽车上路必须办保险，孩子上学也都买保险……中央电视台黄金时间的广告"保险，让生活更美好！"世界名人说保险的一些话也可以引用。像李嘉诚、周润发、丘吉尔、胡适……还有我国历代领导人对保险的说辞。

如果担心保障打折，就告诉她保险是一纸合约，合同上白纸黑字受法律保护。

12. 您如何说服您的客户相信保险，相信您所介绍的险种？

答案在上一提问中也有体现，另补充如下：××人寿是国有企业，今年又升级为副部级央企。保险公司不可以倒闭，因为有《保险法》保障，《保险法》第八十九条明确规定：经营有人寿保险业务的保险公司，除因分立、合并或者被依法撤销外，不得解散。要让客户相信我介绍的险种，首先我必须在客户心目中有比较专业的印象。我可以强调我在公司任职的年限，业务在公司排名情况，还有我为客户的多年如一日的用心服务，在公司所荣获的诸多荣誉。说得直白点，推销保险实际上也是推销我本人。我感觉如果我的客户家庭各方面发展得比我好，或者好很多，那么这个客户相对较难搞定，如果与我发展得差不多甚至不如我，这张保单相对较容易搞定。

13. 您觉得哪种客户最难沟通，甚至觉得很烦？

不懂装懂的、自以为是的、财大气粗的、夸夸其谈的、不可理喻的客户最难沟通；曾经退保的客户也难沟通。我最烦的客户是电话里很赞同保险，见面了顾左右而言他，谈话无边无际，然后你逼急了他还不表态，不说不买，这种人浪费精力和时间，很烦。倒不如那些直接道明不买，哪怕找个不是充分的理由推辞也好，反正我不抱希望也无所谓失望。

14. 您是否有和客户之间不愉快的经历？请详细描述。

有。上面第9题极端冲突就是不愉快的重要经历。当然还有几例：去年9月份，二阿姨婆家一表妹去她家等车，闲聊之间就聊起保险，表姑问阿姨，有没有老人的养老保险，她想给已经70岁的老妈办。当时阿姨就打我电话，我正好在芜湖，我就说70岁的老人肯定买不到任何保险了，但是表姑夫妻可以办养老及医疗，这样老人的遗憾就不会再在他们身上重演。然后我就要了表姑的号码，回家后几天打电话邀请她去参加公司的活动，目的是让她正面了解一下保险是怎么回事。她在××陪读，说那天走不开。我说要么改天我上门去给你介绍吧，她说好。那天周末，我带上电脑，骑着摩托找到她住的地方，她也比较热情，聊了一些孩子的话题，就切入正题，我打开电脑，把养老和医疗的组合险附加意外伤害险详细讲解，当我拿出签单意向书请她签字时，她说必须等老公回来商量再做决定。我本来一般对第一次见面的客户签单不抱多大希望，正收拾准备出门，她老公回来了，她好像很欣喜，男人比较感性，大致听我复述一遍，简单问了几个问题，没提反对意见，只是在我要求的保费上还了10 000元价。就这样顺利签单，去银行缴款。可是还不到一个月，表姑听她哥哥说这种商业保险买了不划算，不如买社保，就坚决要求退保，工作怎么也做不通。我劝她明年这时候退一样，保障毕竟保留一年，她说一天都不能等。我就陪她去公司，领导讲解，劝她别退，损失上万元，她说就当赌钱输了！苦于投保人是其老公，只能等男人回来再办手续。当时她的样子真的很生气，我感觉自己真的很尴尬。其实客户内心怎么都不能接受如此巨大的损失。仅仅一个月时间，我说我当时也跟你说过，不能退保，退保有损失，她没好气地说，你也没有说清楚有这么大损失呀。我知道，她内心恨死我了，我内心也很抱歉，害人家白白损失一万块钱。如果我不做这工作，不上门向她推销保险，她也不至于破这个财的。没办法，挣了人家的钱，只好厚着脸皮勉强陪着人家咯，说一些抱歉的话……还有一次我请我的大客户老客户吃饭，目的还是要她给儿子加保，其实我们电话里差不多都说好了28 000元。可是她条件特别好，我想把保费提高一些，就请了我们公司的两位领导。席间谈到保险设计我就让领导讲，没想到她们太大意，犯了个低级错误，未满18周岁的被保险人规定保额不能超过10万元，造成第二天核保时不能通过。跟客户已经签字，保费已经现金收取，这下麻烦来了。这在客户看来我们首先不负责任，其次不专业，客户挺不高兴。后来我连续短信、电话联系客户，坦诚解释，重新更换险种。客户很重信用，没有反悔。我很感激她。以前在××县缫丝厂我俩做对班，我上班她下班，共用一台机器，厂休时在一块谈心，关系很纯。现在我俩经常联系，像朋友一样。

Appendix V   A Sample Interview of an Agent

Agent:

闲闲地、慢慢地刮,这个东西不能急,人家心情要还好,有时间;如果没时间跟你讲,那天就不要谈了,肯定不行。有一次,去谈,刚好她闲、有空;那人我也认得,就在我们这街道底下。去之前也了解了下子家里情况,有两个小家伙,丈夫在外地开车子;今年准备给小家伙上幼儿园,家里也有点钱;我家里那个他在这场子名誉也还好,人家也相信他;我们平时做人也挺注意。其实那次都没谈多久,一下子就成了。先呢,就是亲朋好友,亲戚啊、朋友啊这些。另外一个,对保险条款要熟悉,不能一问三不知。再热情一点,人家要是有什么需要或者什么事情,那肯定要尽量地帮忙。要是第一次不成,那就多跑几次嘛,反正当朋友来处,时间长了一般都没什么大问题。反正大单子、小单子我都做。小单子也上好厉害哎,三四百的单子我都做,做起来也快得很。要讲真话,反正我不会骗他们的,实事求是的。什么东西清清楚楚在保险合同上写的。要想长期做,这方面不注意肯定不行,要不然就一次性的嘛。再一个根据他家里经济情况;第二个根据自己需求。

2010 年 11 月 19 日

Appendix VI　A Sample Interview of a Client

Client:
　　我买的第一笔单子是他主动找我的，就是人情单，买的是人情单。都是那个圈子里玩的几个人，他人也好，这个人为人好，相当好；一个村子的，又是朋友，我也晓得他做一笔单子得百分之几，是奖励，这个东西反正都有好处，也无所谓。就当是帮助他工作嘛……

2009 年 9 月 4 日

Appendix VII   Confession of an Agent

　　早先开始做保险是摸着石头过河，试试看；后来凭借大家的帮助和自己的不服输精神，工作进展得还算有点成绩；现在对保险工作可以说有点厌倦。一方面我的思想有阶段性波动，最近儿子的陪读问题颇为困扰我，我现在真的非常羡慕那些陪读妈妈，成年成月都可以悠然地、不焦不急地过着陪读生活。幼儿园放假了，不用着急他，可保险公司没有假，每个阶段都有目标推动，层出不穷，没完没了。有时候吧，这阶段经过努力，好不容易达标，甚至超标，刚想喘口气，放松放松，任务就又来了。也许是我这个人上进心强，或者说挣钱欲强，不甘落后，而且还易于服从领导管理，个人荣誉感和集体荣誉感强。环顾周边伙伴有好几个业绩平平，他们对公司的要求也采取无所谓态度，等到季度考核时发现面临被淘汰的危机，再努力一把，或者实在不行就给家人买一点。这种工作作风我不赞同。像我这样吧又太累，也许是我兼职的缘故。如果专门做保险，我想应该不至于这样累的。我们××部大部分都是兼职的，有在职村干部，有退休村干部，以前还有一在职教师（后来因为出现问题保单，客户找他吵，自己也没信心干下去，就离职了），有个体小老板（估计也做不了两年，毕竟他的保单基本都是人情单，又不熟悉条款，没能跟客户讲清楚，不是客户弄懂条款，认可保险才买下的），有家庭妇女，还有好几个跟我一样是幼儿教师。

　　这段时间我们网点业绩不大好，原因是过年前没有发展壮大队伍，也就是招收新人，用公司的话说就是给公司注入新鲜的血液。一般情况下，新人上岗很快能连续出单，老人的客户资源毕竟是有限的，新官上任还三把火呢！半月前，我的顶头上司因为团队业绩低迷，在主任和主管会议上被县支公司经理骂得狗血淋头，当场就哭了，而且主任年纪已五十多岁，七八年来一直为现在的经理鞍前马后效力，帮助她一直坐上××支公司经理的宝座。主任哭着跑回家，闹起情绪说："看我不做保险会不会饿死！"有一个多星期时间她都没怎么过问团队工作。我们去她家看望，她很伤感地说："我很寒心，风风雨雨好几年，没有功劳还有苦劳。寿险太残酷。成者为王，败者为寇。以前我们团队不是没有风光过。"其他网点主任和主管也人人自危，有一老牌主任这样说："只见新人笑，不见旧人哭。"我私下里想，经理她也有她的难处，她也是有上级的，她也有人压她的。怪谁呢？只能怪保险这种经营模式。怪保险公司这个庞大的融资机构。但是工作归工作，会上骂完会后应该做个沟通，私人交情毕竟还有的。在保险公司就是很现实，业绩高，领导都把你捧着，早会不参加都没关系；业绩不好的人最怕开早会，心里不好受啊！我今年在我们网点目前是第二名（那第一名元月份一张保单就签下10万元）。

公司人员流动性太大，入职以来，不断见到陌生面孔，也有很多熟悉的面孔不知哪一天悄悄从身边消失了。回想起他们当初刚入职大部分都做得红红火火，不免感伤。我常常想保险公司和他的营销员之间才真正是"铁打的营盘，流水的兵"。总结他们离司的原因：

（1）最直接原因可能是他们的交际面较窄，做完身边的亲亲友友，便发展不了更多的新客户。

（2）精神不够坚强，受不了被拒绝的打击。

（3）家庭因素，或者小孩需陪读，或者丈夫在外地需照顾。

（4）跟直接领导闹矛盾，工作不愉快，拍拍屁股走人。

（5）脚踏两只船，在其他人寿保险公司挂职，公司警告无效的被公司除名（极少，近一年才发生）。

（6）遇到问题保单，或者退保客户因为损失找业务员吵闹的，感觉太受气，歇了算了。

（7）家人不支持工作、长期反对的，为稳定大局而放弃。

（8）还有极少被别的保险公司挖走的（最近才知道原来在大厅领取单证的内勤员工就跳槽了，大部分原因是别的公司工资高些）。当然，新人一旦成长为熟练的员工，如果想离司，公司会设法挽留，因为培养一位合格的业务员公司也很不容易的，业务员的流失也意味着公司的损失。

在招收新人方面，说实在的，我没有像做业务那样尽心尽力去做，也曾被领导压着去找人，但最后就算把人请到事业说明会上，人家还是拒绝从业，或许是我缺少伯乐的眼光，或者是我眼光过高，我始终认为，宁缺毋滥，免得以后一粒老鼠屎带坏一锅粥，做三天就不干，保险没弄懂却会到处瞎说，破坏农村本来就很困难的寿险市场。还有，招得过多，业务员之间还会存在不良竞争。比如××那一带，前几年业务员最多，可真正留存的却没几个，那些没做得很大原因就是不良竞争。你去他家，我也去了他家，仅仅是巧合，你我都想客户照顾自己，可到头来客户只好谁的都不买，免得得罪人。遇到素质差的业务员甚至还在客户面前损对方，这会给客户留下极差的印象，也有损公司形象。但公司方面却不这样认为，他们认为业务员甚至越多越好，你跑，我也跑。很多人都有从众心理，你买他买，那我也买，人家能买我也能买，人家有，我也要有。员工之间不能"损"而应该"抬"。听起来好像不无道理。

一、如何招收新人

记得刚入司那两年，好像一年就两次发展新人，年底和四五月份各一次，现在好像每季度都在发展。我的主管们经常叫我在下面找合适人，这几天又要大张旗鼓地招兵买马。老业务员跑业务时随时留心身边，有时候征一新人比做一单业务难许多。首先是观念的宣导，他若不相信保险，自己还绝对不买保险，你叫他做业务，那时几乎是不可能的。如果观念不行，他会想：我不能害人啊，或者是我不愿求人啊。记得征我进来的师傅跟我交往了一年多，也就是说她在我身上花的时间和精力不止一年时间。假如某人答应入司了，首先得报名—参加事业说明会—培训（几天）—考试—拿代理人资格证书—从业。报名后要交500元风险金，什么时候不干了，可原数退回。一般在考试前后就可以跑业务，这时都由主管或主任陪访，等资格证出来，就有工号了。我入司时，新人拿3个月底薪，是300元，现在底薪分等级，业绩越好，底薪越高。现在好像已经增长到最高等级能拿1200元，工资肯定不会白拿，必须有相应的业绩支持。新人如有合适人选，可以再征新人，如果征新人达2名，就可以升主管，拿主管津贴，前几个月主管还在新人业绩上拿佣金，有时候公司还设伯乐奖，奖金几百元。记得我师傅当年引荐我入司还奖了一枚金戒指，值几百元。

跃中常常说：你们自己都没有保障，还天天跟客户讲保险。他这话有失偏颇，但也有一定的道理。首先我们不是没有保障而是精英只有意外伤害和医疗保障，属于团体险，保障也不高，像我属于三级精英，意外险有16万元保障。另外，我们只有极少的养老保障，每月在工资里扣一点，实际上并不是真正的企业给员工办的社保，××支公司有近十个农网服务部和两个城区服务部，只有三四个服务部主任享有社保。记得两年前公司曾跟我们签订过一份关于员工保险的合同，具体说的什么，后悔当时也没细看，要是现在我肯定会有一堆问题要问的。现在想来还不知是不是公司应付上面检查才搞的假。现在新《劳动法》明确要求单位替员工买保险，可我们卖的就是保险，自己却不拥有，真是笑话！更感觉委屈。如果哪一天老了，跑不动保险了，我们的养老和医疗还得自己解决。曾经在网上看到这样的话：为什么称呼我们是"跑保险的"？为什么社会对从事保险工作的有一种无形的歧视，他们不受人尊重？因为我们所享受的待遇不公。

二、理赔、退保问题

　　理赔肯定会有问题的，条条框框都有限制。但只要在保险范围，也如实告知了，赔款一般都很顺利。曾经的纠纷听说有带病投保的，已经住过院了，甚至住过几个医院的，然后再买保险，病死后要求理赔肯定赔不下来。新《保险法》出台以后，对客户的利益更侧重保障，明确规定报案3日内必须答复，7日内必须答复理由，30日内必须理赔到位。如果客户对公司不满，可以拨打95519客户服务电话进行投诉。再不行可以起诉公司，法院更侧重保护客户利益。现在我们人寿保险公司的理赔工作在当地算信誉最好的，最差的要算×××，原因主要是他们在××没有公司大厅，只设有一个办事处，如果办事处或者某业务员工作不负责任，问题就来了。而在上海，因为×××本部就设在上海，据说信誉度非常好。

　　关于退保问题，退保的有，但极少，因为大家都清楚退保意味着巨大损失。除非实在失去缴费能力，或者对保险产生深恶痛绝的情绪，或者听某关键人物说保险买了没用。有的客户即使不大情愿再续保，但苦于退保的直接经济损失，还是咬咬牙继续交下去。我目前的一百多位客户，有3人退保；1人没续交也没退保；1人吵着要退，但本人不在家退不了。只要1人退保，往往会影响一片市场，造成一定的负面影响。曾听领导说过，赔到钱的不作声，退保损失的到处喊。今年上半年校园伤害案件频出，校园都要求配保安，曾听公司大厅工作人员开玩笑说："我们在大厅最不安全，以后也要配保安，戴安全帽，那些退保的情绪不好时，骂完了防止打我们。"

Index

communicative purpose 2, 26, 52-55, 66, 73, 75-76, 79-81, 89, 108, 165, 176

discourse analysis 5, 7, 9, 19, 64, 66, 71, 180

discourse system 7-10, 26-27, 29-31, 35-37, 39-41, 48, 53, 58, 64, 71, 112-113, 134, 154, 158-159, 166

discursive pattern 1-2, 26, 29, 52-53, 89, 111, 170-171

dynamics 1, 6, 28-29, 32, 43, 55, 61, 64, 66, 89, 91, 106, 110, 130, 136, 138, 155, 161-162, 165, 167, 172, 178, 191

frame 19, 53, 55, 59-60, 71, 121, 134-135, 148, 159, 162

friendship 14-15, 27-28, 33, 35-36, 46, 60, 64, 96, 112-113, 117-121, 125, 131-132, 134-135, 138, 145-146, 148, 153, 155-159, 161-162, 169

friendship talk 96, 112, 117-121, 125, 131-132, 134-135, 138, 145-146, 155-156, 158, 161-162

genre 20, 32, 52-54, 71, 73-79, 165, 176

Guanxi iii, 4, 19, 23, 29, 41-47, 52, 55, 61-62, 64, 89, 91, 95, 97, 99, 105-106, 108, 110, 130, 134, 136, 148, 154, 161, 163, 165, 167-168, 171-172

identity 1, 10, 19, 22, 26, 29, 31, 34, 52, 56-59, 62, 66, 116, 121-122, 126-127, 145, 149-150, 153-154, 157-159, 161, 163, 165-166

institutional talk 112, 117-118, 121-122, 126, 129-132, 134-135, 138, 145, 149-150, 152, 155-158, 161

insurance sales 1-2, 4, 7-13, 15-17, 19, 21, 24, 26-30, 32-33, 35, 37-39, 41, 52-53, 55, 57, 60-67, 69, 71, 73, 77, 79-82, 89-90, 92, 95, 97-99, 103, 105-106, 108, 110-113, 115-118, 120-122, 125-127, 130, 132, 134-135, 137-138, 147, 152, 155-156, 162-163, 165-167, 171-173

interaction 7-8, 11, 13, 16-21, 23, 29, 36, 42, 47-48, 55-56, 58-60, 62-63, 65, 70-71, 78, 80, 90, 92, 96, 108, 113-115, 119, 122, 126, 134, 136-139, 145, 148, 155, 157-158, 165, 167, 180, 182-183, 187-188, 191

linguistic representation 20, 166

move 54-55, 75, 78, 82, 89-90, 99, 102-103, 105-108, 110, 157, 169-170

negotiation 17, 27, 29, 32-33, 35, 42-43, 51-52, 59, 72, 77, 120, 133-134, 139, 150, 156, 159, 161-162, 165-166, 189

persuasion 2, 16-18, 26-27, 70, 103, 109, 126, 135, 162, 166, 171

socio-cultural 1-2, 4, 6-7, 20, 68, 77, 111, 146, 166, 171-172, 180 task-oriented talk   112, 117, 120, 126, 131, 133-135, 138, 145, 154-158, 162

topic management   1-2, 14-15, 26-27, 29, 63, 112-113, 165, 171

transformational China's rural areas   1-2, 15, 19, 24, 26-27, 51, 53, 55, 61, 73, 79, 89, 95-98, 103, 105, 108, 110-112, 130, 149, 152, 162, 165, 171-173

trust   4, 7, 13, 23, 33, 35, 41-42, 47, 62, 72, 80, 82, 95, 103, 105, 108, 110, 117, 121, 130, 139, 148-149, 154, 164, 168-169, 173